DEMOCRACY AND RIGHT–WING POLITICS IN EASTERN EUROPE IN THE 1990S

EDITED BY JOSEPH HELD

EAST EUROPEAN MONOGRAPHS, BOULDER
DISTRIBUTED BY COLUMBIA UNIVERSITY PRESS, NEW YORK

1993

EAST EUROPEAN MONOGRAPHS, NO. CCCLXXVI

Contents

1. Foreword and Acknowledgments by the Editor   v

2. The Political Right in Eastern Europe
   in Historical Perspective
   Stephen Fischer-Galati   1

3. The Revival of the Political Right in Post-Communist
   Poland; Historical Roots
   Andrzej Korbonski   13

4. What's Right, What's Left and What's Wrong
   in Polish Politics
   Sarah M. Terry   33

5. The Right in Czech-Slovakia
   Sharon Wolchik   61

6. The Role of the Political Right in Post-Communist
   Czech-Slovakia
   Otto Ulc   89

7. Jobbra At! [Right Face!] Right-Wing Trends in
   Post-Communist Hungary
   Ivan T. Berend   105

8. Building Civil Society in Post-Communist Hungary
   Joseph Held   135

9. The Revival of the Political Right in Post-
   Communist Romania
   Michael Shafir   153

10. Strengthening of the Right and Social Changes
    in Croatia and Yugoslavia
    Ivan Siber   175

11. The Political Spectrum in Post-Communist Bulgaria
   Luan Troxel 191

12. Albania
   Elez Biberaj 203

13. Concluding Thoughts on the Revival of the Political
   Right in Eastern Europe
   Ivan Volgyes 223

FOREWORD AND ACKNOWLEDGMENTS

Writing "current history" is an unusually thankless undertaking. The results and conclusions soon tend to become outdated in the near future or even during the present time.

Yet, reflections on current history by experts is a valuable undertaking indeed. If nothing else, these reflections provide insights at particular points in history as seen by contemporaries.

Today, the political Left hardly exists any longer in Eastern Europe. The political and social ideology espoused by various Left-wing groups before World War II has been so completely discredited by the failed communist experiment that very few parties are willing to identify themselves with them. Most new political formations in the region, therefore, consider themselves to be standing to the right or center-right in the political spectrum in the 1990s. This does not mean, however, that they can readily be identified with traditional East European Right-wing movements.

The major ideological elements that made up the baggage of the pre-World War II Right-wing parties included, among others, anti-Semitism, radical, extreme nationalism and, least we forget, a populist version of primitive, peasant socialism. There are very few groups in Eastern Europe today that would openly promote all these ideological constructs. Nevertheless, there are danger signals coming from the countries of the region indicating that the radical Right-wing might reappear, obstructing the development of democratic political systems. There are plenty of historical traditions favoring such a development. This is the danger that led us to the organization of the conference in April 1992 whose proceedings comprise the contributions to this volume.

I want to acknowledge the help provided by many individuals and, above all, the administration of the Faculty of Arts and Sciences at Rutgers University, Camden, for making the conference possible. Professors Andrew Lees and Arthur Klinghoffer, the former the Associate Dean of the Graduate School and the latter a member of the Political Science department, presided over two sessions and participated in others. My secretary, Iris Rodriguez, labored hard to keep participants up-to-date before and during the conference. The fact that the numerous functions of the meeting went off smoothly was due to her dedication and diligence. Mrs. Elizabeth A. Skyta took good care of financial matters, certainly not the least important aspect of such a meeting.

Mrs. Loretta Carlisle typed and organized the manuscript, a major task if there has ever been one, and we all owe her a large "thank you!" I must also thank the participants for their efforts and, not the least, for submitting their presentations for publication on time. I believe that this must be some sort of world-record in scholarly circles.

The volume has been organized on the basis of the assumption that the northern tier of Eastern Europe, including Poland, Czechoslovakia, and Hungary, were farther along their democratization process than the countries of the Southern tier. Each of the former, therefore, are treated by two chapters. The Southern tier's countries are discussed by one contributor each.

The conference proved once again that when there is good will and common effort to understand each other, then East European and American scholars are able to cooperate and consider each others' opinions not as the expressions of hostile positions, but as points of view worth exploring. If only the atmosphere and the spirit of such conferences could be transferred to Eastern Europe! The region would certainly be a better place to live.

Joseph Held

Camden, New Jersey

September 1992

THE POLITICAL RIGHT IN EASTERN EUROPE IN HISTORICAL PERSPECTIVE

Stephen Fischer-Galati

1989 has been hailed as the year when the decades-long struggle of the peoples of Eastern Europe against communist tyranny, for democracy, was won. Since 1945 was similarly hailed as the year when the same peoples' struggle against fascist tyranny, for democracy, was won it seems reasonable to question the optimism of those who hailed the death of totalitarianism and the "yearning for democracy" of the peoples of Eastern Europe.

The revival of the political Right in post-communist Eastern Europe is explicable in more ways than one; yet, all explanations are rooted in the historic realities and experiences of the twentieth century. It would indeed be a grave error to assume—as has been assumed by naive or cynical intellectuals and politicians—that fascism and communism were aberrations incompatible with the democratic convictions and aspirations of the peoples of Eastern Europe. The so-called struggles against authoritarian and/or totalitarian regimes, as demonstrations of implacable opposition to non-democratic orders, was also incorrect. The well-known slogans, applicable on a wider geopolitical scale that "Fascism is dead" and "Communism is dead" have proven to be premature obituaries written by ignorant or self-serving political leaders who, quite frequently, have shouted "Long live Democracy" by necessity rather than by choice.

In fact, the moving force and common denominator of the "peoples' historic struggle for liberation"—equated with national independence and statehood—has been nationalism. With minor exceptions, East European nationalism was by definition anti-imperialist, rooted in the spirit of avenging the humiliations inflicted upon their nations by foreign oppressors. It has also been characterized by intolerance of ethnic and religious diversity and, as such, not committed to the spirit of Wilsonian democracy. Nor was the adoption of market economies, party pluralism, constitutionalism, and guarantees of human and/or minority rights prerequisite for the functioning of the independent states established at the end of World War I. Rather, it was the safeguarding of territorial gains or the recouping of territorial losses resulting from the collapse of the Central and East European historic empires that were the primary concern of the political leaders of interwar Eastern Europe. It is not that the peoples and many of their leaders were necessarily adverse to democracy but democratic forms and practices had to be subordinated to national interests and such interests were defined as a function of historic nationalism.

The imposition of democratic constitutions by the victorious powers, on the one hand, and the threat of communism from Bolshevik Russia, on the other, were regarded as incompatible, if not inimical, to historic nationalism. The socio-economic and political readjustments implicit in democratic constitutionalism, seeking solutions by political compromise that involved organizations representative of all classes in society and of all ethnic and religious groups, was almost as unacceptable to most nationalists as the threat of "bolshevization." Indeed, the reforms in agriculture and industry and unconditional granting of full political and civil rights to ethnic and religious minorities that the successor states undertook under international pressures, solidified the opposition to democratization whether of the Wilsonian or Leninist varieties. It is that very political opposition, comprising initially the conservative nationalist elites and their political organizations, that has been characterized as the "political Right" in interwar Eastern Europe.

Although differences in the constituencies of and specific issues addressed during those years varied from country to country, the "political Right" whether in its extremist, radical authoritarian, quasi-Fascist, form or in the more conventional "Christian-Democratic" one, displayed common characteristics. Albeit within differences in degree of emphasis, the "political Right" was chauvinistic, xenophobic, anti-Semitic, anticommunist, supportive of and supported by the religious and military establishments.

The characteristics attributed to the Right were not generally absent even in centrist or, for that matter, in left-of-center political organizations, not to mention the several "Royal dictatorships" and authoritarian regimes. It seems essential to note that the "political Right" was the dominant force in Eastern European politics before World War II and that its premises and programs were generally, if not necessarily, endorsed, or at least not opposed, by the majority of the peoples of Eastern Europe. That was certainly the case in Hungary and Romania and, perhaps only to a lesser degree, in Croatia and Slovakia. It was also true in post-Stamboliiski Bulgaria, post-Pilsudski Poland, post-Fan Noli Albania and, at least in the 1930s, in Slovenia.

The contention was advanced by apologists of the Right that the abandonment of evolving democracy was the result of the threat of Bolshevism and of the destabilization of the interwar East European political systems by Fascist Italy and Nazi Germany. This contention is generally baseless. The threat of Bolshevism was indeed true in Hungary, Romania, and Poland. It did indeed contribute to the consolidation of the power of Admiral Horthy in the post-Béla Kun period and to the rise in the level of anti-Semitism in Hungary. However, Hungarian irredentism and socio-economic conservatism, both key factors in the success of the moderate Right, antedated and survived the Hungarian Soviet Republic. Nor can it be said that the radical, crudely anti-Semitic, Arrow Cross was the creature of the Bolshevik threat or of Hitler or Mussolini. Similarly in Romania, Bolshevik Russia's irredentism with respect to Bessarabia was less important as a factor in the evolution of the moderate and radical Right than opposition by the moderate Right to the agrarian reforms and the increase in the number of "leftist" political parties. These reforms threatened the monopoly of power of the Bucharest establishment and of the radical Right. The Right was also opposed to the influx of Jews from Bessarabia and Bukovina into northeastern Romania. The radically anti-communist and anti-Semitic League of National Christian Defense and the clearly fascist Legion of the Archangel Michael—the Iron Guard—were home grown, antedated the Nazis, acted independently of any support from Hitler or Mussolini before the mid-1930s and only with minimal support from Nazi Germany thereafter.

The Bolshevik threat for Poland such as it was, ended—at least temporarily—after the victorious Polish-Soviet War of 1919–1920. However, continuing fear of communism, the destruction of the parliamentary system by Pilsudski, and the rise in anti-Semitism caused by social dislocation and economic factors, enabled the Right to take control of the Polish political system in the mid-1930s. It is noteworthy that neither the moderate Right, headed by Roman Dmowski's National Party, nor the radical Right parties such as the National Radical Camp or the *Falanga* were creatures of Nazi Germany. In fact they were both anti-German and anti-Russian. On the other hand, the significance of the close association of both the moderate and radical Right with the Polish Roman Catholic Church was based on shared anti-communism and anti-Semitism.

To an even greater extent than in Poland the role of the Catholic Church as supporter of the political Right was crucial in the interwar years in Croatia, Slovenia, and Slovakia. None of these were threatened by Bolshevism or imperilled by the rise of Fascism and Nazism. The Catholic church in these lands, and for that matter elsewhere in Eastern Europe, was by definition anti-communist and, more often than not, also anti-Semitic, anti-Orthodox, anti-Protestant, and anti-Moslem. It was also invariably conservative and influential in politics. In Croatia it was most supportive of the nationalist opponents of Greater Serbia. The so-called "Right wing" of the Croatian Peasant Party and at least part of the Catholic hierarchy embraced the "clerical fascist" principles which guided the less moderate Frank Party and, for that matter, even the extremist *Ustasha*. And that support, as well as the political organizations themselves, with the exception of the *Ustasha*, antedate and/or were unrelated to either the threat of Bolshevism or the rise of German or Italian totalitarianism.

Opposition to Serbian domination of Yugoslavia's political life was led, in Slovenia, by the Slovene Clerical Party, headed by the Catholic Monsignor Anton Korosek. In Slovakia, political opposition to Czech domination of Czechoslovakia's political and economic life, as well as to Hungarian revisionism, was the *raison d'être* of the Slovak People's Party, headed by Father Andrew Hlinka. Neither the moderate Right Slovene Clerical Party nor the extreme Right Slovak People's Party, were creatures of anti-Bolshevism or of Nazism or Italian Fascism. Their roots were native and reflective of conditions internal to Yugoslavia and Czechoslovakia. Their "Clerical-fascism" was a genuine "organic" political phenomenon comparable with the Clerical Fascist movements of Austria, Spain, and Portugal.

Fear of Bolshevism and direct influence of Italian Fascism did, however, play a role in the evolution of the Right in Bulgaria and Albania. The "peasant democracy" established under Stamboliiski and the presence of an active Bulgarian Communist Party, subservient to Moscow, was feared by the conservative bureaucratic and military forces, as well as by the monarchy, and hated by the extreme Right, ultra-nationalist Internal Macedonian Revolutionary Organization (IMRO). The latter was indeed supported overtly by Mussolini. The military and royal dictatorships that took charge of Bulgarian political life in the mid-1920s were clearly anti-communist, mostly pro-Italian. A contradiction was that they sought to destroy the power of the terrorist IMRO. However, the Bulgarian Right, whether extremist or moderate, was not relying on the support of the Orthodox Church and revealed no anti-Semitic tendencies. Similarly, the Albanian Right, led by Ahmet Zogu (later King Zog I) justified its authoritarian, nationalist regime because of its victory over the "progressive" Monsignor Fan Noli, whose reforms antagonized the landlord beys. The Right maintained itself in power, with support from Fascist Italy, between 1924 and 1939.

It would be incorrect to overemphasize the power of the Right or to dismiss the relevance of democratic, usually centrist, political parties in interwar Eastern Europe. It would also be incorrect to attribute the success of the Right primarily to its anti-Bolshevism, anti-Semitism, xenophobia, and intolerance toward ethnic, national, or religious minorities. It is true, for instance, that socio-economic factors related to urbanization, to the Great Depression, and to unemployment were influential, if not decisive, in the rise of the Right especially in Romania, Hungary, and Poland. Yet, it is also incorrect to suggest that the Right, especially in its extremist forms, was an aberration and that its political power would eventually have been reduced, if not totally obliterated, had the democratic forces been given more time to develop their programs, both domestic and foreign. External factors, related to the power of Nazi Germany and the consolidation of Stalin's power in the Soviet Union, enhanced the legitimacy and power of the Right on the eve of World War II and during the war. But it is also true that, as the "ultimate" exponent of nationalism, the Right had a solid base of support on the eve of the war as well as during the war. And that base did not disappear, albeit for a variety of reasons, even after the war.

It would be difficult to discern any meaningful opposition to the Nazi domination of Eastern Europe during World War II by the leadership or adherents of the centrist or leftist, usually disbanded, political organizations. It is however, easy to prove collaboration of rightist organizations with the authoritarian regimes in power. More significantly, there is evidence of overt support for Nazi Germany and/or Fascist Italy by the radical Right in Romania, Hungary, Croatia, and Slovakia. In Romania, Marshal Antonescu and the Iron Guardists loyal to him justified their support of Hitler in the name of recovering territories illegally annexed by the Soviet Union in 1940. The very legitimacy of the Antonescu regime was, on the other hand, derived from Orthodox Romanianism which, specifically, sought the exclusion of Jews from the Romanian body social and politic if not their phys- ical extermination. No such rationale was evident in Hungary where the Horthy regime justified its pro-Axis stand by common opposition to communism and the USSR.

The Hungarian Arrow Cross, in keeping with its extremist anti- Semitic and anti-communist policies, supported the Nazi goal of ex- terminating "Judeo-Communism" by military means and, in the case of the Jews, by means of the Holocaust. Father Hlinka and his more extremist collaborators were loyal to the Nazis but refrained from the physical extermination of the Jews. In Croatia, however, the *Ustasha* led by Ante Pavelich, while displaying no toleration toward Jews, fo- cussed their attention on the extermination of Serbs. What is more important, however, in terms of assessing the strength of the Right, is the attitude of the masses of Eastern Europe toward occupiers and native leaders during World War II. It seems fair to say that there was genuine support for Antonescu and Pavelich and general acceptance of the Hungarian and Slovak regimes, at least until the collapse of Nazi Germany seemed inevitable.

In view of subsequent developments, it seems essential to con- sider the position of the East European Right outside Eastern Eu- rope proper either in the so-called "governments in exile" or as part of those members of diplomatic, economic, and cultural missions who chose to stay in belligerent or non-belligerent countries during the war years and afterward.

The governments in exile, specifically the Polish and Czech, in- cluded members of the moderate Right. The attitude of the members of these governments toward the Soviet Union varied, and all were united in anti-communism and anti-Nazism. What is less certain is the extent to which their *raison d'etre*—liberation of their countries from fascism and/or communism—entailed the establishment, upon liberation, of truly democratic regimes. More is known about rifts in the ranks of anti-communist diplomats and intellectuals abroad where the anti-communism and anti-Nazism of the majority was based more on violations of their countries' national rights than of those of human, ethnic, minority, or religious rights. In fact, nationalism was the legitimizer of their opposition to Hitler and Stalin.

Generally forgotten in the euphoria generated by victory over the Nazis was the belief that all East European leaders outside Eastern Europe were anti-totalitarian and, as such, at least receptive to democracy. This was hardly the case proven by subsequent events, as a large number of such leaders were either in Germany or Austria during the war. An even larger number had relocated to Franco's Spain, Peron's Argentina, and other Central and Latin American countries after the war. As western suspicions of the intentions of the Soviet Union increased, the true colors of such individuals became discernible. They assumed the posture of champions of democracy or, at least, of liberal nationalism. Living chiefly in Spain and Argentina, they were anti-communists and nationalists of the Right. Thus, the prewar East European Right reemerged as a potential political force by 1945 when Stalin's plans for a communist takeover of Eastern Europe became evident. In that respect the "non-resident" Right assumed the responsibilities of the "resident" Right which shared the common goal of anticommunism and restoration of national independence within the borders of pre-Munich Europe or, in the case of irredentists, of pre-World War I Europe.

Full coordination of external and internal rightist ideologies and programs became possible after 1989. Interaction between emigrant and home-grown rightists became evident, as well as important, as national communism evolved in post-Stalinist Eastern Europe. Initially, as the Kremlin's plan for the communist takeover succeeded in the late 1940s (as well as during the early years of consolidation of communist power in the satellites), the political emigration denounced communism and the communist system as alien to the national historic traditions. However, there were significant differences in the definition of those traditions. They ranged from national independence within the confines of a democratic internal and international order to national independence within an authoritarian, nationalist, ethnocentric system similar to that envisaged, or achieved, by the traditional Right, or even the radical Right, during the interwar years.

The leaders who advocated the restoration of democracy following what they hoped would be the liberation from communism were, in the early years of the Cold War, in the majority. It is evident, however, that the activist extreme Right, located primarily in Spain,

Latin America, and West Germany paid only compulsory lip service to democracy. It revived the shopworn thesis of the radical Right that their countries were victims of the Judeo-Communist conspiracy which the Christian Right had fought since the end of World War I.

During the period of gradual communist takeover and early years of actual communist rule the views of the extreme Right were probably shared by much of the population of Eastern Europe. The Soviet Union was hardly the presumed "liberator from fascism" and the communists were rightly viewed as anything but exponents of the democracy which the Western allies, and especially the United States, were expected to secure for postwar Eastern Europe. The growing resentment toward the communists and their patrons in the Kremlin was enhanced by the fact that much of the leadership, at both the Party and state levels, was Jewish. It is also interesting to note that, although neither anti-communism nor anti-Russianism were tolerated by the new rulers, anti-Semitism was not officially condemned. By the early 1950s, the purging of Jews in both leading and subordinate cadres occurred if not on Stalin's orders at least with his consent. This was followed, after Stalin's death, by the gradual formulation of such doctrines as "socialist patriotism" and "national roads to socialism" which, in essence, reflected the communists' claim of being the executors of national historic legacies. Nationalism officially resurfaced in communist Eastern Europe.

The United States and its European allies showed little inclination to liberate Eastern Europe from communism, as it was most clearly revealed in 1956. Thus, the political emigration which sought restoration of national independence in democratic societies began to lose ground to the political Right. In fact, as "crusades for freedom" and "captive nations' weeks" fell by the wayside in the age of "peaceful coexistence," and as the number of East Europeans allowed to emigrate to the West increased, the Right gained the upper hand. Much of the new emigration was militantly anti-communist but not necessarily pro-democracy. Rather, it joined conationals in the diaspora whose anti-communism and/or nationalism did not necessarily envisage democratization as a prerequisite of post-communist political orders. In fact, more often than not, the recent immigrants reinforced the anti-communism of the diaspora. It validated the Right's interpretation of national traditions which had to be preserved with a view to invalidating the communists' claims to national historic legacies.

The moderate Right, generally supported by such organizations as Radio Free Europe, found no incompatibility between nationalism and democracy in a liberated Eastern Europe. The radical Right, on the other hand, pretended to equate anti-communism with democracy while, in fact, embraced neo-fascist positions. It denounced the communists as instruments of the Judeo-Bolshevik, anti-national conspiracy, as well as of Russian imperialism, mortal enemies of the national Christian traditions of Eastern Europe. In turn, the East European communists themselves, particularly in Romania and Poland, adopted increasingly more nationalistic stands emphasizing historic international animosities and conflicts, as well as anti-Semitism. Concurrently, the Catholic and Orthodox churches became more involved in politics. Their leaders encouraged if not supported those aspects and elements of communist nationalism that were compatible with historic national traditions as expounded by the historic moderate and extremist Right. For instance, in the 1980s anti-Turkish, pro-Macedonian, and anti-Yugoslav policies became *de rigueur* in Bulgaria; the Transylvanian question in both internal and external aspects was back on the front burner in Romania and, though somewhat more moderately, also in Hungary; Croat-Serbian relations took a turn for the worse while Slovak nationalism, in both its anti-Czech and anti-Semitic garb reared its head. Thus, the convergence of the traditional nationalism of the Right and the new one of the Left became increasingly more evident on the eve of the collapse of the communist regimes in 1989.

The legitimacy and/or validity of communist nationalism was questioned by both the moderate and the extreme Right. The blueprint for political and social change in post-communist Eastern Europe also differed in the case of the moderate and extremist anti-communist nationalists of the Right. It is evident that in both cases historic nationalism was the indispensable legitimizer of any political program that would replace the communist system in "liberated" Eastern Europe. And it is also fair to say that in the competition for power among exponents of nationalism, the political Right had a distinct advantage over other political organizations after 1989.

The expectations, or hopes, of idealists that the collapse of communism would lead to the rapid democratization of the East European states proved illusory. And there were good reasons for that. Anti-communism did not necessarily envisage democracy as an alternative either in Eastern Europe itself or in the East European political emigration abroad. The denial of allegiance to communism and the professing of a commitment to democracy by members of the former apparats and bureaucratic establishments often was a subterfuge for insuring political survival. So was the effort to equate anti-communism with a commitment to democracy. Both were used by seekers of political power from inside and outside Eastern Europe. These were devices used primarily because the "restoration of democracy" became a prerequisite for securing economic aid from the United States and Western Europe. This is not to say that the elimination of the onerous restrictions on freedom of speech, of the press and, above all, of religion was resisted by the first post-communist regimes. These essential elements of democracy were desired by the majority of the peoples of Eastern Europe. It is also true that party pluralism was reinstated together with freely elected parliaments. But these freedoms were often used for nondemocratic purposes primarily by communist or opportunist converts to "democracy" as well as by neo-fascists who were to gradually shed their democratic garb.

The notion of "restoration of democracy" implied the existence of democracy, or at least of democratic parties, prior to the advent of communist totalitarianism. The western democracies lent their support to "historic parties" whose pre-1948 leaders had either been active abroad or survived the communist era at home, as well as to East European politicians who could persuade the West of their democratic proclivities. The litmus test was anti-communism, a firm commitment to a market economy, and respect for minority and religious rights, constitutionalism, and for other normal prerequisites for democratic societies. As it turned out, and not surprisingly, the very notion of "restoration" was in fact baseless since it was founded on wrong assumptions and misinterpretations of historic realities.

The leaders of the "historic parties" who returned to Eastern Europe were soon to realize that they were alienated from the population both because of their prolonged absence from their native countries and because of the obsolescence of their ideas. And that was true, albeit to a lesser degree, also for the members of historic parties who sought to revive the ideas and programs of the 1920s and 1930s. Other political organizations, with names similar to those of the historic parties, or committed to the democratic principles advocated by the West, fared better only in countries such as Czechoslovakia, Hungary, and Poland. The population in these countries perceived that direct western economic support was presumably to be secured because of their commitment to the development of market economies.

However, what may have proved decisive for the political evolution of postcommunist Eastern Europe was the insistence of the West, in the cases of the favored Czech, Hungarian, and Polish "democratic" regimes, on the rapid introduction of market economies as prerequisite for economic assistance. In selected cases, the West made economic assistance contingent on the granting and guaranteeing of unlimited rights to national, ethnic, and religious minorities.

It may well be asked whether the linking of the requirement for a market economy with that of respect for human and minority rights was reflective of a commitment to democracy or of stratagems based on the political interests of the United States, Germany, Great Britain, and France. The equating of anti-communism with democracy, of market economies with democracy, of respect of minority and human rights with democracy was at best unrealistic. The fact that these precepts were applied selectively tends to lead to the questioning of the commitment of the Western nations to the establishment of viable democratic states throughout the former Soviet empire.

Democracy in Eastern Europe was not to be reinstated, not even to be born again; it was to be introduced gradually in societies exposed for generations to relentless nationalism under authoritarian and/or totalitarian regimes, whether "fascist" or "communist." But that would have entailed recognition of the historic reality that "democracy" and democratic political organizations were a rare commodity in Eastern Europe both before and after World War I. It would have required the realization that nationalism was the legitimizer of the East European states and political organizations of the interwar, wartime, and even communist periods. Nationalism was by definition if not intolerant of ethnic, national or religious diversity at best only marginally tolerant. What is less certain is whether massive economic assistance, in the form of a Marshall Plan for Eastern Europe, would have lessened the pains of transition from communism to an eventual democracy. However, in the absence of such economic assistance and in the presence of massive poverty and rising economic expectations the insistence on the introduction of market economies, with corollary massive inflation and unemployment, was to lead to distrust of the free economies and their advocates. It also led to renewed support for the defunct command economy which at least guaranteed job security and a minimum subsistence level. The situation was right for the rebirth of xenophobia, and particularly of anti-Semitism through the traditional association of Jews with economic matters. It led to considerable support for the historic positions of the Right, both moderate and immoderate.

The radical Right in post-communist Romania bears a striking resemblance to that of the interwar period; the Right in Hungary has not abandoned its chauvinistic and anti-Semitic stance of earlier years anymore than has the Polish Right. The Slovak secessionists, although presumably leftist, are the heirs of the Slovak nationalist Right; the Croat nationalists have the support of the old and new *Ustasha*. What is more alarming for the future of democracy is the renewed acceptance by the vast majority of political parties of the need of identification of their plans and programs with the national historic legacy. Once again nationalism is the *sine qua non* for political success in Eastern Europe. The exponents of East European nationalism have seldom made market economies and toleration of ethnic, national, and religious diversity a prerequisite for the achievement of the national historic legacy. It is quite likely that in the event of further deterioration of the economic and political crises of Eastern Europe the Right, old and new, moderate or extreme, will at least consolidate its present gains. It may even become the dominant force in East European politics. This could be all the more likely because of the convergence of the interests of the supporters of nationalist, anti-democratic, causes of the former Left and the traditional and new Right.

THE REVIVAL OF THE POLITICAL RIGHT IN POST-COMMUNIST POLAND: HISTORICAL ROOTS

Andrzej Korbonski

What is a political Right? How can it be defined and located on a political spectrum? What is its ideology and program and who are its supporters? These are just some of the questions that need to be answered prior to a discussion of the political Right within a specific national environment.

It is clear that posing the question is much easier than answering it. For example, the *International Encyclopedia of Social Sciences*, traditionally a reliable source of information for scholars seeking definitional enlightment, does not even contain an entry for the Right. One of the co-editors of a classic work on the subject, *The European Right – A Historical Profile*, devotes 28 pages in an attempt to find an acceptable definition, alas, without much success.[1] A search of other political dictionaries and almanacs yields equally unsatisfactory results.

The definitional problem is further compounded by the fact that the concept of political Right is a broad one and it embraces both the extremist, violent branch, symbolized by German Nazism and its Hungarian and Romanian variants, and the conservative, Right-of-center parties, essentially committed to democratic principles, with different fascist and authoritarian movements in-between.

In light of this, one is tempted to define the Right simply as being at one end of the political continuum in sharp opposition to the Marxist or non-Marxist Left, which seems to be easier to conceptualize. An alternative would be to apply the notion of self-definition: a party or a movement is Right when it says it is right. Failing all this, one can always claim that the meaning of the Right, like pornography, lies in the eye of a beholder.

Narrowing the discussion to Poland does not help matters. The previously mentioned study of the European Right includes chapters on Hungary and Romania but excludes both Poland and Czechoslovakia. In Poland itself, until relatively recently, there were precious few scholarly studies of the Right and only the past few years witnessed the appearance of monographs discussing case studies of Right-wing movements and parties in interwar Poland. Other than that, the *tabula* remains *rasa*.

Historical Antecedents

It is generally agreed that the political Right, especially in its extremist or radical version, is very much a twentieth century phenomenon. It is also a well-known fact that during the first eighteen years of this century, Poland did not appear as an independent state on the map of Europe and instead formed a part of three empires: Tsarist, German and Austro-Hungarian. This imposed some *a priori* restrictions on the ability of the Poles to organize themselves politically.

The record shows that these restrictions proved most effective under the German empire. While the German electoral law, reasonably liberal for its time, allowed the Polish minority to vote in the elections to the *Reichstag*, until the eve of World War I there was only sporadic organized political activity, and the voters, as well as the emerging Polish political elite tended to support the existing German parties, especially the *Zentrum* and the *SPD*, [The Socialist Party of Germany].

The situation was quite different in Austrian-ruled Galicia where the Poles enjoyed considerable political freedom, alongside other minorities, such as the Czechs, Slovenes, Croats, and others. Prior to the outbreak of World War I, the political landscape was dominated by two parties: the Peasant Party and the Polish Socialist Party, representing the moderate Left and Center of the political spectrum.

The political Right, in its first reincarnation, was born in the Russian part of Poland toward the end of the nineteenth century.[2] Following the lifting of the ban on organized political activities and the elections to the first Duma in the wake of the 1905 revolution, a new political organization, known as the National Democrats or *Endecia*, preempted the Right wing of the political arena. Headed by Roman Dmowski, who remained the undisputed leader of the Polish Right until his death in January 1939, the National Democrats resembled to some extent the German National Liberal Party of the post-Bismarckian period: it was a party of *Bildung und Besitz*; it was strongly nationalistic, and both anti-Semitic and anti-German. It saw the future of Poland as being in close association with Tsarist Russia as the only country capable of erasing the eighteenth century partitions and uniting all territories of historic Poland, including those held by Austria and Germany.

The National Democrats were fiercely opposed to both the Left, represented by the Social Democracy of the Kingdom of Poland and Lithuania (*SDKPiL*) and the left wing of the Polish Socialist Party, as well as to the pro-Austrian nationalist movement, spearheaded by Jozef Pilsudski and his legionaries. Until the collapse of the Russian Empire in 1917 they were fully confident about assuming a leading political role in independent Poland.

This was not to be, however, and, at least during the first, democratic phase following the declaration of Polish independence in November 1918, it was the Left and the Center which dominated both the executive and legislative branches of the new republic. The moderate Left gained strength as a result of the victorious Polish-Soviet War of 1919–1920, which discredited the newly formed Polish Communist Party and forced it underground where it remained throughout the entire interwar period. The Center was firmly anchored in two peasant parties and in an incipient Christian Democratic organization. The Right made a valiant bid to capture the Presidency of the Republic in 1922, trying to raise the nationalist banner against the ethnic minorities that accounted for about one-third of the country's population. When that failed and after the assassination of the first, democratically elected president by a member of a nationalist extremist group, the political fortunes of the Right began to wane.

The Revival of the Right

By hindsight, the single most important event which, first arrested the decline of the right, and, ultimately, proved responsible for its revival, was the military coup of May 1926, which marked the beginning of the end of parliamentary democracy in Poland. The parliamentary system continued to linger, albeit in a restricted way, for a few years, coming to an abrupt end in 1930 with the arrest of several prominent leaders of the moderate Left and Center parties.

The coup, led by Marshal Pilsudski, was supported by the Left— both the Social Democrats and the Communists—who erroneously interpreted it as being directed against the Right. Yet, paradoxically, it was the Right which, in the final analysis, greatly benefitted from the aftermath of the coup, which created conditions favoring its revival.

To begin with, the coup could be viewed as an attack on parliamentary democracy and party politics. In the second half of the 1920s, it was clear that a growing segment of the Polish population was becoming disenchanted with the parliamentary system and inter-party strife. The frequent, revolving door changes in the government and party coalitions, resulting in the failure to enact important pieces of legislation, began to alienate the electorate. The game of governmental musical chairs could also be observed elsewhere in Europe and, as the record shows, it also led in most countries to the demise of democracy and a rise of authoritarian systems.

In almost all instances, the democratic breakdown led to the resurgence of the Right, both moderate and extreme, and Poland was no exception. It is clear that by that time the Polish political culture was still in the process of formation and, as such, it provided little support for democracy. Quite the opposite. If one were to identify the most telling element in the Polish attitude toward government and politics, it was most likely the near obsession with national unity as a guarantor of the survival of the country, squeezed between the two traditional enemies, East and West. Anything that threatened or disrupted that unity—be it parliamentary politics, inter-party conflicts or ethnic strife—was condemned as weakening the fabric of that unity and exposing Poland to its perennial adversaries. The obvious answer was the destruction of the parliamentary system to be replaced by some, largely undefined, Right-oriented authoritarian regime.

The second important aspect of the coup was the discrediting of the Left. Its support of the coup alienated many of its adherents and the subsequent arrest of its leaders meant that, at least for the next decade or so, covering most of the 1930s, the Social Democrats disappeared from the political arena and did not stage a comeback until the eve of World War II. With the Communist Party outlawed and, on top of that, unable to abtract much support among the Poles—in contrast to national minorities—the political spectrum was, in a sense, truncated with only the Center remaining relatively unscathed.

Although the organized Left no longer counted as a formidable political force, the specter of the Communist threat continued to haunt the country. The memories of the Polish-Soviet War remained as fresh as ever and having both a long common border with the

USSR and a large Ukrainian and Belorussian minority, made Poland particularly sensitive to developments within the Soviet Union. It was the Right which saw itself as the only political force capable of mobilizing the masses against Communism and, at the same time, filling the existing vacuum in the political arena.

The third consequence of the coup which, in time, benefitted the Right, was the gradual development of a kind of "personality cult" around Pilsudski, even after his death in 1935. While Pilsudski himself had hardly endeared himself to the Right, if only by his treatment of its leader, Dmowski, the old Marshal's ability and willingness to destroy the parliamentary system and his attempt to create a national umbrella-like organization standing above the political parties, appealing to national unity and trying to enhance the role of the state versus society at large, must have struck a sympathetic chord among the actual and potential supporters of the Right. To a considerable degree, Pilsudski's cult resembled a nascent *Führerprinzip*, so dear to the hearts of the Right. The willingness to use violence to overthrow democracy was also, most likely, applauded by the Right.

Thus, it may be argued that already prior to the Nazi takeover in Germany in January 1933, which provided a powerful boost to the fortunes of the Right all over Europe, conditions existed in Poland that accelerated the resurgence of Right wing movements of various hues. In addition to anti-parliamentarism and anti-communism, there was growing contempt for party politics, inclination to hero worship, and potential use of violence to solve political disputes. There was also the impact of the Great Depression which hurt Poland as much as, if not more than, many other countries in East Central Europe.

In looking at the impact of the crisis in Poland, it is easy to discover the same phenomena that led to a Nazi victory in Germany. The rapidly deteriorating economic situation generated high unemployment and declining living standards. This resulted in a progressive polarization of society, characterized by an emergence of a growing group of *declassé* elements. They were equally opposed to the status quo and felt threatened by the inroads of the Left. This was accompanied by a rapid rise of ethnic antagonisms and nationalist chauvinism, directed against the Jews and national minorities, with the result that a growing number of people began looking to the Right for the solution of all their problems.

Thus, the so-called Lipset phenomenon, which tried to explain the rise of Nazism in Germany with reference to the middle class, feeling squeezed by both the proletariat and the upper bourgeoisie, applied to some extent to Poland.[3] The emerging Polish professional and business class found itself competing for increasingly scarce opportunities with the mostly Jewish middle class, further fueling rampant nationalism and anti-Semitism. Moreover, many young people, unable to complete their education and find employment, began to swell the ranks of the *declassé*. They also directed their ire primarily against the national and ethnic minorities, insisting on the introduction of *numerus clausus* and other restrictive devices limiting access to institutions of higher learning.

The government of the day, firmly in the hands of the Pilsudski clique, both explicitly and implicitly encouraged the drift to the Right. It succeeded in April 1935 in pushing through a new constitution which, *de facto*, firmly institutionalized a Right wing authoritarian system. It also tried, albeit with relatively little success, to create still another front or umbrella-like organization, known as the Camp of National Unity, whose program contained a hefty dose of nationalism, etatism and anti-Semitism.[4]

Hence, it is not surprising that the Nazi victory in Germany found a sympathetic echo in some segments of the Polish population and greatly contributed to the rise of the Right. But even here the reaction was far from simple and uniform. Perhaps the most significant was the fact that in the second half of the 1930s the Polish Right was sharply divided between a reasonably moderate National Party (*Stronnictwo Narodowe* or *SN*) and several extremist parties and groupings, such as the National Radical Camp (*Oboz Narodowo-Radykalny* or *ONR*) and the *Falanga*.[5]

Not surprisingly, the National Party, born out of a 1928 merger of several National Democratic parties and groups, and led by the venerable, long-time leader of the Right, Dmowski, inherited many of the programmatic ideas and priorities from its predecessors. It was, above all, strongly nationalistic, anti-Semitic, and both anti-German and anti-Soviet. Anti-Semitism, long a trademark of the old *Enjecia*, was given additional fuel by the impact of Hitler's policies in Germany, by the persistent economic conflict, and by a tacit encouragement of it by the post-Pilsudski regime. The anti-German sentiments, also part and parcel of the program of the old National Democratic Party, received a powerful stimulus from the growth of the Nazi irredenta which was making significant inroads within the German minority concentrated in Western Poland which, prior to 1918, belonged to

Germany. Not surprisingly, the strongest support for the National Party came from the same region.

The anti-Sovietism was a synthesis of the old animosity toward the Left and the new fear of the Soviet Union. Whereas the National Democrats looked toward Tsarist Russia for protection, the Nationalists, not unlike similar parties elsewhere in East Central Europe, viewed the communists as their worst enemies.

The economic program of the National Party did not offer any striking changes in the *status quo*, except by emphasizing the role of the state as a major regulator of economic policy and guarantor of full employment.

Rather surprisingly, the more radical Right wing groups which began to emerge in the second half of the 1930s, never managed to attract much popular support. While it would be tempting to brand them as belonging to a lunatic fringe of Polish politics, the radicals never approximated the violent, neo-Nazi character of the Iron Guard in Romania or Arrow Cross in Hungary. If anything, they were modelled primarily on the Spanish *Falange*, which assumed a dominant position in Spain, following Franco's victory in the Civil War.

In fact, many of the ideological pronouncements of the Spanish *Falange* could most likely be adopted verbatim by the Polish National Radicals or *Falangists*.[6] They included, above all, emphasis on national unity of Poland and suppression, even elimination, of separatists tendencies advocated by minorities, and the establishment of national dictatorship and one party rule. In the economic realm, private property was to be maintained and respected, but the state was to continue playing an important role as coordinator of economic policy.

In light of the most recent developments in today's Poland, it is important to note that the Polish Right has accorded special recognition and provided strong support to the Roman Catholic church, which has traditionally enjoyed preferential status among the various religious denominations in the country. It was this close association with the Church that gave the Right, both moderate and radical, its special standing, closely resembling its Spanish counterpart. The strongest link between the Right and the Church was, of course, anti-Semitism. While the Church strenuously denied it, the Catholic clergy and the Catholic media tended to propagate anti-Semitism, sometimes in a rather crude form.

The final characteristic feature of the Polish Right, especially of its extremist wing, was its unabashedly expansionist character, directed at Germany. Its leaders talked openly about extending Poland's western border to the river Oder and their favorite national hero was King Boleslaw the Brave, under whose rule, spanning the first quarter of the eleventh century, the Oder did indeed, albeit for a short time, form the Polish-German frontier.

Thus, on the eve of World War II, the Right made a rather spectacular recovery from the doldrums of the mid-1920s. Because of the nature of the political system, being firmly in the hands of the epigones of Pilsudski together with the Left and Center, it did not play a major role on the national scene. On the other hand, the National Party managed to score significant successes in local elections, especially in Western Poland, and appeared to be well on the way to becoming an important political actor in the years to come.

While the government, for a variety of reasons, was forced to tolerate the growth of the moderate Right, it was becoming increasingly concerned with the activities of the extreme Right and its advocacy of violence directed against the Jews and other adversaries. Faced with a threat of an impending war with Germany, the top priority for the regime was to mobilize the people and strengthen the nation's unity. Any activities that disrupted that process were condemned. In the final analysis, the government did not hesitate to outlaw some of the extremist organizations and send their leaders to the newly established concentration camp in North Eastern Poland. They were released shortly before the outbreak of the war.

The defeat in September 1939 was almost immediately followed by the creation of two centers of political activity: the government-in-exile, first in France and, after June 1940, in London, and an underground national political council in German-occupied Poland.

With the prewar regime thoroughly discredited, both institutions included representatives of political parties opposed to the post-Pilsudski government. The National party was represented in both bodies, alongside the Social Democrats, the Peasant party, and Christian Labor party. Despite frequent disagreements, their coalition managed to survive almost until the end of the war.

The situation within the military branch of the anti-German resistance diverged rather sharply from the overall consensus on the civilian side. Although some of the best known leaders of the prewar extreme Right joined the military underground organization, which ultimately began to call itself the Home Army (*Armia Krajowa* or

AK) and remained loyal to the London exile government throughout the war, others refused to do so and created their own independent military organization, known as the National Armed Forces (*Narodowe Sily Zbrojne* or *NSZ*).

The disagreement between the mainstream military leadership and the Right wing defectors concerned the attitude toward the Soviet Union. Between 1941 and 1943, the exile government in London maintained diplomatic relations with Moscow, despite the Soviet annexation of Eastern Poland in September 1939, in the wake of the Ribbentrop-Molotov treaty. The Nationalist fringe condemned what they called a surrender to the Kremlin, and their own military organization adopted a theory of "two enemies"—Germany and the Soviet Union—rather than Germany alone.

Even from a perspective of fifty years, the activities of the National Armed Forces remain highly controversial. Because of far-reaching secrecy surrounding their organization and operations, relatively little is known about them. Nonetheless, it is known that in addition to fighting the German occupation troops, the Nationalists also fought against the Red Army and Jewish partisans operating on Polish territory. The most controversial single act perpetrated by the National Armed Forces came toward the end of the war, when its largest and best known operating unit, the so-called Holy Cross Brigade (*Brygada Swietokrzyska*), retreating from the advancing Soviet army, received a right of passage from the *Wehrmacht* and, together with German units, managed to reach American forces in Eastern Bavaria, shortly before VE-Day in May 1945.[7]

This clear-cut example of collaboration with the enemy was almost universally condemned by all the Poles who prided themselves as being the only German-occupied people who did not produce a Quisling and, for all practical purposes, it discredited the extreme Right for many decades. While the passage of time managed to defuse some of the controversy, I would argue that even today, half a century after the fact, more people condemn rather than justify this particular act of the extreme Right.

As mentioned earlier, the National Party representatives remained within the exile government, although some of them opposed the reestablishment of diplomatic relations with the USSR in 1941. Below the government level, the most interesting aspect of activities sponsored by the Nationalists was the beginning of a propaganda campaign in favor of a postwar extension of Poland's western frontier to reach the Oder river.[8] Strongly reminiscent of the prewar agitation of the radical Right, this campaign appeared to make an impact on the postwar plans of the exile government leaders.

Following the break-off in diplomatic relations between the London government and the Kremlin, in the wake of the discovery of the Katyn massacre in April 1943, Moscow proceeded to organize a separate Polish army on Soviet soil and also established something called the Committee of Polish Patriots, viewed as a nucleus of a future communist government of Poland. This was not an easy task, especially in the absence of a sufficient number of Polish officers who had to be replaced by Red Army officers. In order to downgrade the Soviet input and to make the new army as Polish as possible, everything was being done to emphasize the strongly national character of the army. Indeed, some of the ideological pronouncements, produced by the Committee of Polish Patriots, appeared to have taken a leaf straight from the program of the prewar Right.[9] Similarly, the debates concerning the character of future Poland, conducted among the politruks of the so-called Berling Army, sounded surprisingly similar to the discussions conducted before the war by the leaders of the Right. Additional piquancy was provided by the fact that several of the leaders of the Patriots Committee as well as the high ranking political officers were Jews.

Communist Rule and the Right: 1945–1988

To no one's surprise, the Right was excluded from participation in the discussions leading to the formation of the Polish government which received Western recognition in July 1945. The National Party tried hard, but failed to obtain legal status in Poland in order to participate in the country's political life, despite receiving green light from the Soviets.[10] The few remaining detachments of the National Armed Forces continued to resist the communists but, by 1947, they, together with similar *Armia Kraiowa* units, which defied orders to stop fighting, were defeated. At the same time, several show trials of civilian National Party leaders resulted in a virtual decapitation and destruction of the organized Right. All signs pointed to the Right being permanently eliminated from the postwar Polish political landscape.

And yet, paradoxically, the circumstances surrounding the birth of the new, communist Poland, provided a potentially fertile ground for a future revival of the Right. The newly acquired former German territories pushed the country's western frontiers far beyond the limits envisaged by the extreme Right. The Holocaust, on the one hand, and the expulsion and/or the evacuation of both Germans and the Ukrainian and Belorussian minority, resulted in Poland, for the first time in its long history, becoming an almost 100 percent homogenous national state, a dream of the Nationalists. In the absence of other institutionalized resistance to communist rule, the role of the Catholic church, a traditional ally of the Right, was visibly enhanced. Finally, the imposition of communist rule generated mass resistance which, although passive, was bound to benefit any future attempts at the resurrection of the Right. While all these factors might be described as positive, there remained one phenomenon that could only be branded as negative, if not vicious: it was the persistent anti-Semitism, which survived the Holocaust and which manifested itself early on in the infamous Kielce program of the summer of 1946.

Still, officially at least, the Right was "excommunicated" and pronounced dead, especially after 1948, when in the wake of Tito's expulsion from the Cominform, "right wing, nationalist deviation" was proclaimed a cardinal sin in the communist book. A relatively little noticed fact was that the well known leader of the prewar Right wing extremist group, *Falanga*, Boleslaw Piasecki, was allowed to organize and lead a new Catholic lay organization. It was known as PAX; yet this did not seem to affect the overall picture in which there was no room for the political Right.[11]

Even today it is difficult to pinpoint the beginning of a turnaround in the fortunes of the Right in People's Poland. I am prepared to argue that it coincided with the re-emergence of anti-Semitism in 1955, fueled by the purges in the secret police apparatus. The highly publicized ouster and subsequent trials of mostly Jewish secret police officials, followed in early 1956 by the widely quoted anti-Semitic remarks of Nikita Khrushchev on the occasion of the selection of a new communist party leader, culminated in the resignation of the two most prominent Jewish members of the Politburo, Jakub Berman and Hilary Minc. The crucial two-month period preceding the upheaval of the "Polish October," witnessed a significant increase in anti-Semitic attacks orchestrated by hard line *apparatchiki* in the party, who tried desperately to blame the Jews for the excesses of the Stalinist period.

The outburst of anti-Semitism ended almost as quickly as it erupted, as the new Polish leader, Wladyslaw Gomulka, managed to restore order in the name of party unity. However, only a few years later, in the mid-1960s, there was a new wave of anti-Semitic attacks which coincided with the emergence within the party of a new, rather distinct faction, known as the "Partisans."

Headed by a self-proclaimed hero of the wartime communist military resistance, Mieczyslaw Moczar, the "Partisans" managed to attract some following within the Party. They appealed particularly to the younger generation of party members who were becoming increasingly disenchanted with Gomulka's policies. There is little doubt that the economic stagnation which became the trade mark of Gomulka's policies in the mid-1960s, resulting in a significant decline in social and political mobility, played a major role in the process of alienation. In addition to blaming Gomulka for the declining opportunities for advancement, the "Partisans" singled out the intelligentsia and the Jews as being largely responsible for their plight. Presumably, in order to attract greater following, they also occasionally criticized the leadership for being over-dependent on the Kremlin and tried to capitalize on traditional Polish patriotism by demanding preferential treatment for the veterans of World War II, regardless of their political coloration.

Although there is substantial evidence suggesting that the "Partisans" ultimately fell victim to their own propaganda and that they never succeeded in attracting a mass following, it is also clear that Gomulka felt sufficiently threatened. He decided to settle the score with both the "Partisans" and other opposition groups within the Party, by launching a vicious anti-Semitic and anti-intellectual campaign that reached its zenith in March 1968.

By now, there is a considerable body of literature devoted to the examination of March 1968 and hence there is no need to recapitulate the various developments.[12] Suffice it to say that Poland, at the time of March 1968, came closer to becoming a neo-Fascist state than at any time during its independent existence. The extreme Right, long presumed dead and buried, returned with a vengeance.

Looking back at the situation preceding the events, one is struck by its similarity to the conditions existing in the country in the mid-1930s, which spawned the revival of the Right. In both cases, the government in power was clearly highly inefficient and unable to sustain economic growth and social advancement. Although the economic situation in the 1960s was a far cry from the post-depression period of the 1930s, one could postulate in both cases the emergence of a "revolution of declining expectations." While the pseudo-Fascists of March 1968 were not unemployed, their living standard either remained constant or grew very slowly, in contrast to the dynamism of the 1940s and 1950s. Moreover, the aspirants to the exalted status of intelligentsia, recruited primarily from the peasant and working class millieus, found their opportunities for advancement in shorter and shorter supply.

Clearly, someone was at fault. In addition to blaming the Gomulka regime for its indecisiveness, the neo-Fascists focused their anger on the two traditional scapegoats: the Jews and the intellectuals. As the record shows, the viciousness of anti-Semitic attacks in the mass media closely resenbled the anti-Jewish propaganda in the early years of Nazi rule in Germany, and the same applied to a large extent to the treatment of the intellectuals.

One may speculate that if left undisturbed, the March 1968 movement could have led directly to the creation of a new political system in Poland, combining the worst features of both the extreme Right and the extgreme Left. This possibility was apparently too much to contemplate for the Gomulka regime, which untimately managed to re-establish some semblance of stability. In this Gomulka was strongly supported by the Kremlin which has always harbored serious doubts about Moczar and his "Partisans," and faced with the "Prague spring" in Czechoslovakia, Leonid Brezhnev was not willing to become directly involved in restoring normalcy in Poland.

It took almost a decade for the fortunes of the Right to turn around once again. In the second half of the 1970s, the creation of the Workers defense Committee (*Komitet Obrony Robotnikow* or KOR) was paralleled by the emergence of a Movement for the Protection of Human and Civil Rights (*Ruch Obrony Praw Czlowieka i Obywatela* or *POPCiO*) which, together with one of its splinter groups, the Confederacy for Independent Poland (*Konfederacia Polski Nieoodlealei* or *KPN*) adopted a stance definitely Right of center. Right from the start it became clear that there was little love lost between *KOR* on the one hand, and the two other organizations on the other, the latter of which soon introduced a note of anti-Semitism in their attacks on the Workers Defense Committee.[13] Perhaps not surprisingly, the anti-Semitic tone was also picked up by the Catholic church, which also criticized *KOR* with an apparent *imprimatur* of Cardinal Wyszynski, basking in the new glory bestowed on the church by the election of the Polish Pope.

The dramatic events of 1980–1981, which began with the birth of "Solidarity" and terminated with the imposition of martial law, seemed to overshadow the escalating conflict between *KOR* and *KPN*, as both of them disappeared from the political scene. Still, the bacillus of anti-Semitism, so carefully nurtured by the Right, managed to survive. It soon found two powerful supporters—once again, the Catholic church and a new, conservative faction within the Communist Party, led by Stefan Olszowski, a prominent member of the ruling oligarchy. The Catholic hierarchy, possibly stung by a criticism of its attacks on *KOR*, became more nuanced in its attacks on "Solidarity," which it accused of being dominated by Trotskyites and other Left wing extremists. Although the church, headed after Wyszynski's death in 1981 by cardinal Jozef Glemp, was very careful to avoid any references to anti-Semitism, the true meaning of the various pronouncements and declarations was unmistakable and resembled similar criticism of organized labor voiced by the Right in the interwar period.

Olszowski's brainchild was something called the Patriotic Association "Grünwald," which surfaced out of nowhere in 1981.[14] Although initially dismissed as a crude joke, *Grünwald* survived for several years, even during the period of martial law, generously funded out of Communist Party funds. It represented a throwback to March 1968 and it was clearly intended to attract and mobilize the same elements in Polish society that participated in the March excesses. It was virulently anti-Semitic and anti-intellectual, but this time, in contrast to March 1968, it gained very few adherents and ended the same way it began, as a rather bizarre joke. Thirteen years after March 1968, it was becoming clear that an overwhelming majority of the Polish population was beginning to have second thoughts about the anti-Semitic campaign which it saw as causing a major international embarrassment, tarnishing Poland's image abroad.

The turbulent eight-year period following the imposition of martial law in 1981, has been extensively examined in the literature and there is no need to discuss it again. With the lifting of military rule in 1983, the stage was set for what turned out to be the final confrontation between the decaying communist regime and the opposition, spearheaded by "Solidarity," which although outlawed, has succeeded in creating and maintaining an effective underground organization. In time, the growing anti-communist resistance was strengthened by a groundswell of intellectual opposition, including university students, most visibly illustrated by a phenomenal increase in the volume of illegally published newspapers, journals, books and pamphlets.

The record shows that the Right's role in the anti-communist resistance campaign of the 1980s was marginal. To be sure, *KPN* did engage in some sporadic grandstanding, such as organizing demonstrations on Poland's traditional national holidays, while periodically launching *ad personam* attacks on "Solidarity" leaders, often tinged with anti-Semitism, but for all practical purposes, the leadership of the anti-communist opposition remained firmly in the hands of individuals closely identified with former *KOR* and "Solidarity." Thus, not surprisingly, the Right was not represented in the "Round Table" negotiations in the spring of 1989, which paved the way to the semi-free parliamentary elections in June of that year. The elections themselves represented a clear triumph for Lech Walesa and "Solidarity" and it appeared that both *KPN* and some Right wing lunatic fringe groups would be confined to playing a minor role in post-1989 Polish politics.

This was not to be, however. On the one hand, the postelection period began to witness a veritable explosion in the number of political parties and groupings of various hues, stretching across the entire spectrum, from Left to Right. On the Right, *KPN* was joined by the resurrected National Party (*SN*) and a newly formed Christian-National Union (*Zjednoczenie Chrzescijanski-Narodowe* or *ZChN*). *SN* proved to be only a shadow of its former self and succeeded in attracting few members in contrast to *ZChN* which, from the beginning, enjoyed the support of the Church and managed to build up considerable following. It should be made clear that although all the parties—*KPN, SN,* and *ZChN*—were clearly located Right of center, none of them could be classified, at least in 1989–1990, as radical or extremist. Still, their presence provided a guarantee that the traditions of the Polish Right, going back more than a hundred years, would be preserved in post-communist Poland.

On the other hand, while a revival of the Right after the collapse of communism could have been easily anticipated and, as such, did not raise many eyebrows, the outcome of the first round of presidential elections in November 1990 was most surprising and created considerable concern about future political stability in the country. The defeat of Prime Minister Tadeusz Mazowiecki, representing the political center, by a virtually unknown, Stanislaw Tyminski, whose campaign was heavily sprinkled with Right wing populist if not neo-fascist overtones, illustrated the fragility of Polish politics in the aftermath of the collapse of communism which made it highly vulnerable to Rightist demands.

The fact that the official candidate of *KPN*, Leszek Moczulski, attracted little support, did not invalidate the fear and suspicion that the end of forty-odd years of communism unleashed forces in Polish society that could be easily manipulated by the Right, using the traditional slogans and appeals to rampant nationalism, xenophobia, anti-Semitism and anti-intellectualism. Although Tyminski was soundly beaten by Walesa in the second round of the elections, the year 1990 ended on a sour note which greatly dampened the enthusiasm of the previous year. The highly publicized split within "Solidarity" and the low rate of voters participation in the elections, did not help matters.

The question still remained whether the vote in support of Tyminski reflected a permanent realignment of Polish politics in favor of the Right, or whether it was simply a vote of protest against the high cost of post-communist transition, comparable to the 1954 French elections which introduced the concept of *Poujadisme* to political vocabulary.

By hindsight, it was the latter interpretation that turned out to be correct. After tying to capitalize on his remarkable showing, Tyminski quickly discovered that his support proved ephemeral and soon both he and his party "X," which he created, disappeared from the Polish political map. Undoubtedly, the decision of the Catholic church to throw its support behind Walesa—after a rather lengthy ambivalent stance—appeared to be decisive. Still, the episode showed very clearly that despite the setback there was potential reservoir of support for the Right that could be tapped in the future by a demagogue smarter and more attractive than Tyminski.

Conclusions

Looking back at the seventy-year long history of the political Right in Poland, one can distinguish several cycles in its fortunes. The Right started reasonably strongly in the early days of the Second Republic, only to fade away following the May 1926 coup. It came back about a decade later but its revival was then interrupted by World War II. Seemingly eliminated for good from the Polish political arena under communist rule, it staged another comeback in the mid-1950s, continued to linger on for another ten years or so, and then exploded in March 1968. During the next two decades the Right maintained a rather low profile but, as shown above, it did not disappear entirely from the political landscape.

Considering the odds against it, the Right proved to be most resilient and skillful at overcoming the various obstacles and surviving both the dozen or so years of bureaucratic-military regime between the wars and more than forty years of communist rule after the war. The obvious question to be asked at this stage concerns the secret of the Right's success at surviving.

Looking for an explanation, one can identify several factors that have nurtured Rightist tendencies in Poland throughout the last seven decades. In many respects they are identical to, or closely resemble, the conditions favoring the Right in other countries of Eastern Europe. There is little doubt that radical nationalism, traditionally present in countries, which for a variety of reasons makes some people feel insecure within the existing international environment, is one of the factors. Another one is, most likely, a reaction against a broadly defined process of modernization which, as a rule, destroys the traditional, mostly peasant-rooted social and economic links and attachments, exposing an individual to an uncertain future. Disenchantment with the brief democratic interludes as well as the fear of the extreme Left also played a role.

In addition there is, as always, the impact of *differentio specifica*, the national specificity, which in the case of Poland means the prominent political and social role played by the Roman Catholic Church. Moreover, the carefully preserved memories of the past glory of Poland stretching "from [Baltic] sea to [Black] sea" also made their contribution as did the presence of many national and ethnic minorities on the territory considered by the Poles to be their historic homeland.

If true, then it can be rather easily seen that many of the conditions survived essentially unscathed during the past seventy years. Nationalism is still very much present and the process of the communist-sponsored economic and social transformation created many dislocations that will need time to be resolved. More than forty years of communist rule ended with the Left being discredited, at least for some time to come. Finally, the Catholic Church at the end of the 1980s appeared as strong as ever and has not hesitated to let everyone know it.

Hence, in conclusion, it is not really surprising that the Right in Poland survived rather comfortably, despite many obstacles in its path. The question that still must be posed concerns the future of the Right in post-communist Poland, but the answer to it deserves a separate treatment that, if only for reasons of space, cannot be accomplished here.

NOTES

1. Eugene Weber, "The Right: An Introduction," in Hans Rogger and Eugene Weber, eds., *The European Right* (Berkeley and Los Angeles: University of California Press, 1965), pp. 1–28.

2. Piotr Wandycz, *The Lands of Partitioned Poland, 1795–1918* (Seattle and London: University of Washington Press, 1974), pp. 288–295.

3. Seymour Martin Lipset, *Political Man* (Garden City, NY: Doubleday & Co., 1960), pp. 131–137.

4. For details, see Edward D. Wynot, Jr., *Polish Politics in Transition: The Camp of National Unity and the Struggle for Power, 1935–1939* (Athens, Georgia: University of Georgia Press, 1974), *passim.*

5. For excellent brief accounts, see Andrzej Micewski, *Wspolrzadzic czy nie klamac* (Paris: Libella, 1978), pp. 13–19, and Zbigniew S. Siemaszko, *Narodowe Sily Zbrojne* (London: Odnowa, 1982), pp. 11–28.

6. Stanley G. Payne, "Falangism," in David L. Sills, ed., *International Encyclopedia of Social Sciences* (n.p.: The Macmillan Company and the Free Press, 1968), pp. 288–291.

7. Siemaszko, *Narodowe Sily Zbrojne*, pp. 153–172.

8. Sarah M. Terry, *Poland's Place in Europe: General Sikorski and the Origin of the Oder-Neisse Line, 1939–1943* (Princeton, NJ: Princeton University Press, 1983), pp. 66–79.

9. Krystyna Kersten, "Wladza - Komunizm - Zydzi," *Polityka* (Warsaw), No. 27, July 6, 1991.

10. Krystyna Kersten, *Narodziny Systemu Wladzy: Polska, 1943–1948* (Paris: Libella, 1986), pp. 161–163.

11. Lucjan Blit, *The Eastern Pretender* (London: Hutchinson, 1965), *passim.* See also, Micewski, *Wspolrzadric czy nie klamac*, pp. 25ff.

12. For a recent comprehensive study, see Jerzy Eisler, *Marzec 1968* (Warsaw: Panstwowe Wydawnictwo Naukowe, 1991).

13. Jan Jozef Lipski, *KOR* (London: Aneks, 1983), pp. 106–107.

14. For origin of Grunwald, see Tadeusz Szafar, "Anti-Semitism: A Trustry Weapon," in Abraham Brumberg, ed., *Poland: Genesis of a Revolution* (New York: Random House, 1983), pp. 109–122.

WHAT'S RIGHT, WHAT'S LEFT, AND WHAT'S WRONG IN POLISH POLITICS?

Sarah M. Terry

Introduction

Six months after Poland's first fully free parliamentary elections in October 1991, the seemingly endless rash of unsettling headlines about the country's perilouss political and economic conditions underscores the timeliness of the topic of this volume. For most of their brief existence, the fragile minority coalition and fragmented parliament have been locked in a state of near paralysis over core issues of economic policy. Following two years of bruising recession, industrial production and real incomes continued to fall in the first quarter of 1992. The public mood was so dyspeptic that nearly 50 percent of eligible voters sat out last October's elections. And now, as spring prepares to give way to summer, Warsaw is rife with rumors about the intentions of world-be strong-man President Lech Walesa, including even the possibility of a Pilsudski-style military coup or some other form of dictatorial rule.

As alarming as these developments may seem, do they necessarily reflect the emergence of a powerful, even dominant, Right-wing authoritarian orientation in Polish politics? I think not. Indeed, the central thesis of this paper will be that it is premature to speak of a resurgence of the political Right in Poland in the traditional sense of that word, and will be argued along these lines. In Section I, using data from recent public opinion polls, I will attempt to show that, although some elements of the essential social basis for a Right-wing domination do exist, they are offset by a variety of countervailing tendencies. In am referring to an overwhelming preoccupation among virtually all strata of the Polish population with economic issues that typically underpin a centrist or social-democratic orientation. Section II will examine the October 1991 parliamentary elections with an eye toward demonstrating, first, that the present post-communist/post-Solidarity party structure cannot easily be analyzed along a traditional Right-Left spectrum and, second, that the election results did not show a popular preference for "Rightist" political values. In the concluding section, I will address what I see as the most serious threats to continuing democratization in Poland–namely, political fragmentation and institutional paralysis, with predictable consequences for the country's painful economic transition—which, if they persist,—could make a return to authoritarianism (of whatever political coloration) an increasingly attractive option.

1. Polls of Poles: The Social Basis of Post-Communist Politics

This section is based on two sets of polling data. The primary source is an extensive public opinion survey conducted by the Times Mirror Center for the People and the Press in May/June 1991 in twelve European countries.[1] I will draw here mostly on the Polish results but, where relevant, will use comparisons from the other East European countries included in the survey (Bulgaria, Czechoslovakia, and Hungary). This data will be supplemented by a second set, consisting of a series of polls commissioned by the United States Information Agency between April 1990 and September 1991, plus partial data from a January 1992 poll. Although less comprehensive than the Times-Mirror survey—with the exception of the 1992 data, they deal only with Poland and cover a more narrow range of issues–the USIA polls provide both broad corroboration of the Times-Mirror findings and perspective over time.[2]

Before proceeding with the data, two caveats are in order. The first concerns the potential problems of interpreting polling results from Eastern Europe. Any public opinion survey is obviously a snapshot that records society's attitudes at a given point in time. While in a more or less stable-state situation popular moods tend to shift slowly, in the tumultuous political and socio-economic climate that has characterized Eastern Europe since 1989, public moods may be much more volatile (hence the utility of the USIA series as a control). The second caveat, in the context of the focus of this volume, concerns the definition of the "political Right." Are we talking primarily about the radical authoritarian, quasi-Fascist Right (emphasizing chauvinistic, xenophobic and militaristic values)? Do we have in mind a more moderate Christian-Democratic orientation (emphasizing Catholic fundamentalism, a big-business bias and a less chauvinistic form of nationalism)? Or do we also include the liberal Right of the classical Adam Smith/Milton Friedman stripe (emphasizing more or less unregulated free-market capitalism)? Because the first two categories have an infinitely longer genealogy in Eastern Europe than the third (a recent importation represented by the Balcerowicz/Bielecki team in Poland and Vaclav Klaus in Czechoslovakia), the following discussion will focus on the authoritarian-chauvinistic and Christian-national variants.

These two caveats when considered together with the volatility of the public mood, not only in Poland but throughout Eastern Europe, suggest a cautionary approach to all polling data. The results of any particular survey must be read in a specific timeframe; in addition, in light of the enormous complexity of the post-communist transitions, it is crucial that indicators of unrealistic expectations or frustrations with the process not automatically be construed as evidence of antidemocratic or authoritarian tendencies. In the case of Poland, it is also important to keep in mind that this was the first East European country to embark on the course of democratization and economic "shock therapy." Thus, by the time of the *Times-Mirror* survey, the Poles were further into the deflationary spiral, psychological as well as economic, than the others. With these considerations in mind, let me proceed to highlight the data.

From the point of view of Poland's vulnerability to Right-wing chauvinistic tendencies, the most damning aspects of the Times-Mirrow poll concerned attitudes toward other ethnic groups, where the Poles emerged by far as the least tolerant of the East European countries surveyed. Presented with the statement "I do not have much in common with people of other ethnic groups and races," an astonishing 74 percent agreed, compared with 17 percent of the Bulgarians, 31 percent of the Czechoslovaks, and 27 percent of the Hungarians [see Table I.1 for a detailed breakdown]. When asked to rate various ethnic groups in Poland, the results were overwhelmingly unfavorable, and distinctly more negative than for similar questions asked in the other East European countries. Although ethnic minorities comprise only a small fraction of the Polish population, only the Lithuanians came out with a "favorable" rating of more than 50 percent [Table I.2]. This might be partially explained by the possibility that many responses were less a reflection of attitudes toward minorities within

Poland than of anxieties about relations with neighboring countries to which they belonged. In this case, Lithuanians would have scored relatively high in the spring of 1991 because of their stalwart resistance to Soviet bullying.[3] Whatever the reasoning, the Poles scored low on ethnic tolerance. (In the other three countries, groups receiving less than a 50 percent favorable rating were the exception rather than the rule).

Other categories of questions that could be construed as indicators of Right-wing tendencies concerned attitudes toward patriotism, national security and defense. Here the results suggested a marked degree of anxiety over Poland's security but were not out of keeping with geopolitical realities and, on balance, certainly could not be described as reflecting a bias toward "militarism" (as the preliminary *Times-Mirror* analysis suggested.) When asked if they were patriotic, 76 percent of the Polish respondents agreed (only slightly more than for the other East European countries); asked if parts of neighboring countries "really belong to us," 61 percent said "yes" (fewer than for Hungarians but ahead of Czechoslovaks and Bulgarians); asked if "we should be willing to fight for our country . . . right or wrong," 48 percent of the Poles agreed (fewer than the Bulgarians but well ahead of the Czechoslovaks and Hungarians).[4]

Where the Poles diverged most sharply from their neighbors was in reference to their assessment of external threats and how best to ensure national security. Both the Times-Mirror and USIA polls showed a significant level of concern with a potential Soviet (or post-Soviet) threat. According to the former (taken two and one-half months before the abortive August coup), 58 percent said the Soviet Union was having a "mostly bad or very bad influence" on Polish affairs, with another 24 percent expressing ambivalence (both "good and bad influence"); the latter show an even higher level of concern, with "unfavorable" opinions rising steadily from 58 percent in April 1990 to a high of 77 percent in May 1991, before slipping back to 69 percent just after the failed August coup. On the specific issue of troop withdrawls, 61 percent thought the transfer of Soviet troops from the former GDR to the USSR might present serious security problems, while 44 percent thought there was a chance Moscow would change its mind about the withdrawals (with another 14 percent uncertain). According to USIA data, the failure of the August coup somewhat diminished Poles' fears of external aggression (from 65 to 60 percent from May to September 1991); but concern over the impact of the breakup of the USSR remained high. In the September poll, 70 percent named Soviet instability, nuclear proliferation or mass migration as the "most serious threat" to Polish security.[5]

In addition to perceiving a greater threat from the former Soviet Union, the Poles were alone among the East Europeans in seeing Germany also as a potential military threat, with 40 percent voicing this concern in September 1991 (although other data show rather mixed attitudes toward Germany).[6] As to how best to ensure national security, the Poles were well ahead of others in stating (despite the dire economic situation) that too little was being spent on national defense, and that "the best way to ensure peace is through military strength" [Tables I. 4-5]. They were also more likely to favor some form of association with NATO over a regional defense alliance [Table I.3].

Rather than try to draw conclusions about how the above opinions and perceptions could influence political orientations, it might be more useful to recall the peculiarities of the situation in which the Poles found themselves in this period. In May/June 1991, Poland was still excluded from the "Pentagonale" (originally "Alpine/Adria") regional security grouping—ostensibly because it belonged geographically to the Baltic region, but more likely because the other East European countries were reluctant to assume the baggage of Poland's historically troubled relations with its two powerful neighbors. In addition, Poland was the only East European country that had not yet negotiated an agreement for Soviet troop withdrawal—and where, in the prelude to the abortive August coup, the Soviet side was proving demanding and truculent. Small wonder, under the circumstances, that the average Pole saw NATO association and a high level of defense spending as keys to national security. (It is interesting to note that following Poland's inclusion in the "Pentagonale" group in July 1991, favorable ratings of Hungary and Czechoslovakia, suggesting a more positive attitude toward a regional security arrangement, rose significantly.)[7]

In another area that could presage a swing of popular opinion toward some form of authoritarianism, a number of questions elicited evidence of growing frustration with the political system. Walesa's performance as President received only a 43 percent approval rating (a mere 6 percent indicating "strong" approval) versus 45 percent disapproving (15 percent "strongly") and 12 percent expressing no opinion. The USIA data were somewhat more negative; in both the

May and September 1991 surveys, two-thirds of respondents thought Walesa was doing a "fairly bad" or "very bad" job. Parliament fared even worse: In the *Times-Mirror* poll, 33 percent said it was having a "good" influence (only 2 percent "very good"), 41 percent a "bad" influence (10 percent "very bad"), with the remaining 26 percent indicating ambivalence or expressing no opinion. Again, the latest USIA data are more negative: In both the May and September 1991 surveys, only 26 percent expressed confidence in parliament, with 69 percent indicating "not much" or "no" confidence. Moreover, the USIA data show a sharp decline in popular approval from the April 1990 poll, which showed a 56 percent "confidence" rating of parliament and a 63 percent positive rating of the government (while confidence in the army rose from 59 to 71 percent in the same period).[8]

When asked, in the Times-Mirror survey, about the electorate's ability to influence the work of government, the responses were overwhelmingly negative. To the statement "people like me don't have any say about what the government does," 87 percent agreed (61 percent "completely"). To "generally speaking elected officials lose touch with the people pretty quickly," 89 percent agreed (49 percent "completely"). To "most elected officials care what people like me think," 68 percent disagreed. To all three questions, the Polish responses were more negative on the performance of the political system than in the other three East European countries surveyed, but only marginally so. To a fourth question, whether "voting gives people like me some say about how the government runs things," the Polish responses were slightly less pessimistic; 41 percent agreed, compared to 52 percent who disagreed and 7 percent who had no opinion. Nonetheless, the total of the 52 and 7 percent who lacked faith in the power of the ballot came eerily close to the percentage of the electorate that failed to vote in the October parliamentary elections. By the time of the January 1992 USIA poll-three months after the elections and three months into the ensuing governmental crisis—a mere 28 percent of respondents believed voting gives people a say.[9]

A final category of issues that might indicate susceptibility to Right-wing views, especially of the isolationist/xenophobic variety, concerns attitudes toward foreign investment and economic activity. Of the four East European countries surveyed, Poland showed a relatively high level of resistance to foreign economic involvement: 29 percent cited "economic domination by the West" as one of their greatest fears (ahead of "military attack by a neighboring country," "the economic collapse of the Soviet Union" and "a flood of refugees into our country.[10] Only 46 percent thought foreign investors were having a "very good" or "mostly good" influence (vs. 66 percent in Hungary), while 15 percent expressed negative views, 39 percent had no opinion or voiced uncertainty; 25 percent (far above levels elsewhere) disapproved of companies based in other countries selling their products in Poland.[11] In all three cases, however, the responses should be read in the context of the specific situation. On the first two questions, "West" should be read in the first instance as "Germany"; by Spring 1991, Germans (private individuals as well as corporate entities) were actively buying assets (especially land and especially in former German territories in western Poland) at highly favorable exchange rates. On the third question, Polish farmers and some industrial producers could well have felt their interests were being sacrificed to subsidized West European producers by Poland's open-borders trade policy, in contrast to the EC's strict quotas on Polish exports. Indeed, by the summer of 1991, the need to reintroduce trade barriers to protect domestic producers was the subject of active debate and subsequent policy revision.

But all of the above provides only a partial and very incomplete image of the current state of Polish public opinion. The other more important part of the picture shows an overwhelming preoccupation with personal economic and general social welfare concerns that are typical of a centrist to center-Left orientation. In other words, if you ask a Pole a specific question implying some variant of a rightist orientation, the answer may well be in the affirmative. But ask what concerns him most, then questions of ethnic relations, xenophobia, national pride and security, lost territories, etc., fade into secondary, even tertiary importance. Asked various open-ended questions—for instance, what is the most serious problem facing your country, what do you like most/least about recent changes, etc.—the overwhelming preponderance of responses in the *Times-Mirror* survey related to the economic uncertainities of transition. Similarly, the USIA data show that seven out of ten Poles (along with similar majorities of Czechs, Slovaks and Hungarians) defined democracy primarily in economic terms. Asked what is "the most important characteristic in a democracy, 42 percent said "economic prosperity in the country," another 14 percent each answered "a government that guarantees economic equality among its citizens" and "a government that guarantees. . . basic economic needs of its people."[12]

The problem with these answers and with those to questions targeted on specific economic issues is not that they demonstrate inclinations of either a Left-or Right-wing variety, but that they demonstrate profound confusion over what can and should be expected in the transition from a Soviet-style centrally-planned economy to some form of free-market or mixed-market economy. By now, it has become a post-communist cliche that East Europeans expect their new governments to provide the best of both worlds: on the one hand, the efficiency and prosperity of the free market combined, on the other hand, with the social safety net promised (but never really delivered) by their defunct "socialist" systems. Few observers of the contemporary East European scene would deny that there is some truth to this characterization; but it is also an oversimplification that masks a complex reality in which anxieties and pessimism about the present and near-term future mix with hopes for the longer term.

At the macro level, 80 percent of Poles (the same as for Hungarians and Czechoslovaks, slightly more than for Bulgarians) approved of efforts to establish a free-market economy, although they were almost evenly divided between those who felt the pace was too fast, too slow, or about right.[13] Beyond that, responses indicated a high level of ambivalence over the direction of systemic change, with a lack of control over personal success and continued reliance on state responsibility for social welfare correlating positively (and incongruously) with approval of free market principles. On the one hand, 66 percent agreed that success in life is determined by forces outside one's own control; 64 percent that hard work offers little guarantee of success; 86 percent that the state should guarantee everyone food and basic shelter; 89 percent that everyone should have equal opportunity for success; 91 percent that it was the responsibility of the state to take care of the very poor.[14]

On the other hand, 85 percent admired people who get rich from working hard; 62 percent agreed that people who run their own businesses have a good influence (with 24 percent ambivalent); 57 percent believed that large private companies have a good influence (32 percent ambivalent); 57 percent that prices should be allowed to increase to make more goods available, even if everyone cannot afford them; 56 percent that unemployment must be accepted if that's what it takes to improve and modernize the economy; 51 percent that people who start private businesses should be allowed to make as much profit as they can (vs. 41 percent who said government should set limits to profit). Asked what role the state and private sectors should play in various areas of the economy, Poles opted for a mixed economy, with a larger role for the state sector in heavy industry, infrastructure and health care, and for the private sector in agriculture, services and light industry.[15]

Another important indicator of resistance to the Rightist orientation in Poland concerns attitudes toward the role of the Catholic Church in politics. Despite continued high levels of religious observance, Poles have reacted very negatively to the Episcopate's shift from supporting the anti-communist opposition to pushing its own social/clerical agenda. For instance, to the open-ended question "What do you like least about the way things have changed," 11 percent volunteered "the incredible influence of the Church in political life (vs. 64 percent who cited economic issues). Asked whether the Church was a generally good influence, only 45 percent agreed, 39 percent said "bad," while 16 percent were ambivalent or had no opinion; among the East European countries, the Church's favorable rating was lowest in Poland and the unfavorable rating was highest. But the most striking finding came in answer to the question "Does the Church play too great a role in the political life of this country," 70 percent of Poles agreed, two to four times more than in the other East European countries; only 1 percent said "too small a role." Moreover, two-thirds supported a woman's right to an abortion in the early stages of pregnancy.[16]

Finally, despite the evidence cited earlier that most Poles lack faith in their ability to influence government, responses to a number of questions in the *Times-Mirror* survey demonstrated a considerable degree of maturity and flexibility on political issues. On the touchy issues of how to deal with the old regime, Poles took a relatively tolerant attitude. Fifty percent agreed that officials responsible for past policies should be identified and held accountable (vs. a high of 63 percent in the former GDR and a low of 41 percent in Hungary), while 42 percent said "look to the future and forget"). At the same time, fully 79 percent (the high for the region) said that top-level people at state enterprises and agencies should be kept if they were "doing a good job"; and, asked the open-ended question "What do you like least about the way things have changed," only 3 percent cited "not settling accounts with the former *nomenklatura.*"[17] On more general political issues, "only" 66 percent approved of the change to a multiparty system (a low among the East Europeans), with another 16

percent unsure; but perhaps this was due to confusion over the proliferation of political parties following the break-up of Solidarity. To
the statements "Good political leaders are willing to make compro-
mises in order to get the job done" and "It's necessary for the future
of our country to be involved in world affairs" (implying a balanced
and moderate international posture), 69 and 83 percent respectively
answered in the affirmative.[18]

If there is a danger lurking behind these inconsistent data, it is
not that a coherent social base exists for the resurgence of a powerful
Right. The real danger is that underlying support for political and
economic reform will be eroded by a combination of prolonged and
deep recession and governmental gridlock. Indeed, two years into the
transition, there is growing evidence that this is precisely what is
happening. I will return to this issue in the concluding section.

II. The 1991 Elections: the Cacophony
of (Unaccustomed) Democratic Choice

Several months prior to the October 1991 parliamentary elections, the following satirical comment on political orientations appeared in the most influential Warsaw daily:[19]

At last, slowly, we are beginning to discover what differenti-
ates the Right from the Left in Poland. To clarify matters,
we present the basic features of both orientations:

The RIGHT	The LEFT
Opposes the binding legal order; calls for rejecting the law and applying in its place the principle of social justice.	Regards the letter of the law as holy and sees every violation of it as a violation of the natural order
Recognizes the principle that all money and wealth derive from dishonest sources and have been acquired at the expense of others. Those who have amassed wealth should be subject to confisca- or, at least, investigation.	Strives by every means to establish propertied groups in Poland, seeing in them the basis of social well-being. Regards the source of wealth as the private matter of the individual acquiring it.

Declares itself for the rapid removal of various properties from present owners and placing them in other hands.	Declares itself for the inviolability of the right of ownership.
Categorically opposes the inflow of foreign capital.	Demands the acceptance of all forms large-scale capital investment.
Favors subsidies for state industry.	Favors the wrecking of state industry.
Unions are the closest allies of the Right. They call for guaranteeing the legitimate rights of the working people, as well as raising the living standard of wage-earners.	Union activity is recognized as a factor in the destabilization of the economy.
Takes on the fate of working people; warns against social pauperization, tearfully recalls the fate of the peasantry. Supports strikes.	Sees workers and peasants as demoralized by the existing system of privileges; is for controlled unemployment and a limit on the right to strike.

As is clear from the above, the program of the Right in Poland is presently the program of the *PPR*. In turn, the Left has accepted the program of the Central Union of Polish Industry, Trade and Finance 'Leviathan.'

The above passage is admittedly a whimsical (and oversimplified) version of "what's right and what's left" in the contemporary Polish political spectrum. But it also attests to the extensive degree of disorientation in post-communist politics, not only in Poland but in much of Eastern Europe, with most parties seeking to disassociate themselves as much as possible from the legacy of the communist past, while still appealing to the populist, social-welfare expectations of that legacy. Before looking at the orientations of the parties that participated in the October elections, however, let me take brief note of two problems of a historical and institutional nature that have impeded the emergence of a functional party system.

In an insightful essay on "A Political System under Construction," Miroslawa Grabowska, a researcher at the Institute of Political Studies of the Polish Academy of Sciences, compared the context of political transition in 1918 with that in 1989/90. In the earlier period, a reborn Poland emerged from partition and war with a well-defined and more or less complete spectrum of political parties. The key players—from Right to Left, the National Democrats (or *"Endecja"*), the Polish Peasant Party (*PSL*), the Polish Socialist Party (PPS), and the Social Democracy of the Kingdom of Poland and Lithuania (*SdKPiL*, which together with the *PPS*-Lewica would form the first Polish Communist Party)–could all trace their beginnings back to the 1890s. Each had a leadership experienced in political and social activism, a distinctive program, and its own press. She notes, in addition, that the southern European countries that experienced transitions from authoritarian to democratic rule in the late 1970s and early 1980s also benefitted from well-developed party structures and that

> the degree of organization of political forces was an important factor in the very process of creating a democratic order–and, especially, the durability of that order.

By contrast, the transition process may begin "in a situation in which political options have not yet been articulated, and political groupings do not exist or are poorly organized and uninstitutionalized." In such a situation, it is the "process itself that becomes the formative factor," while "political parties react to events and changes rather than shape them"; the transition then "resembles an airplane with no one at the controls. . ."[20]

Clearly, the current transition more closely approximates the latter scenario, beginning as it did with the progressive unravelling of the two central elements of the Polish political landscape over the preceding decade. The first was the old communist-led ruling coalition— the Polish United Workers' Party (*PZPR*) itself plus its junior (often malcontent) partners, the United Peasant Party, the Democratic Party, and several small regime-oriented Catholic groups (most notably PAX). The second of course, was the opposition Solidarity movement which–despite (or perhaps partly because of) its survival through a decade of acute crisis, martial law and harassment—had always been a broad-based organization riddled with fault lines, along both ideological and personality vectors, that could be kept in check only so long as it was facing a more or less cohesive adversary. Within a year of Solidarity's stunning sweep of the seats it was allowed to contest in the June 1989 parliamentary elections (see discussion below), and spurred on by Walesa's attempt to reclaim the political spotlight by declaring a "war at the top," the movement splintered into at least a dozen parts.

The resulting fragmentation of the political spectrum has led to a cacophony of parties—many little more than *"partie kanapowe"* [couch parties], so called because all of their members can fit on one sofa–that defies analysis along a traditional Right-Left lines. As an alternative, Dr. Grabowska has provided a three-dimensional grid on which to track political orientations. The first dimension concerns the attitude of a given party toward the future economic system, including the extent of free-market reforms, the pace of reform, and the role of the state in protecting weaker strata of society. The second concerns the structure of political power, including such contentious issues as presidential vs. parliamentary rule and the type of electoral system (majoritarian vs. proportional representation). The third, at least in Poland, concerns the "spiritual" realm, especially the divisive issue of Church-state relations as well as whether politics should be defined in terms of "nation" ("us" vs. "others") or in terms of civil society. Parties that support a "Rightist" position on one dimension often take a "Leftist" stance on another, with the result that political coalition-building has become a moving crap-shoot in which potential alliances on one set of issues come unglued over irreconcilable differences on others.[21]

Ironically, the second structural problem is a direct outcome of the "historic compromise" that led to the formation of the first non-communist government in Eastern Europe. The April 1989 Roundtable Agreement extended the "leading role" of the *PZPR*-led coalition, while giving the Solidarity-led opposition a minority voice in parliament—an imperfect bargain agreed to by the latter in the belief that communism was historically a spent force and that this would only be an interim (if necessary) arrangement. Accordingly, the former was guaranteed 65 percent of seats in the *Sejm*, the lower and more powerful house; the latter was allowed to contest the remaining 35 percent of *Sejm* seats (161 out of 460), plus all 100 seats in a reconstituted Senate (abolished in 1947) the latter with only limited veto and advisory powers. As a counter-weight to potential parliamentary opposition, the Roundtable Agreement also created an enhanced presidency with carefully circumscribed emergency powers that were intended, on the one hand, to reassure Moscow of Warsaw's continued loyalty but, on the other, to impede the arbitrary exercise of presidential power.

By the end of the year, with communist regimes toppling elsewhere in the region and Moscow watching from the sidelines, the compromise that had seemed so daring when it was struck began to look more like a millstone around the neck of Poland's fledgling democracy. Although General Jaruzelski never used his presidential powers to influence the policy of the Mazowiecki government, the delicate constitutional balance between President and parliament created the potential for political gridlock. Equally serious, with nearly two-thirds of the deputies to the "contractual *Sejm*" from parties belonging to the defunct *PZPR*-led coalition, it was a foregone conclusion that they would try to shape the law governing the next (and first truly free) elections to maximize chances for their own political survival. After a bruising six-month battle (in which the ex-communists were joined by several small post-Solidarity groupings with similar motives), the *Sejm* scrapped the majority system used in the 1989 elections in favor of a *PR* system with no threshold for representation in parliament—an outcome that only encouraged the proliferation of parties. Thus, to Dr. Grabowska's three dimensions outlined above, we must add an unwelcome fourth fault line in the form of personality conflicts (often among rival Solidarity leaders) which have further fragmented the political scene by preventing cooperation among individuals and groups that would otherwise appear to be ideologically compatible.

More than 100 parties and other political organizations participated in the 1991 elections, of which 27 succeeded in registering national lists.[23] The results of the election, which drew out only 43 percent of potential voters and in which no party received more than 12 percent of valid votes, are shown in Table II.1. In all, 29 parties and groups won at least one seat in the *Sejm* (11 only one each!). The top five vote-getters, which accounted for just over 50 percent of the valid votes (21 percent of eligible voters) and 57 percent of seats won, were spread so widely across the political spectrum as to make a majority coalition virtually impossible. Looking only at those parties that did or were expected to make a strong showing, the more or less "pure plays" in terms of political orientation and program were few and far between.

Among the most consistent parties were those on the former communist and social democratic Left, all of which focused to varying degrees on continued support for a large state sector or softening the transition process by a gradual phase-out of subsidies to large state-owned enterprises and retaining the redistributive functions of the state. Of these parties, the Social-democracy of the Republic of Poland (*S-dRP*, the main successor to the *PZPR*) was the most important element in the electoral "Alliance of the Democratic Left" (*Soiusz Lewicy Demokratycznei* or *SLD*). Although early polls showed it attracting only 3 to 5 percent of the vote,[24] it came in just shy of 12 percent of votes cast and a close second to the "winning" Democratic Union. At the same time, the *SLD* appears to have drawn out its maximum constituency, mostly from the former nomenklatura and other white-collar beneficiaries of the old regime, while the negative baggage of the past left it unable to attract significant support among its alleged natural working-class constituency, except in areas especially hard-hit by the recession.[25]

The situation on the social-democratic Left provides a more complicated and perhaps more instructive example of the structural weaknesses in Polish politics. Three parties vied for voters attracted by a traditional Western-style social-democratic program focused on establishing a regulated market economy while retaining a strong social safety net: "Solidarity of Labor" (*Solidarnosc Pracy* or *SP*), the "Democratic-Social Movement" (*Ruch Democraty-czno-Sooleczny* or *RD-S*), and the Polish Socialist Party (PPS). Of the three, the last was internally (and fatally) splintered along historical lines–with one faction linked to the old *PZPR*, a second to the long-suppressed Right wing of the original *PPS*, a third emerging from the Solidarity movement; the *SP*, despite its late entry into the race, was thought to have the most promise. Early polls gave the three together as much as 9 percent of the vote. However, on-again, off-again attempts to form an electoral alliance foundered two months before the elections, mostly due to personality conflicts. In the end, the SP won only 2 percent of the vote and 4 *Sejm* seats, the *RD-S* less than one percent and one seat; the *PPS* was completely shut out.

On the Right, it was more difficult to find a "pure play." Perhaps the closest, each in its own very different terms, were the ultra-right National Party (*Stronnictwo Narodowe* or *SN*) and moderate Liberal-Democratic Congress (*Kongres Liberalno-Demokratyczny* or *KLD*). The former—a quasi-Fascist, explicitly anti-Semitic fringe group with

a narcissistic focus on the "*narod*"—failed to register visible support in
pre-election polls and won no seats. On the other hand, the *KLD*, the
party of Poland's second non-communist Prime Minister Jan Bielecki
(January-November 1991), reflected his unflinching commitment to
secular politics and a rapid shift to a free-market economy—and thus
to a continuation of the IMF-supported "shock therapy" program
inaugurated by the Mazowiecki/Balcerowicz team at the beginning of
1990. Despite the growing unpopularity of the government's reform
program, the KLD showed a relatively strong 10 percent support in
early polls and ended up with 7.5 percent of the vote; it has found
additional support in the *Sejm* from the strongly pro-business wing of
a small party with the unlikely name of Polish Party of Beer Lovers.[26]

Other key players on the Right reflected a mish-mash of ideological and programmatic metaphors—a fact that contributed to the
inability of the post-election coalition government to broaden its parliamentary base. The self-defined center-Right parties that formed
the core of that coalition included: The Christian-National Union
(ZChN), which campaigned under the banner of the "Catholic Electoral Alliance" (*Wyborcza Akcia Katolicka* or *WAK*); the "Center
Citizens Alliance" (*Porozumienie Obywatelskie Centrum* or *POC*), a
coalition of the Center Alliance formed in 1990 by Walesa to spear-
head his presidential campaign and remnants of Citizens' Committees
that guided Solidarity to its 1989 parliamentary victory; plus several
factions of the agrarian movement (discussed below). Although all
subscribed to conservative policies on social and religious issues, their
economic platforms were unmistakably Leftist. The *WAK* and *POC*
came in third and fourth respectively, each receiving just short of 9
percent of the vote. This represented a major gain for the Catholics
(the *ZChN* drew only 2 percent in early polls) but a disappointing loss
for the Center Alliance and Citizens' Committees, which saw their
combined support shrink about 40 percent from earlier indications.

The agrarian camp was initially split along lines similar to the
PPS with pre-communist, former pro-communist and pro-Solidarity
factions all claiming title to the legacy of the original Polish Peasant
Party (*Polskie Stronnictwo Ludowe* or *PSL*). After failed attempts
at unification—which, had they succeeded, would have led to a first
place finish in the elections—the movement went into the campaign
divided between a reconstituted *PSL* (combining the reformed pro-
communist peasant party and remnants of its pre-1948 nemesis) and
the Solidarity-based Peasant Alliance (*Porozumienie Ludowe* or *PL*).

Although both parties tended to be conservative on national and social issues, the former was able both to distance itself from the *ancien regime* and to capitalize on its opposition to the austerity policy of the Mazowiecki and Bielecki governments which had squeezed the farm sector especially hard. The PSL came in fifth (a hair behind *WAK* and *POC*) with just over 9 percent of the vote; the PL, unable to shed the burden of "guilt by association" with two years of Solidarity-imposed austerity, came in eighth with 5.5 percent (and quickly fell apart along lines of personal rivalry).

Finally on the Right, the Confederation for an Independent Poland (*Konfederacia Polski Nieoodlealei* or *KPN*) is one of the oldest opposition movements, predating Solidarity by about a year. Having lost its main issue with the collapse of the Soviet bloc, *KPN* shifted its focus to a combination of opportunistic and populist issues. Rejection of political domination by Moscow has been replaced by opposition to economic assistance from the West and defense of the rights of workers in state-owned enterprises. In addition, it benefitted both from the fact that it bore no responsibility for the unpopular economic programs of the first two post-communist governments and from its lack of a strong link to the Episcopate (unlike the *ZChN*). For voters who wanted to express rejection of the communist past, fear of future dependence on the West, skepticism of the Church's social agenda, and support for a Leftist economic program, *KPN* provided a convenient vehicle. It placed sixth in the election, with 7.5 percent of the vote (and 10 percent of *Sejm* seats), or about twice the level of support shown in early polls.

In the middle, the Democratic Union (*Unia Democratyczna* or *UD*) continued to occupy a broad spectrum ranging from the socialdemocratic Left (close to the *SP*) to the free-market Right (close to the *KLD*). Led by Poland's first non-communist Prime Minister, Tadeusz Mazowiecki, its distinguishing feature in the 1991 campaign was its style, unique in the Polish context, which emphasized consensus politics with a determinedly secular and pragmatic bias. Thought to be the front runner (with early forecasts running from 18 to as much as 25–30 percent of the vote), the *UD* was nagged by a combination of the unpopularity of the austerity program first introduced by the Mazowiecki government in 1990, the lack of a clear ideological profile, ambivalence over the possibility of Mazowiecki seeking the premiership again, plus voter confusion and apathy. In the end, it won a narrow victory over the former communist alliance (with 12.3

percent of the vote), but by most accounts was considered to have lost the election, the biggest victim of the non-voting majority.

One other party merits brief mention–less because it figured large in the election than for what its fortunes tell us about the current state of Polish politics–namely, Party "X," the creation of the mysterious Polish-Canadian businessman, Stanislaw Tyminski, who came from nowhere to defeat Prime Minister Mazowiecki in the first round of the 1990 presidential election.[27] Tyminski's initial appeal was based on his demagogic style and eclectic image as "Polish boy who made good in the West" (of dubious accuracy), as defender of state-owned enterprises and opponent of foreign investment (which he warned would leave Poland hostage to the West), and, perhaps, above all as a way to vote for "none of the above" in an election in which most of the better known candidates had several strikes against them. The fact that he could draw 20–25 percent of the electorate was interpreted as a sign of the immaturity of Polish voters and their vulnerability to extremist tendencies. As more information came out about Tyminski's checkered past, including links to Poland's former communist secret police, Party "X"s political fortunes waned, falling from 7–8 percent in early polls to a paltry 0.5 percent of the final vote and three seats in the *Sejm*.

III. "*L'etat, c'est Lech*" and Other Conundra[28]

The dictionary definition of a conundrum is "a problem admitting of no satisfactory solution."[29] Approximately eighteen months into Walesa's presidential term and six months into the life of the new parliament and government, this would seem a more appropriate characterization of the current state of Polish politics than trying to find some elusive center of gravity on a traditional Right-Left scale.

The first such "program admitting of no satisfactory solution" was (and remains) the issue of fashioning a workable government from the fractious parties described in the preceding section. With no one willing to include the former communists in a coalition, and most right-of-center parties unwilling to join a government led by the *UD* due to deep differences both over the pace of economic reform and the role of the Church in political life, the two largest parties in the *Sejm* were effectively relegated to the opposition. At the same time, neither of the remaining alternatives seemed much more promising. The first was the cluster of smaller, self-defined Rightist parties to form a coalition; the problem with that was that, to control even a bare majority of deputies, such a coalition would have to include parties with widely disparate agendas. A more coherent center-Right coalition could routinely command at best 40 percent of the votes in the Sejm. The second alternative was to concede that no party or orientation had won the election, that the *Sejm* was too fragmented to form a working coalition, and that the best solution was to transfer primary responsibility for appointing the government to the presidency and enhance the powers of the government *vis-à-vis* parliament. This was clearly the course preferred by Walesa who, during the immediate post-election turmoil, proposed a set of constitutional amendments (the so-called "little constitution") that would have had precisely this effect. The problem here was that most in the Sejm saw Walesa's proposals as a transparent grab for power, rather than as a sincere attempt to give Poland a stable government capable of keeping the reform program on track as the president himself claimed.[30]

After nearly two months of wrangling, the *Sejm* seemed ready to confirm something close to the broad version of a Right-wing coalition—including (in order by size of its *Sejm* caucus) *WAK, KPN, POC, KLD* and *PL.* Then two of the potential partners withdrew their support, the far-Right populist *KPN* over the proposal of the other four to continuing the previous two governments' fast track toward a market economy. Thus, Poland ended up with the minimal version, a minority three-party center-Right coalition, with POC leader and former Solidarity lawyer Jan Olszewski as Poland's third non-communist Prime Minister (much to Walesa's chagrin). This put the new government in the unenviable position of being dependent for its survival on its ability to cobble together transient majorities with non-coalition parties on an issue-by-issue basis.

Not surprisingly, the new government quickly found itself caught between parliament and the president over core economic issues. Hence, the second conundrum: how to reconcile the campaign promises of the coalition partners (as well as other parties), which were based on a significant easing of the austerity program pursued by the Mazowiecki and Bielecki governments, with the need to meet commitments made by those two governments to international funding agencies and Western creditors. This was Poland's main, perhaps only, hope of keeping its struggling economy afloat and attracting badly needed foreign investment. Thus, almost immediately on taking office the Olszewski government found itself embroiled in a protracted crisis over the state budget for 1992 in which the most serious stumbling blocks were the size of the budget deficit, subsidies for state-owned enterprises, wages for public-sector employees, and pensions. The pressures on Olszewski were enormous. Not only did renewal of a multi-billion dollar aid package from the International Monetary Fund depend on limiting the deficit to 5 percent of gross national product, but fulfillment of an agreement negotiated in 1991 for a 50 percent reduction in Poland's debt to Western governments was contingent on meeting the IMF target. In the end, the government had little choice but to renege on its promises and submit a budget that met the deficit limit (in part by eliminating pay increases and trimming pension benefits)—and that was promptly and decisively rejected by the *Sejm* in early May.[31]

The budget impass has only fueled the political tug-of-war between parliament and president. The latter repeatedly and with increasing force demanded Olszewski's resignation and emergency powers for himself, and the former just as often refused him the necessary two-thirds vote. Again, the options look ominously like more problems "admitting of no satisfactory solution." Even were Walesa to succeed in ousting the government and installing himself as another Pilsudski or a "Polish de Gaulle," he would be risking what remains of his waning political support by taking direct responsibility for increasingly unpopular policies. Moreover, he lacks the backing of the military or of a strong political party essential to make either role credible.[31] The alternative, at least theoretically, of using his powers under the present constitution to dissolve parliament and call new elections is even less promising. First, with few parties inclined to change the electoral law (for most an act of voluntary suicide), any new elections would be held under the same law that produced the current *Sejm*; second, there is the very real risk that voter turnout would be as low or lower than in 1991, further eroding the legitimacy of the institution. Third, and perhaps most seriously, new elections would mean yet another period of uncertainty in which the reform process is placed on hold (or worse, subjected to another round of demagogic campaign rhetoric), while potential investors, both foreign and domestic, sit on their money waiting to see what the policy of the next government will be.

What does all this tell us about Right and Left in Polish politics? Mostly it tells us what's wrong—the fragmentation and over-personalization of the party system and an electoral system that encourages more of the same; a constitutional division of powers designed for specific circumstances that no longer exist and which now impedes effective government. These are compounded by sagging public confidence in all institutions charged with managing the transition. Does this accumulation of conundra presage a resurgence of the Right, even a return to some form of Right-wing authoritarianism? Although such a scenario cannot be excluded, especially should the downward economic spiral continue, it is more likely in the near term that center and Left-of-center parties will benefit from six months of budget gridlock under the Olszewski government. From this gridlock no parties on the Right have emerged unscathed (with the exception of the moderate *KLD*, the one Right-wing party that could accommodate itself to a coalition with the centrist but strongly pro-reform Democratic Union). Perhaps the one bright spot on the horizon is the slight upturn in industrial production in March and April 1992, fueled by a dynamic private sector even as the dominant state sector continued to decline.[33] At a certain point in the transition process, economic recovery can become self-sustaining even though the political institutions that must initially program the transition are still dysfunctional. Whether that stage has been reached in Poland is still in question, but at this point in time I remain a cautious (if nervous) optimist.

TABLES

Table I.1 [Q. 402(0)]:

"I don't have much in common with people of other ethnic groups and races."

	Poland	CSFR	Hungary	Bulgaria
Completely agree	36	12	9	7
Mostly agree	38	19	18	10
Mostly disagree	15	37	32	29
Completely disagree	6	22	23	50
Don't know	5	10	18	4

Table I.2 [Q. 208]:

"I'd like you to rate some different groups of people in Poland according to how you feel about them. For each group, please tell me whether your opinion is very favorable, mostly favorable, mostly unfavorable or very unfavorable."

	Ukrainians	Germans	Jews	Lithuanians	Byelorussians
Very favorable	2	1	2	5	2
Mostly favorable	29	36	38	50	42
Mostly unfavorable	34	37	27	16	18
Very unfavorable	8	10	8	2	2
Don't know*	27	16	25	27	36

[* In the review session with the *Times-Mirror* analysts, it was generally agreed that most "don't know" responses to this question represented hidden unfavorable opinions.]

Table I.3 [Q. 313]:

"Thinking about national security, which one of the [following] arrangements . . . would be the best policy for our country?"

	Poland	CSFR	Hungary	Bulgaria
Signing individual defense treaties with neighboring countries	34	32	23	27
Joining a regional defense alliance	12	28	37	27
Membership in, or association, with NATO	30	15	17	23
Don't know	24	25	23	23

Table I.4 [Q. 314]:

"Do you think that our country spends too much, too little or the right amount for our national defense?"

	Poland	CSFR	Hungary	Bulgaria
Too much	13	38	27	8
Too little	27	2	15	14
Right amount	25	31	35	31
Don't know	35	29	32	47

Table I.5 [Q. 400(u)]:

"The best was to ensure peace is through military intervention."

	Poland	CSFR	Hungary	Bulgaria
Completely agree	23	6	15	13
Mostly agree	35	14	19	13
Mostly disagree	22	40	26	27
Completely disagree	5	29	29	31
Don't know	15	11	11	16

[On this question, Poles showed a greater belief in the efficacy of military strength than any of the other countries surveyed; the next highest was France, where 43 percent agreed.]

Table II.1: Results of Poland's Parliamentary Elections (October 27, 1991)

Party	% of Vote	% of Sejm	#of Deputies Seats
Democratic Union (UD) [S]	12.31	13.48	62
Alliance of the Democratic Left (SLD) [C]	11.98	13.04	60
Catholic Electoral Alliance (WAK) [S]	8.73	10,65	49
Center Citizens' Alliance (POC) [S]	8.71	9.56	44
Polish Peasant Party (PSL) [C]	8.67	10.43	48
Confederation for an Independent Poland (KPN)	7.50	10.00	46
Liberal Democratic Congress (KLD [S]	7.48	8.04	37
Peasant Alliance (PL) [S]	5.46	6.09	28
Solidarity Trade Union [S]	5.05	5.87	27
Polish Beer-Lovers' Party (PPPP)	3.27	3.48	16
Christian Democracy (ChD) [C]	2.36	1.09	5
Union of Real Politics (UPR)	2.25	0.65	3
Solidarity of Labor (SP) [S]	2.05	0.87	4
German Minority	1.70	1.52	7
Party of Christian Democrats (PChD)	1.11	0.87	4
Party "X"	0.47	0.65	3
Silesian Autonomy Movement(RAS)	0.35	0.43	2
Polish Western Union (PZZ)	0.23	0.87	4
Other*	10.32	2.39	11
Totals	100.00	100.00	460

Source: Based on official results released by the State Election Commission, reported in David McQuaid, "The Parliamentary Elections: A Postmortem, " *Report on Eastern Europe*, Vol. 2, No. 45 (November l8, 1991), p. 16.

[S] post-Solidarity parties; [C] former communists and communist allies

*Eleven groups were elected to one seat each; these included the post-Solidarity Democratic-Social Movement and the post-communist Democratic Party.

NOTES

1. The twelve countries in the *Times-Mirror* survey consisted of five West European (including both parts of Germany), four East European and three then Soviet republics. A preliminary analysis of the results was summarized in a supplement to the *Los Angeles Times*, September 17, 1991; a final report, under the title *The Pulse of Europe*, is scheduled to be published in book form in 1992. The author served as a consultant in the review of the East European data. Results from this survey will hereafter be cited as "T/M, Q[uestion] 000."

2. The results of the USIA-sponsored polls were published in a series of Research Memoranda by the Agency's Office of Research. Those used here were: M-175-91: "Poland: The Perils of Development," October 28, 1991; M-177-91: "Poles Want to Emulate U.S. and Germany," October 31, 1991; M-178-91: "Instability in the Soviet Union Troubles Polish Public," October 31, 1991; M-183-91: "Poles Prefer 'Few Economic Worries' to 'Freedom to Express Views'," November 8, 1991; and M-38-92: "Coping with Freedom and Uncertainty: public Opinion in Hungary, Poland, and Czechoslovakia, 1989–1992," March 12, 1992. They will hereafter be cited by memorandum number, followed by table or page reference.

3. The USIA polls did not ask about ethnic minorities but about attitudes toward selected countries (or Soviet republics than seeking independence). With the exception of Germany, where a number of crosscutting factors colored views, the results were broadly comparable to those in the *Times-Mirror* poll. The data on attitudes toward Lithuania are especially interesting as they show a steady decline in the number of respondents expressing a "favorable" opinion from 68 percent (April 1990) to 50 percent (May 1991, about the same time as the *Times-Mirror* poll) to 40 percent (September 1991, with only 3 percent saying "very favorable"); this would appear to correspond to the rise in tensions between Warsaw and Vilnius over the Polish minority in Lithuania, especially immediately after the failed August coup. USIA, M-177, pp. 9, 11–12.

4. *T/M, Qs.* 400 (t, v,x).

5. *T/M, Qs.* 207(a-b), 316 and 317; USIA, M-178-91, Tables 1 & 5.

6. USIA, M-178-91, Table 6. The question asked "which foreign country, if any, . . . represents the *most* serious military threat

to our country?" Respondents were allowed to name more than one country; 32 percent answered "don't know" or "no country." Of the remaining 68 percent, nearly three-fifths named Germany, although it is not clear how many listed it first; 54 percent, or fourfifths of those perceiving a military threat, named the USSR, Russia, or Ukraine.

7. USIA, M-177-91, pp. 12–13. The "Adria-Alpine" group was founded in the early 1980s as an informal consultive group of contiguous provinces in Austria, Hungary, Italy and Yugoslavia; by the fall of 1989, consultations had been raised to the level of foreign ministsers and, with the admission of Czechoslovakia 1990, it was renamed the "Pentagonale." With respect to the high level of support for defense spending, it is important to note that a consistent 70 percent said that military force should be used solely for the defense of Poland; U8IA, M-178-91, Table 10.

8. *T/M, Qs.* 104 and 206(e); USIA, M-175-91, Tables 6 and 9.

9. *T/M Qs.* 400(a-d); USIA, M-175-91, pp. 19–21, and M-36-92, pp. 22–23.

10. *T/M, Q.* 214; Bulgarians put "military attack" first (the poll was conducted in a period of high tension over the Turkish issue), which Czechs, Slovaks and Hungarians by wide margins cited a "flood of refugees."

11. *T/M, Qs.* 206(m) and 227. The USIA data fully confirm this skepticism toward foreign investment, especially toward ownership of real estate by foreigners (with only 13 percent approving in the September 1991 poll); M-183-91, Tables 19 and 20.

12. *T/M, Qs.* 201 and 202. USIA, M-36-92, Table 12.

13. *T/M, Qs.* 204 and 205.

14. Ibid., Qs. 400 (e,f,m,n,o).

15. Ibid., Qs. 400 (fl), 206 (b,n), 218, 219, 220 and 217 (a-m).

16. Ibid., Qs. 202, 206(g), 203 and 402(1). USIA data show a slightly higher level of "confidence in the Church in its September 1991 poll (53 percent), but also demonstrate a dramatic decline from 79 percent in April 1990, with all of the decline coming among those expressing" a great deal of confidence in the Church (down from 44 to 18 percent). They also confirm the high level of disapproval of Church meddling in politics, with 75 percent agreeing in both the November 1990 and September 1991 polls that the Church was too invoived in politics and is losing sight of its main spiritual role. M-175-91, Tables 9 and 10.

17. *T/M, Qs,* 215, 216 and 202.

18. Ibid., Qs. 203 and 400(p and w).

19. "New Political Orientations," *Komentarz Ogorka* [Ogorekls Commentary], *Gazeta Wyborcza*, July 6/7, 1991.

20. Miroslawa Grabowska, "*System partyjny–w budowie*," *Krytyka* (Warsaw), No. 37 (1991), pp. 24–33.

21. Ibid.

22. Concerning the battle over the electoral law, see David McQuaid, "The 'War' over the Election Law," *Report on Eastern Europe*, Vol. 2, No. 31 (August 2, 1991), pp. 11–28.

23. There were varying estimates of how many political organizations participated in the elections. See, e.g., David McQuaid, "The Parliamentary Elections: A Postmortem," *Report on Eastern Europe*, Vol. 2, No. 45 (November 8, 1991), pp. 15–21; also Krzysztof Jasiewicz, "From Solidarity to a Fragmented Parliament" (unpublished manuscript, 1992).

24. Early poll results for the *S-dRP* and other parties were reported in *Gazeta Wyborcza*, July 5, 1991. Analysis of party orientations and election results is based largely on the two sources cited in note 23, plus: David Warszawski [Konstanty Gebert], "The Elections: Don't Let's be Shocked," and Wojciech Maziarski, "The Powerlessness of the Powerful: Walesa Now," both in *Gazeta Wyborcza*, November 3, 1991, and translated in *East European Reporter*, Vol. 5, No. 1 (January-February 1992), pp. 19–23; also "Right-About: Interview with Jaroslaw Kaczynski," *Polityka*, January 18, 1992, and Jerzy Wysocki, "Left Behind," *Zycie Warszawy*, February 2, 1992, both translated in *East European Reporter*, Vol. 5, No. 2 (March-April 1992), pp. 49–53.

25. The *SLD* was supported by just short of 5 percent of eligible voters and won only 4 percent of seats in the Senate, where a simple plurality system was used; see Jasiewicz, *op. cit.*

26. The Beer Lovers' Party (*Polska Partia Przyiaciol Piwa* or *PPPP*) began as a joke but caught the fancy of some anti-establishment voters; financed in part by businessmen in exchange for places on the ballot, the party won 16 seats (10 of which went to probusiness candidates). Once in the *Sejm*, the latter split with their less serious colleagues to form a separate parliamentary caucus ("Big Bear") and often votes with the *KLD*.

27. Concerning the Tyminski presidential campaign, see the chapter by Andrzej Korbonski in this volume.

28. The title "*L'etat, c'est Lech*" was taken from the London

Economist, May 2, 1992, p. 60.

29. *The American Heritage Dictionary of the English Language* (Boston: Houghton Mifflin Co., 1969), p. 290.

30. See, e.g., Louisa Vinton, "After the Elections: A 'Presidential government'?" and "Five-Party Coalition Gains Strength, Walesa Proposes 'Little Constitution'," in *Report on Eastern Europe*, Vol. 2, No. 45 (pp. 22–28) and no. 49 (pp. 5–12).

31. For running analyses of the mounting government and budget crises, see the following articles in *RFE/RL Research Report*; Louisa Vinton, "Poland: Government Crisis Ends, Budget Crisis Begins" (Vol. 1, No. 3 [Jan. 17, 1992], pp. 14–21), and "The Polish Government in Search of a Program" (Vol. 1, No. 13 [March 27, 1992], pp. 5–12); and Anna Sabbat-Swidlicka, "Poland: Weak Government, Fractious *Sejm*, Isolated President" (Vol. 1, No. 15 [April 10, 1992], pp. 1–7). On the final defeat of the government's budget proposal, see Stephen Engelberg, "Poland's Parliament Rejects Austerity Budget Cuts," *New York Times*, May 7, 1992, p. A11.

32. Concerning Walesa's Gaullist pretensions, see Anthony Robinson, "Politician Walesa trapped by harsh economics," *The Financial Times*, April 29, 1992, p. 3; and "Poland: L'etat, c'est Lech," *The Economist*, May 2, 1992, pp. 60–61. See also the scathing six-page indictment of Walesa's presidency in the form of interviews with some of his former and present aides published by Poland's leading daily; Jaroslaw Kurski, "*Wodz–Przedostatni Rozdzial*," *Gazeta Wyborcza*, April 22, 1992, pp. 8–13.

33. "Polish Monthly Economic Monitor (Premier Issue)," *Plan-Econ Report*, Vol. 8, No. 22 (June 4, 1992).

THE RIGHT IN CZECH-SLOVAKIA

Sharon Wolchik

The reemergence of the political Right as a viable political force throughout Central and Eastern Europe is one of the more interesting aspects of the repluralization of politics that has followed the collapse of communism in the region. It is interesting in part because the development of a system of political organizations to channel mass political preferences and demands is one of the central features of stable democratic political systems. It is also significant because, in contrast to the area of institutional and legal change where a good deal has been accomplished since 1989, the party system is still very much in flux throughout the region. The reemergence of Rightist parties and movements also highlights another important aspect of the transition, namely, the reappearance of attitudes that citizens were unable to express openly under the old system.

After a brief analysis of Rightist parties and traditions in pre-Communist Czech-Slovakia, the pages to follow analyze the evolution and fortunes of Rightist parties and movements since 1989, and citizen attitudes toward a number of important political and economic issues. We will then examine several of the factors that influence the role of Rightist forces in post-Communist Czech-Slovakia including the legacy of communist and precommunist political cultures and traditions; the intersection of nationalist and partisan politics; and the characteristics of transitional politics at present. They conclude with an evaluation of the future outlook for Rightist parties.

Rightist Parties and Movements Defined

At the outset, it is important to distinguish among several kinds of Rightist parties and movements. As the discussion to follow and other chapters in this book make clear, any effort to examine the role of Rightist parties and movements immediately runs into definitional problems. These differences arise from a number of sources. First, the term typically encompasses a wide variety of groups. In the Czechoslovak case, this problem is illustrated by the fact that individuals and groups from supporters of free-market economics and liberal democratic institutions such as those espoused by Prime Minister of the Czech Republic Vaclav Klaus to groups of "skinheads" whose activities include attacks against minorities and gypsies all consider themselves to be Rightist groups. Thus, the antidemocratic attitudes of certain interwar extreme Rightist groups, which were also anti-Semitic and intolerant of members of other ethnic groups, are reflected in the priorities of a number of extreme Rightist organizations in Czech-Slovakia at the present time. However, many of those most supportive of liberal democracy today also consider themselves to be Rightists. Further difficulties arise from the fact that in many of the countries of Central and Eastern Europe the terms "Right" and "Rightist" as they apply to political attitudes and positions today differ to some extent from their use in the pre-communist period. The political importance of particular types of Rightist groups also varies from one country to another. There are also important differences in the meaning and understanding of the term from country to country.

As the section to follow will illustrate, the fluidity and lack of consistency still evident in the political values and preferences of citizens also contribute to the difficulty of defining Rightist political forces. Many citizens who define themselves as Rightist or sympathize with Rightist parties also hold certain values and political orientations that are not consistent with such orientations. Thus, while many citizens in Czech-Slovakia think that the Left-Right continuum makes sense and, in fact, define themselves and political groups along this continuum,[1] any effort to categorize groups on a single Left-Right dimension fails to capture the complexity of political orientations and positions evident today. As the section below will argue in greater detail, in Czech-Slovakia this continuum must be supplemented by the national dimension. Thus, parties are differentiated not only by their position on the Left-Right continuum, defined primarily in terms of policies toward economic reform and the move toward the market, but also by their commitment to a national or civic principle of citizenship.[2] At the same time, although most parties that consider themselves to be Right of center and are seen as such by others, support the recreation of a market economy. There are also important differences in the economic policies of these groups, Finally, as the situation in Slovakia illustrates, the difficulty of defining Rightist groups and movements is compounded by the fact that certain Leftist groups currently espouse many of the antiliberal and nationalistic attitudes that have generally been associated with Rightist movements and parties in the past.

For the purposes of this paper, I will distinguish among three kinds of Rightist groups and movements. The first of these are what I term "mainstream" Rightist parties. These are secular and Christian parties that support the move to a market economy and profess respect for the norms and values of democratic political life. Their leaders also view the development of greater links to the rest of Europe as a high priority.[3] The second are what might be termed "extreme" or "radical" Right-wing groups and movements. Although these parties compete in elections and participate in the political process, they espouse certain values that are at variance with democratic norms. Finally, there are less organized mass movements, such as the "skinheads," whose members hold antidemocratic, anti-Semitic views and also engage in sporadic attacks on minorities and gypsies. Although groups of the second and third variety exist in Czechoslovakia as elsewhere in the region, they encompass only a small minority of the population. Much of the analysis to follow, then, will focus on the emergence of the mainstream right of center groups which currently are very significant players in the country's political life.

The Right in Historical Perspective

The role of Right of center political forces in Czechoslovakia during the interwar period was conditioned by several factors. These include the fact that, in contrast to the situation in many of the other countries in the region, a democratic, multiparty political system remained in effect in Czechoslovakia until it was ended by outside forces. The fortunes of Rightist parties were also influenced, as at present, by the ethnic composition of the state. Although Right of center forces, as well as more extreme Rightist movements, existed in all parts of the country, they were markedly more powerful in Slovakia and among certain minorities, including the Sudeten Germans, than among Czechs. There were also significant differences in political values among different ethnic groups.

At the national level, the dominance of the five Czech parties known as the *Pětka* for much of the interwar period colored the government's policies. Comprised of the Social Democrats, the Socialists, the National Democrats, the Czechoslovak Populist Party, and the Agrarians, the *Pĕtka* included moderate, Right of center parties. However, all members of the coalition supported the maintenance of democratic institutions and the enactment of progressive social and labor legislation.[4]

In the Czech Lands, support for antidemocratic parties was centered primarily on the Communist Party, which received between 10 and 13 percent of the vote during this period.[5] Several small parties on the extreme right, including the Fascist National Front, and Czechoslovak National Democracy led by Karel Kramář, existed in the Czech Lands during this period. However, the political climate in the Czech Lands did not favor their development and they had few followers. The Fascist Party of General Rudolf Gajda, for example, polled less than one percent of the vote in the 1929 elections and two percent in the 1935 elections.[6] It was only among the Sudeten Germans, who shared a number of economic and other grievances, that significant support existed for extremist groups on the right. Influenced by developments in Germany under Hitler, many Germans in the Sudeten land came to support the numerous nationalist, extremist organizations and parties that developed, including the Sudeten German Party led by Konrad Henlein.[7]

Rightist political forces also exploited nationalist sentiment in Slovakia during the interwar period. Drawing on popular resentment of what was perceived to be domination from Prague and economic hardship, nationalist Slovak parties, including the Slovak People's Party founded by Father Andrej Hlinka, gained support. Members of Hlinka's party participated in the government of the country in the late 1920s. However, the party soon came to reflect the views of more radical nationalist leaders such as Vojtech Tuka, who steered the party in more extreme directions and developed links to Germany and Italy. The activities of these groups, which paved the way for the establishment of the Slovak state under Hitler's auspices in March 1939, contributed to the break-up of the interwar state in the name of Slovak national interests.[8]

There were similar differences in political culture in different parts of the country during this period. As Gordon Skilling has noted, the political culture of Czechoslovakia between the world wars can best be characterized as a dual one.[9] Thus, although belief in political pluralism and attachment to democratic procedures was widespread, a sizeable portion of the electorate supported the Communist Party or other authoritarian groups and movements. In the Czech Lands, the dominant democratic political culture included support for social democratic traditions, such as a high degree of egalitarianism and a commitment to social justice, as well as belief in the value of democratic institutions. Most citizens of Bohemia and Moravia who did not share the belief in liberal democracy or were disaffected supported the Communist Party. Support for values associated with the extreme Right, including radical nationalism and anti-Semitism, thus, was found largely in areas with sizeable German concentrations. In Slovakia, on the other hand, dissatisfaction with the political system and the economic situation, which was far worse than in the Czech Lands, found its expression primarily in nationalist movements that eventually took on many of the trappings of and adopted many of the policies of Hitler's Germany.

The Czech Lands and Slovakia entered the period of renewed political pluralism that followed the end of communist rule with very different legacies in terms of Rightist values and traditions. In Bohemia and Moravia, there was a history of political activity by moderate Rightist parties, but these were often overshadowed by parties to the Left of center. The values of the extreme Right were associated primarily with the German minority, which was expelled after World War II. In Slovakia, mainstream center Right parties were also weak. But, by way of contrast, the extreme Rightist traditions associated with the People's Party and the independent Slovak state were linked in the minds of many to Slovak national aims. The heritage of extreme Rightist groups was thus more pervasive in that part of the country.

The Emergence of Rightist Political Groups after the Collapse of Communism

The reemergence of the political Right as a legitimate force in politics in Czechoslovakia as elsewhere in post-communist Europe is one of the most striking aspects of political life in the region. This was evident in the reaction against Leftist parties and movements that were identified with the communists in the period immediately following the fall of the communist system in 1989. The dominance of parties to the Right of center was also reflected in the results of the June and November 1990 elections. To a certain extent, this phenomenon parallels that which occurred in other Central and East European countries after the fall of communist systems.[10]

The emergence of Rightist parties as legitimate and powerful political forces in Czechoslovakia took place within the context of the recreation of pluralistic political life after the collapse of communist rule. As in other post-communist countries, the fortunes of such parties and movements, as of others that are currently active, also have been shaped by the characteristics of transition politics. However, there are a number of ways in which the position and role of these groups differ in Czechoslovakia. These differences reflect the country's previous political history and political traditions, and the reemergence of ethnic conflict.

In Czechoslovakia as in other communist states, the end of the Communist party's monopoly of power was followed by a rapid repluralization of politics. Once the Communist party's monopoly of political power was broken, there was a proliferation of political associations, interest groups, and political parties. The more than 100 such groups that had been formed prior to the June 1990 parliamentary elections included old parties that had been allowed to exist under the tutelage of the Communist party during the communist period, such as the Peoples' party and the Socialist party in the Czech Lands and the Democratic party in Slovakia, and allegedly reformed versions of the Communist party in both the Czech Lands and Slovakia. They also included a variety of ethnically based groups, such as the Movement for Self-Governing Democracy-Association of Moravia and Silesia, Coexistence-Hungarian Christian Democratic Movement, Hungarian People's party, Hungarian Civic party, and the Slovak National party. New non-partisan groups and movements, such as the Civic Forum and Public Against Violence, as well as more exotic political groupings such as the Beer Drinkers' Party, also emerged. The early post-communist period also saw the reemergence of a number of political parties, including the National Socialist party, that had been banned after World War II.[11] Many of these groups were winnowed out as viable political forces. This was the result of threshold provisions. They required parties to receive 5 percent of the vote in the federal and Czech legislatures and three percent in the Slovak National Council in 1990, and three percent in 1992, in order to seat deputies.[12] The party system that is emerging in Czechoslovakia will clearly be a multiparty system in which a number of political forces will be significant. In the first year after the end of communist rule, the dominant political forces in Czechoslovakia, as in Poland and Hungary, were the umbrella movements that emerged from the former opposition to lead the revolutions. These groups, whose non-partisan emphasis was symbolized by their initial leaders, Vaclav Havel and Fedor Gal, were united by a rejection of the communist system. Many of the early activists of these groups also rejected socialism in any form. Vaclav Havel, for example, noted when asked about socialism, that the country had tried it once and that he was not eager to experiment with it again.[13] However, although the message of these groups, captured succinctly in their 1990 campaign slogans that promised the re-creation of democracy, the market, and a return to Europe, was clearly anti-communist and anti-socialist, they were not Rightist political groups at the outset.[14] Rather, as the debate concerning economic policy and the proper role of the state continued until the fall of 1990, the programs of these groups reflected the heterogeneity of their leaders and supporters.

The impact of this legacy was evident in the results of the June 1990 parliamentary elections. Led by former dissidents and activists who had spearheaded the fight against the old system, Civic Forum and Public Against Violence won easy victories in the 1990 June and November elections.[15] With 49.5 percent for the Czech National Council, 50 percent in the House of Nations and 53.2 percent to the House of the People, Civic Forum emerged as the strongest political force in the Czech republic. Public Against Violence, won with 29.3 percent of the vote for the Slovak national Council, 37 percent for the House of Nations, and 33 percent for the House of the People in Slovakia. Jan Čarnogursky's Christian Democratic Movement emerged as the second strongest party in Slovakia, with 19.2 percent of the vote for the Slovak National Council, 19 percent of the vote to the House of the People, and 17 percent of the vote for the House of Nations.[16]

The victory of these coalitions did not in and of itself lead to the clear dominance of the political Right in Czechoslovakia. Although the Social Democrats and Socialists did very poorly in both the Czech Lands and Slovakia in the 1990 elections and failed to win enough votes to seat representatives in the Federal Assembly, the Communist party received significant levels of support in both parts of the country. The approximately 13 and 17 percent of the vote the party obtained in the June 1990 Parliamentary and November 1990 local elections were, in fact, similar to the levels of support the party had won in the free elections of the interwar republic.[17] The strength of the party after the fall of communism in Czechoslovakia reflects a number of factors. These include the fact that, in contrast to the situation in a number of other countries such as Poland and Hungary, where communism was clearly imposed from outside, the Communist party had indigenous roots in Czechoslovakia that dated from the interwar period. The party could also draw on the more general tradition of support for socialist ideals during that period. The size of the Communist party and its apparat, as well as the sudden nature of the change of regime in Czechoslovakia in 1989 also undoubtedly help to account for the party's support.

As developments in early 1991 were to illustrate, there were significant differences of opinion on economic policies and on other critical aspects of the transition within both Civic Forum and Public Against Violence. Although the governments chosen as the result of the 1990 elections adopted many policies and programs that could be labelled Right of center, particularly in terms of economics, the movements themselves were very loose organizations that united people with a variety of policy perspectives and preferences. The lack of common political ideals or a shared vision of the future, beyond a common opposition to communism, as well as personal antagonisms and disagreements, led to the break-up of both of these groups in the first half of 1991. This process of political differentiation, which has occurred in other post-communist societies and appears to be a necessary part of the creation of a new party system, occurred in January 1991 in the Czech Lands, and in April 1991 in Slovakia.

In the Czech Lands, disagreements within the Civic Forum came to a head when opponents of Vaclav Klaus broke away from the hierarchically structured political party that was emerging under Klaus's guidance. They formed Civic Movement, a more loosely organized, non-partisan group dedicated to preserving some of the original positions of Civic Forum. The creation of the Civic Democratic party led by Klaus was followed in February 1991 by the formation of a third group, the Civic Democratic Alliance.

This process had its parallel in Slovakia in April 1991. At that time, Vladimir Mečiar's supporters left Public Against Violence to form the Movement for a Democratic Slovakia after relations between two groups within Public Against Violence became acrimonious. Mečiar's opponents then worked with PAV's primary electoral rival at that time, the Christian Democratic Movement, to remove

Mečiar from his position as Prime Minister of Slovakia. It is only after this time, that the Rightist tendencies evident in some of the policies and actions of representatives of Civic Forum and Public Against Violence solidified into political forces. They clearly identified themselves as mainstream Rightist political parties. The outcome of this process of political differentiation, in terms of public support, has been quite different in the two parts of the country.

In the Czech Lands, Klaus's *Obcanske demokratické strana* or (*ODS*), or Civic Democratic party quickly emerged as the strongest of the parties created from the Civic Forum. Public opinion polls conducted in the last half of 1991 and first half of 1992 found that *ODS*, with approximately 20 percent support, was consistently the strongest political party in the Czech Lands prior to the June 1992 elections. Committed to a continuation of the government's economic policies as well as the development of closer links to the rest of Europe, ODS received 33.4 percent of the vote to the House of Nations and 33.9 percent to the House of the People, in coalition with Vaclav Benda's small Christian Democratic party in the June 1992 elections.[18] Its leader, Vaclav Klaus, became Prime Minister of the Czech Republic and represented the Czech side in the negotiations with the Slovaks that led to the decision to divide the state.

Civic Democratic Alliance, the second clearly Right of center party that emerged from the Civic Forum, adheres to many of the positions of *ODS*, such as the move to the free market economy support for democratic liberties and values, and the development of closer ties to the rest of Europe.[19] As the result of the June 1992 elections in which *ODA*, with 4.08 percent of the vote for the House of Nations and 4.98 percent for the House of the People did not receive enough votes to seat any deputies[20] illustrate, *ODA* is far weaker electorally than *ODS*. Nonetheless, the party played an important role in defining the terms of public debate and discussion, given the prominence of the intellectuals who are its leaders and supporters. Despite the differences that continue to exist between the two groups, *ODS* and *ODA* representatives often cooperated in the Federal Assembly. With nearly 6 percent of the vote in the Czech National Council, *ODA* has 14 seats in the CNR and has joined Klaus's *ODS* coalition in that body.[21]

Citizen's Movement (*Obcanské hnuti*, or *OH*), the third group that emerged from the former Civic Forum, also portrays itself as a center-Right party. However, most voters appear to agree with a sample of political analysts and experts who in 1991 classified this movement as Left of center.[22] This classification in all likelihood stems from both the large number of reform communists among the leaders of the movement and its support of efforts to buffer the impact of the transition on individuals and maintain a stronger safety net during the transition to democracy. Although individual leaders, such as Jiři Dienstbier, former Foreign Minister, and Dagmar Burešová, former Chair of the Czech National Council, continue to be popular with voters, *OH* received less than 5 percent of the vote to both chambers of the Federal Assembly and to the Czech National Council and did not seat any deputies in either body.[23]

The Right of center political parties that emerged from the former Civic Forum in the Czech Lands joined several other smaller Right-wing parties already active in the region. The most important of these is the People's party, which attempted to change its image and overcome the impact of its subservience to the Communist party during the communist period. Hurt by allegations made public just prior to the June 1990 elections that its leader, Josef Bartončik, had collaborated with the secret police, the People's party won 8.7 percent of the vote to the Federal Assembly and 8.4 percent to the Czech National Council in June 1990 and 12.1 percent in the November 1990 local elections.[24] Depending on support primarily among older, religious voters, it espouses a political program based on Christian values and is also supportive of a strong social policy. In the 1992 elections, the party received 5.98 percent of the vote to the House of Nations, 6.08 for the House of the People and 6.3 percent to the Czech National Council as part of a coalition with other Catholic parties.[25]

Two other Right of center parties, the Party of Entrepreneurs and Private Farmers and the Club of Engaged Nonparty members also ran in the 1992 elections. However, neither party received enough votes to seat deputies in the Federal Assembly or the Czech National Council.[26]

In Slovakia, by way of contrast, the break-up of Public Against Violence has been followed by a steep decline in support for moderate Right of center politicians and parties. The Movement for a Democratic Slovakia (*Hnutia za demokratické Slovensko*, or *HZDS*) formed by Vladimir Mečiar and his supporters in April 1991 considers itself and is considered by voters to be Left of center on economic issues. It has also become a champion of Slovak national interests. This party, which received from 25 to 35 percent support in surveys conducted in the year before the June 1992 elections, emerged as the strongest political force in Slovakia. With 33.85 percent of the vote to the House of the Nations and 33.53 percent to the House of the People of the Federal Assembly and 37.3 percent of the vote in the Slovak National Council, Mečiar's party was by far the most popular party in the June 1992 elections. As Table 1 illustrates, Leftist and nationalist parties also emerged as the second and third most powerful parties in the June 1992 elections.[28]

The Civic Democratic Union, (*Občanska demokratická unie*, or *ODU*), which was formed in October 1991 by Mečiar's opponents in Public Against Violence on the other hand, has become a very marginal force in Slovak politics. Espousing a program similar to that of *ODA* in the Czech Lands and supporting the maintenance of a common state, *ODU* received from two to four percent of popular support in the months prior to the June 1992 elections.[29] With 4.04 percent of the vote to the House of Nations and 4.0 percent to the House of the People, *ODU* did not seat any deputies in the Federal legislature. Similarly, the party's percent of the vote to the Slovak National Council (4.03 percent) did not allow it to seat any deputies in that body.[30]

Given the high level of representation of members of Public Against Violence in the government of Slovakia prior to the June 1992 elections, and the prominence of certain of its leaders, including Martin Porubjak, *ODU* was a more powerful force in Slovak political life than its level of popular support alone would suggest. The intellectuals associated with the party will undoubtedly continue to play a role in shaping public debate in Slovakia. However, the party's direct role in Slovak politics will be limited as the result of the June 1992 elections.

The Christian Democratic Movement, led by Jan Čarnogursky fared somewhat better in the 1992 elections. The KDH (*Krest'ansko-demokraticke hnutie*), which is also Slovakia's main Christian political party, received from 8 to 17 percent of popular support in public opinion polls in 1991 and the first half of 1992. Internal divisions within *KDH* came into the open in March 1992 when followers of Jan Klepač, former deputy Chairman of the Slovak National Council, broke with Čarnogursky over the movement's position in regard to Slovak independence and formed the Slovak Christian Democratic Movement (*Slovenské krest'anskodemokratické hnutie*, or *SKDH*). In the June 1992 elections, KDH received 8.8 percent of the votes for the House of Nations and 9.0 for the House of the People; it also received 9.0 percent of the vote for the Slovak National Council.[31] The breakaway *SKDH*, which espoused a more nationalistic program, was supported by 3–4 percent of citizens in Slovakia in polls conducted prior to the 1992 elections[32] and received 3.3 percent of the vote for the House of Nations and 3.5 percent for the House of the People. The party obtained 3.1 percent of the vote for the Slovak National Council and thus did not seat deputies in either the federal or the republic legislatures.[33] A coalition of Hungarian parties, including Coexistence, the Hungarian Christian Democratic Movement, and the Hungarian people's party obtained 7.4 percent of the vote to both the Federal Assembly and the Slovak National Council and obtained 12 and 14 seats in these bodies. (see Table 1) However, although leaders of these groups support the creation of a market economy and certain other positions of center-Right parties, their main emphasis is on issues that affect the situation of the Hungarian minority.Independent Initiative, received less than one percent of the vote to the Federal Assembly and only 2.3 percent of the vote. It thus will not seat deputies in either body. Another small Right of center party, the Republican Party of National Democratic Union, also failed to win enough support to seat deputies.[35]

Thus, in this area as in many others, there are important differences in political developments in the Czech Lands and Slovakia. As the results of the June 1992 parliamentary elections illustrate (see Table 1 for a summary), there is clearly more support for Right of center political parties in the Czech Lands than in Slovakia. The victory of Right of center forces in the Czech Lands and Left of center parties in Slovakia was the catalyst for the negotiations that appear to have sealed the fate of a common state of Czechs and Slovaks. There has been a tendency in commentaries about the break-up of the federation to attribute its demise primarily to the decisions of political leaders in both regions. However, the different outcome of the elections in the two parts of the country in fact reflects broader, long-standing differences in popular preferences and attitudes towards important political and economic issues.[36]

The Extreme Right

The end of the communist system has also seen the revival of extreme Right-wing groups and movements in Czechoslovakia. However, in contrast to the situation in certain other postcommunist countries, in Czechoslovakia these are generally weak. The Republican Party-Association for the Republic is the only significant extreme Right political party. Led by Miroslav Sladek, a former engineer who once described Vaclav Havel as a murderer, an alcoholic, and a drug addict,[37] this party captures the support of those who are most fearful of and disgruntled by the disruptions caused by the transition to the market in the post-communist period. Leaders of the party have advocated many of the policies espoused by the "skinheads," including the deportation of foreign guest workers and policies against the gypsies. Party leaders have been among the most adamant supporters of measures to bring former members of the Communist party to account. The Republicans also have called for the return of Subcarpathian Ruthene and the reorganization of the country along a system of lands.[38] Support for this party, which won less than 1 percent of the vote in the 1990 elections as part of a coalition, reached

Table 1

Czech Lands	House of the People	House of Nations	*Czech* National Council
Civic Democratic Party,	seats	seats	seats
Christian Democratic Party	33.9%(48)	33.4%(37)	29.7%(76)
Left Bloc (Communist party of Bohemia and Moravia, DLCSFR)	14.3%(19)	14.5%(15)	14.1%(35)
Czechoslovak Social Democratic Party	7.7%(10)	6.8%(6)	6.5% (16)
Republican Party	6.5(8)%	6.4%(6)	6.3%(15)
Christian Democratic Union - People's Party	5.8%(7)	6.1%(5)	6.3%(15)
Liberal Social Union	5.9%(7)	6.1%(5)	6.5%(16)
Civic Democratic Alliance	4.98% -	4.8% -	5.9%(14)
Association for Moravia - Silesia	4.9% -	4.2% -	5.9%(14)
Civic Movement	4.4% -	4.7% -	4.6 -

Slovakia

Movement for a Democratic Solvakia	33.5%(24)	33.9%(33)	37.3% (74)
Party of the Democratic Left	14.4%(10)	14.0%(13)	14.7%(29)
Slovak National Party	9.4%(6)	9.4%(9)	7.9%(15)
Christian Democratic Movement	9.0%(6)	8.8%(8)	8.9%(18)
Coexistence/Hungarian Christian Democratic Movement	– –	– –	7.42%(14)
Coexistence/Hungarian Christian Democratic Movement/Hungarian People's Party	7.4%(5)	7.4%(7)	– –
Social Democratic Party	– –	6.1%(5)	– –
Civic Democratic Union	4.0% –	4.0% –	4.0% –
Hungarian Civic Party	3.7% –	2.4% -	2.3% –
Democratic Party-Civic Democratic Union	3.7% –	3.4% –	2.3% –

Source: Jiri Pehe, "Czechoslovakia's Political Balance Sheet, 1990–1992," *RFE/RI Research Reoorts*, Vol. 1, No. 25, 19 June 1992, p. 29. and "Volby 1992," *Respekt*, 8-14 June 1992.

a peak of 7 percent in mid-1991, but declined to approximately 4 percent by December 1991 and remained at approximately that level throughout the first half of 1992.[39] The party received 6.37 percent of the vote for the House of nations, 6.48 percent for the House of the People of the Federal Assembly, and 5.98 percent of the vote for the Czech National Council. It, thus, holds 14 seats in both the Federal Assembly and the Czech National Council.[40] The Republicans did particularly well and won over 10 percent of the vote in the Northern Bohemian region, which has been very badly hurt by the changes associated with the economic reform and has the highest levels of unemployment in the Czech Republic. Anti-Semitic and other extreme views have also been propagated since January 1991 by the weekly *Politika*. Published by editors who were formerly affiliated with a publication of the Czechoslovak People's Party, the weekly's circulation has increased to 10,000.[41]

The post-communist period has also seen the emergence of "skinheads" in Czechoslovakia. Few in number, members of these groups nonetheless have attacked gypsies and foreign workers in a number of cities.[42] They have also taken part in demonstrations and protests organized by the Republican party. Although representatives of the Republican party deny any direct link to the skinheads or any responsibility for the violence they have used, the two groups share many of the same attitudes toward gypsies, minorities, and foreign workers.

The development of these groups is an indication of the degree of strain the changes have produced for certain groups of the population. However, given the relatively small number of people involved in the activities of these groups, they do not pose a serious threat to political stability at the present time.

The Nationalist Dimension

There has also been a revival of certain of the policies and symbols associated with extreme Right-wing traditions and movements in Slovakia. However, given the present weakness of Rightist political forces in Slovakia, many of the symbols and attitudes that historically have been associated with Right wing movements are currently espoused by political forces that call themselves and are seen by others as being Left of center. This phenomenon is particularly evident in regard to the extreme nationalism often associated with Right wing parties and movements in the region. Thus, while representatives of the mainstream, or moderate Rightist parties, including the *ODU*, or Civic Democratic Union, and Ján Čarnogursky's Christian Democrats, differed in terms of their emphasis on the need for greater autonomy for Slovakia prior to June 1992, most remained committed to the principle of a common state with the Czechs. Vladimir Mečiar's Movement for a Democratic Slovakia and the Slovak Nationalist Party, by way of contrast, adopted many of the symbols, as well as the emphasis on Slovak nationalism, that characterized the extreme Right-wing movements that supported the creation of the Slovak state in 1939. The creation of the Slovak Christian Democratic Party led by Jan Klepac in March 1992 added a Right-wing nationalist party to the spectrum in Slovakia, but, as noted above, the following of this party to date remains limited.

Mass Attitudes and Values

The differing fortunes of Rightist parties in the two parts of the country are paralleled by important differences in public opinion. Popular attitudes toward key aspects of the current transition, including privatization and the role of the state in ensuring the material well-being of citizens, and the political values of the population, differ in the Czech Lands and in Slovakia. Citizens in the Czech Lands are more supportive of privatization and the notion that individual citizens should bear more responsibility for ensuring their futures than are citizens in Slovakia. Respondents in the Czech Lands also are more positive in their evaluation of the political changes since 1989 along a number of dimensions. These differences, which became evident soon after the end of communist rule, intensified in the course of 1991 and were among the factors that fueled support for nationalist and Left of center parties in Slovakia.[43]

The results of the June 1992 parliamentary elections give credence to the view that citizens in the two halves of Czechoslovakia indeed adhered to dramatically different political perspectives. However, although the outlines of this picture may be correct, the situation in fact is not quite so simple.

First, it is important to keep in mind the fact that the dominance of the Right of center parties in Bohemia and Moravia is tempered by continued support for the Communist party in those areas. As Table 1 illustrates, the Communist Party received the second largest number of votes after Klaus's Party in the 1992 elections; support for the Social Democrats also increased in the months prior to the election. The Left of center Liberal and Social Union, a coalition of Agrarians, the Green party, and the Czechoslovak Socialist party, was the fourth most popular political force in public opinion polls in early 1992 and received from 5.8 to 6.5 percent of the vote in June 1992, (see Table 1.)

Ethnicity has proved to be a potent focal point for political identification in the Czech republic as well as in Slovakia. This tendency has been particularly evident in Moravia. There, what was primarily a secondary, cultural identity until 1989 has taken on increased significance. Thus, the Movement for Self-Governing Democracy-Association for Moravia-Silesia, (*Hnuti za samosoravnou demokracii*

- *Společnost pro Moravu a Slezsko, HSD-SMS*) which received 10.3 percent in the 1990 elections, was the second most popular political party in Moravia in the months leading up to the 1992 elections. Although Klaus's Civic Democratic Party received the largest number of votes in Moravia, the *HSD-SMS* came in third, after the Leftist block coalition.

A further factor that prevents a simple division of politics in the country into Right and Left along republic lines is evident in the results of public opinion polls and studies of popular political attitudes and preferences. As noted earlier, substantial numbers of citizens continued to support a positive role for the state in providing social welfare, employment, education, housing, low cost medical care and other benefits. There is also a growing apprehension of and dissatisfaction with the results of the shift to the free market economy on the living standards of families. Political life also continues to be characterized, to some degree, by positive attitudes toward social justice and a fair degree of egalitarianism. Support for these policies, which once again reflects the legacy of the interwar as well as communist periods, is more widespread than electoral support for the Communist party and is further fueled by the new hardships. As in the case of support for Left of center parties, there is a greater attachment to these values in Slovakia than in Bohemia and Moravia. However, there are also sizeable groups of the population in Bohemia and Moravia who share these attitudes.

Surveys conducted by the Association for Independent Social Analysis in 1990, for example, found that 47 percent of respondents in Slovakia and 32 percent in the Czech Republic thought that the state should bear complete responsibility for finding employment for every citizen. Approximately equal percentages (46 and 34 percent) felt that the state should retain complete responsibility for ensuring a decent standard of living for the whole population. Most citizens wanted the state to continue to finance basic health care and pensions as well (84 and 80 percent).[45] The results of a survey conducted by ASIA in November 1991 further illustrate these tendencies. Thus, half of those surveyed in the Czech Lands, but only a third in Slovakia agreed with the idea that it was all right for some people in society to get rich.[46]

As Table 2, which is based on the results of public opinion polls conducted by the Association for Independent Social Analysis in May 1992, indicates, the majority of citizens in both parts of the country preferred the current system to that which existed before November 1989. However, approximately 20 percent of those surveyed in the Czech Lands and a third in Slovakia preferred the communist system. Similarly, although a majority of all citizens felt that the current difficulties created by the change of the social system were unavoidable, over 40 percent felt that another, less costly path to democracy and economic prosperity could be found. Levels of satisfaction with overall political developments since the 1990 elections were low, as only 31 percent of all citizens (and 21 percent in Slovakia) were either very satisfied or satisfied. Sixty-eight percent, and 79 percent in Slovakia, were either dissatisfied or very dissatisfied.

Table 2

Views toward Various Aspects of Political and Economic Changes

	Total	CR	SR
In terms of the current situation and developments since November 1989:			
Prefer current system	71	75	63
Prefer pre-November 1989 system	22	18	30
The difficulties which the overall change in social system have created			
Are unavoidable	54	58	44
Could be avoided; another less costly way could be found	43	38	51
Attitude toward political developments since the 1990 elections			
Very satisfied	1	1	2
Rather satisfied	30	36	19
Rather dissatisfied	48	45	54
Very dissatisfied	20	17	25
Don't know/no answer	1	1	1

Source: Association of Independent Social Analysis, *Vyzkum politických postoju*, 15-24 dubna 1992 (Prague: ASIA, May 1992), pp. 1–2.

Surveys conducted by the Institute for Public Opinion Research in Prague found similarly low levels of satisfaction with the overall political situation prior to the June 1992 elections. Only 1 percent of citizens in both the Czech and Slovak republics were very satisfied; over twice as many respondents were satisfied in the Czech republic as in Slovakia (26 and 13 percent). Fifty and 51 percent were rather dissatisfied and 23 percent of those surveyed in the Czech Lands, as well as 35 percent of those in Slovakia, were very dissatisfied.[47]

As these surveys illustrate, despite the rejection of communism and positive attitudes toward the recreation of democratic political life that characterized the early months after the fall of the communist system, the impact of communist rule on the attitudes and values of the population persists among sizeable groups. Many of these attitudes and values are not espoused by the mainstream Right-wing parties.

The Impact of Transitional Politics

The fortunes of Rightist political parties in Czechoslovakia are also influenced by several other factors related to the nature of transitional politics. The first of these is the volatility of voter preferences at present. As in many other post-communist countries one of the legacies of the communist past has been a marked reluctance on the part of many citizens to join political parties. With the exception of parties that were in operation prior to the Revolution of 1989, few political parties have large numbers of members. Klaus's Civic Democratic Party, for example, which was consistently the most popular political party in the Czech Lands in 1991 and the first half of 1992, nonetheless had a membership of approximately 20,000.[48] The low levels of party identification mean that Czechoslovakia does not have the benefit of this device that serves to simplify political decision-making for citizens and structure and mediate political conflict in more established democratic political systems. Political preferences, thus, are still volatile, and citizens available to be mobilized are not numerous. The relatively large number of voters who indicated that they were undecided concerning their voting preferences in March 1992, which included a third of the voting population in Bohemia and Moravia, and 17 percent in Slovakia[49] provides further evidence.

The voluminous public opinion data available since the fall of the communist system also illustrate a further trend that may influence the fortunes of Rightist parties. Thus, numerous surveys conducted by different organizations have documented the increase in dissatisfaction and political alienation that have occurred in the course of the first two years of post-communist rule. Evident in the growing number of citizens who perceive the revolution to have been stolen, or derailed, popular disillusionment with the political system is also reflected in the increase in popular distrust of political leaders and institutions. President Vaclav Havel, who was trusted by 81 percent of those surveyed in Bohemia and Moravia in March 1992, was partially immune to this trend. However, even he suffered a loss of trust in Slovakia prior to the June 1992 elections. Thus, although approximately 50 percent of those surveyed in Slovakia trusted Havel in December 1991 and March 1992, an almost equal proportion (46 percent), did not trust the President in March 1992.[50] Trust in political institutions, including the federal government and parliament, was lower in both parts of the country, and particularly low in Slovakia, where only 29 percent of the population trusted the federal government and 28 percent the federal parliament by May 1992. Trust in the Slovak government and Slovak National Council was equally low (30 and 26 percent). In Bohemia and Moravia, 48 percent of those surveyed trusted the Federal government and 27 percent the Federal parliament.[51] In Slovakia, these attitudes are coupled with extremely negative attitudes concerning the federation. Thus, while there was considerable variation in the opinions of Slovaks concerning the best form of state arrangements, it is significant that only 8 percent of those surveyed in late 1991 were satisfied with the federal arrangements of the time.[52]

Their attitudes are paralleled by those concerning economic developments and expectations for the future. Although a majority (51 percent) of citizens surveyed in April 1992 by the Association for Independent Social Analysis indicated that they preferred a market economy, a sizeable proportion of respondents (39 percent) indicated that they preferred a mixed economy with market and socialist attributes. Support for a mixed economic system was substantially higher in Slovakia (46 percent) than in the Czech Lands (36 percent). Sizeable numbers of respondents in both republics also felt that a market economy in the long run would allow only a small portion of people to become wealthier rather than lead to a better living standard at all. This view, which was held by 64 percent of all those surveyed, was far more dominant in Slovakia (74 percent). However, it is significant that 58 percent of citizens in the Czech Lands also expressed these sentiments.[53] The same survey found that a majority of respondents (57 percent) agreed or strongly agreed that economic developments in their country were leading to prosperity, and a better standard of living. However, forty percent disagreed or strongly disagreed. Negative evaluations were strong in Slovakia, where 40 percent disagreed and 14 percent strongly disagreed, but a quarter of respondents in the Czech Lands also disagreed, 8 percent strongly disagreed. A study of popular attitudes toward privatization conducted by the Center for Social Analysis in January 1992 found a similar degree of ambivalence toward privatization, particularly in Slovakia. Seventeen percent of respondents in the Czech Lands and 35 percent in Slovakia wanted less privatization. Sixty-seven percent of respondents in Slovakia, and 43 percent in the Czech Lands, thought that privatization would strengthen "mafias."[54] Thus, although negative attitudes are most prevalent in Slovakia, many citizens in Bohemia and Moravia also hold extremely negative views of the current economic situation and of their own economic prospects in the near future.

Future Prospects

As the pages above have illustrated, the demise of communism in Czechoslovakia has been followed by the reemergence of the political Right as a significant force in mainstream political life. Political figures who are affiliated with Right of center political parties dominated the governments of both republics and the federal government in the first two years of the post-communist period. However, this dominance was short-lived in Slovakia, where Leftist and nationalist parties emerged as the victors in June 1992. Vaclav Klaus's Right of center party received the largest share of the vote in June 1992 in the Czech Lands and dominated the government of the Czech Republic. However, the political Right is far from dominant, even in Bohemia and Moravia. Given this fact, the victory of nationalist political parties that are also Left of center and formation of a Left of center government in Slovakia, and the prevalence of certain Left of center values and expectations on the part of many citizens in both parts of the country, it is premature to speak of the victory of the political right.

There are many elements of the current economic and political situation that are similar to those that have given rise to extreme

Right wing movements in other countries. The growing disillusionment of many with the workings of democratic government, coupled
with nostalgia for the security of the past, and the uncertainty that
continues to pervade many areas of life all provide fertile soil for the
growth of anti-democratic, extremist movements. The growth in popular dissatisfaction and the other features of the transitional period
discussed above, then, may well prove problematic for the political
Right in Czechoslovakia. Perceived to be the architects of the current
economic reform, mainstream Right of center politicians may well
suffer as a result of the economic dislocations and social and psychological hardships the population is experiencing during the transition
to a free market economy. The impact of such factors on political life
and the fortunes of political parties has been particularly evident in
Slovakia, where economic dissatisfaction fueled nationalist sentiments
and resulted in Meçiar's victory in the June 1992 elections. The fact
that the Communist party and the Social Democrats were the second
and third most popular parties in Bohemia and Moravia for much of
1991 and 1992 and the June 1992 elections indicates that such factors
are also important in the Czech Lands despite the victory of Vaclav
Klaus's party. Although a Right-wing government in the Czech Lands
has been formed as a result of the 1992 elections, it is too early to
rule out an eventual return to a Left of center government. This
possibility, which would be consistent with certain elements of the
pre-communist political culture in the Czech Lands, is given credence
by the fact that to date there is little real social base for mainstream,
Right of center parties. This problem, of course, is one that Vaclav
Klaus and other Right of center politicians have been working very
hard to remedy by means of policies designed to create a group of
private entrepreneurs. The initial success of the "voucher" privatization plan, which saw over 8 million citizens buy coupon books to
be redeemed for ownership shares, bodes well for this effort. The
massive numbers of citizens who are participating in this effort may
well have an increased personal interest in keeping the forces that
support privatization in power. But the long-range political impact
of this method cannot be assessed at this time.[55] In the meantime,
the responsibility of Right of center parties for economic policies in
the Czech Republic and the inevitable hardships that these policies
will continue to create for many groups of the population, at least in
the short run, may spark a backlash against those most responsible
for these policies. The break-up of the federation will also cause eco-

nomic dislocations in the Czech Lands, as well as in Slovakia, even though they are likely to be less severe. While this situation may increase support for more extremist Right wing parties among certain groups of the population, it is more likely that Leftist parties and groups in Bohemia and Moravia, and nationalist parties and policies in Slovakia will be the beneficiaries. Independence and experience with the impact of Mečiar's economic policies may also eventually renew support for center Right political forces. But such a shift is likely to take some time, given the attitudes and political preferences of the population in Slovakia.

NOTES

1. See, for example, Lubos Rezler, "An attempt to Identify the Background of Political Left and Right Continuum in Czechoslovakia 1990," Prague, MS, February 1991, and Jaroslav Hudeček, "*Polus 0 identifikaci stran no 'levo-pravem' kontinuu*," *Socioloqický časopis*, 1992, Vol. 28, No. 2, pp. 275–82.

2. I am indebted to Miloslav Petrusek, Dean of the Faculty of Social Sciences of Charles University, for this classification scheme.

3. These parties resemble those that Sternhell terms "radical" or "revolutionary" Rightist parties; but in contrast to these, they advocate a rapid move to recreate the market.

4. See Vaclav L. Beneš, "Czechoslovak Democracy and Its Problems, 1918–1920," in Victor S. Mamatey and Radomir Luža, A *History of the Czechoslovak Reoublic, 1918–1948* (Princeton, NJ: Princeton University Press, 1973), pp. 39–98; Jósef Korbel, 1977, pp. 67–78; Richard F. Nyrop, ed., *Czechoslovakia: a Country Study* (Washington, D.C.: The American University (Foreign Area Studies), pp. 28–34.; Josef Anderle, "The First Republic, 1918–1938," in Hans Brisch and Iván Völgyes, eds., *Czechoslovakia, the Heritage of Ages Past* (New York: Columbia University Press, 1979), pp. 89–112; Victor S. Mamatey, "The Development of the Czechoslovak Democracy, 1920–1938," in Mamatey and Luža, pp. 99–166; Věra Olivova, *The Doomed Democracy: Czechoslovakia in a Disrupted Europe, 1914–1938.* (London: Sidgwick and Jackson, 1972); and Josef Korbel, *Twentieth-Century Czechoslovakia: The Meanings of Its History* (New York: Columbia University Press, 1977), pp. 58–71.

5. See Korbel, p. 71.

6. See Korbel, pp. 74–78; Bruce Garver, "The Czechoslovak Tradition: An Overview," in Brisch and Völgyes, *Czechoslovakia: The*

Heritage of Ages Past (New York: Columbia University Press, 1979), especially pp. 40–42; and Josef Anderle "The First Republic, 1918–1938," in Brisch and Völgyes, pp. 100–103.

7. See Olivová, Chps. 2–4; Joseph Rothschild, *East Central Europe Between the Two World Wars* (Seattle, WA: University of Washington Press, 1974), pp. 122–129; Josef Korbel, *Twentieth-Century Czechoslovakia*, pp. 116–120; and Luža, 1964, pp. 24–184 and F. Gregory Campbell, *Confrontation in Central Europe: Weimar Germany and Czechoslovakia* (Chicago, IL: University of Chicago Press, 1975), chaps. 3–6.

8. See Rothschild, *East Central Europe Between the Two World Wars*, pp. 117–121; Vera Olivová, *The Doomed Democracy*, Chaps. 5 and 6; Korbel, *Twentieth-Century Czechoslovakia*, pp. 153–156; Yeshayahu Jelinek, *The Parish Republic: Hlinka's Slovak People's Party* (Boulder, CO: East European Monographs, 1976); and Samuel Harrison Thomson, *Czechoslovakia in European History*, Second Edition (Princeton, NJ: Princeton University Press, 1953), pp. 416–419 for discussions of these parties and the Slovak state. See also Edita Bosak, "Slovaks and Czechs: An Uneasy Coexistence," in H. Gordon Skilling, ed., *Czechoslovakia 1918–88: Seventy Years of Independence* (London: Macmillan, 1991).

9. See H. Gordon Skilling, "Czechoslovak Political Culture: Pluralism in an International Context," in *Political Culture and Communist Studies*, Archie Brown, ed. (London: Macmillan, 1984), pp. 117–120.; H. Gordon Skilling, "Stalinism and Czechoslovak Political Culture," in *Stalinism: Essays in Historical Interpretation*, Robert C. Tucker, ed. (New York: W. W. Norton & Co., 1977); Archie Brown and Jack Gray, eds., *Political Culture and Political Change in Communist States*, Second Edition (London and New York: Holmes and Meier Publishers, 1979); David W. Paul, *The Cultural Limits of Revolutionary Politics: Change and Continuity in Socialist Czechoslovakia* (New York: Columbia University Press, 1979), and "Czechoslovakia's Political Culture Reconsidered", in Brown, pp. 134–148; and Sharon Wolchik, *Czechoslovakia in Transition*, Chapters 1 and 2 for discussions of Czechoslovakia's political culture prior to and during communism.

10. See Wolchik, "The Crisis of Socialism in Central and Eastern Europe and Socialism's Future," and other essays in Cristiane Lemke and Gary Marks, eds. *The Crisis of Socialism in Europe* (Durham, NC: Duke University Press, 1992) for discussions of this reaction.

11. See Wolchik, *Czechoslovakia in Transition*, Chapter 1 for information on the party system immediately after World War II and pp. 77–96 for a more detailed discussion of the party system in the early post-communist period.

12. See Jiri Pehe, "The Electoral Law," *RFE Report on Eastern Europe*, March 16, 1990, pp. 15–18; and Wolchik, *Czechoslovakia in Transition*, pp. 77–79; Jiri Pehe, "Czechoslovak Federal Assembly Adopts Electoral Law," *RFE/RL Research Report*, Vol. 1, February 14, 1992, pp. 27–30.

13. See Wolchik, "The Crisis of Socialism in Central and Eastern Europe and Socialism's Future," pp. 84–113 for a discussion of the reaction against socialism in the early post-communist period.

14. An incident that took place during the mass demonstrations in November 1989 illustrates this point quite clearly. Václav Klaus was originally asked to speak to the crowd at the massive demonstration at Letna Plain on November 27, 1989. However, when the organizers of the rally learned that Klaus was planning to speak on the need to recreate a free market economy, he was removed from the speakers' list.

15. See Wolchik, *Czechoslovakia in Transition*, Chaps. 1 and 2; and Jan Obrman "Civic Forum Surges to Impressive Victory in Elections," *RFE Report on Eastern Europe*, Vol. 1 No. 25, June 22, 1990, pp. 13–16.

16. See Wolchik, *Czechoslovakia in Transition*, pp. 51–52; and *Výsledky voleb do FS a ČNR podle jednotlivych kraju, Svobodne slovo*, June 12, 1990, p. 4.

17. See Jiři Pehe, "Changes in the Communist Party," *Radio Free Europe Report on Eastern Europe*, Vol. 1, No. 48 (November 30, 1990), pp. 1–5; Wolchik, *Czechoslovakia in Transition*, Chaps. 1 and 2; Sharon Wolchik, "Czechoslovakia in Transition," in *Instability in Eastern Europe in the Post-Communist Era* (Boulder: Westview Press, forthcoming).

18. "Volby 1992," *Respekt*, June 8–14, 1992.

19. See *"Strany, hnuti a koalice," Hospodařské noviny*, April 21, 1992, p. 9; Jan Obrman, "The Czechoslovak Elections: A Guide to the Parties," *RFE/RL Research Report*, Vol. 1, No. 22, 29 May 1992, 10–16; and CSTK, *1992 Elections in Czechoslovakia, Election Results*, Bulletin No. 4, Prague, 1992.

20. See "Volby 1992"; Jiři Pehe, "Czechoslovakia: Parties Register for Elections," *RFE/RL Research Report*, Vol. 1, No. 18, (May

1, 1992), pp. 20–25; and "*Strany, hnuti a koalice,*" p. 9.

    21. "Volby 1992."

    22. See Hudeček.

    23. The party received 4.74 percent of the vote to the House of nations, 4.39 percent to the House of the people, and 4.59 percent to the Czech National Council, "Volby 1992."

    24. See Wolchik, *Czechoslovakia in Transition,* p. 92.

    25. "Volby 1992."

    26. "Volby 1992."

    27. Information from Institute for Public Opinion Research, Prague, and Association for Independent Social Analysis.

    28. "Volby 1992."

    29. From information from surveys conducted by the Institute for Public Opinion Research in Prague January-April 1991 and Association for Independent Social Analysis in 1991 and the first half of 1992. See "Nationwide Survey on Expected Voting Patterns," *FBIS-EEU-92-059,* March 26, 1992, p. 12; Pehe, "Election Preview," p. 25; and dr, "*Stale věři prezidentovi,*" *Lidové noviny,* January 10, 1992; "*Vyvoj voličskych sympatii v ČR,*" *Rude právo,* January 10, 1992.

    30. "Volby 1992."

    31. "Volby 1992."

    32. "The Elections on Trial," *Norodná obroda,* April 24, 1992, 14, as reported in FBIS "HZDS Still Ahead in Slovak Opinion Polls," FBIS-EEU-92-084, April 30, 1992, 9.

    33. "Volby 1992."

    34. See Alfred A. Reisch, "Hungarian Coalition Succeeds in Czechoslovak Election," *RFE/RL Research Report,* Vol. 1, No. 26, 26 June 1992, 20–22.

    35 "Volby 1992."

    36. See Sharon L. Wolchik, "Ethnic issues in Post-Communist Czechoslovakia," paper presented at Conference on Nationality and Ethnicity in Eastern Europe, Center for European Studies, Harvard, December 6, 1991.

    37. OC, "Will There Be Shooting Next," *Občansky denik,* August 19, 1991, 7, as reported in "Sladek Verbally Attacks President Havel," FBIS-EEU-91-165, 26 August 1991, 14.

    38. See Jiři Pehe, "The Emergence of Right-wing Extremism," *RFE Report,* June 28, 1991, Vol. 26, pp. 1–5 for an overview of the policies of this party.

39. From information in Institute for Public Opinion Research report, Prague, January 31, 1992.

40. "Volby 1992" and Pehe, "Czechoslovakia's Balance Sheet," 29.

41. Jan Brabee, *Respekt*, No. 5, 3–9 February 1992, 7–9.

42. See "Skinheads Clash with Anti-Fascists in Prague," FBISE-EU-92-051, 16 March 1992, 4.

43. See Wolchik, *Czechoslovakia in Transition*, Chap. 2, and Wolchik, "Ethnic issues in Post-Communist Czechoslovakia."

44. Marek Boguszak and Vladimir Rak, "Czechoslovakia - May 1990 Survey Report," (Prague: Association for Independent Social Analysis, 1990), Table 1; Boguszak and Rak, *"Společnč, ale každy jinak, Lidove Noviny*, June 28, 1990, p. 4: and Jan Hartl, Michael Deis and Jill Chin, "Czech and Slovak Views on Economic Reform," *RFE/RL Research Report*, Vol. 1, No. 23, 5 June 1992, 64–65. See also Wolchik, *Czechoslovakia in Transition*, Chaps. 2 and 4.

45. Boguszak and Rak, "Czechoslovakia - May 1990 Survey Report," Table 1; and Boguszak and Rak, *"Společně, ale každy jinak."*

46. See Deis and Chin, p. 65.

47. From information from Institute for Public Opinion Research, Prague, June 1992.

48. See Jiři Pehe, "Czechoslovakia's Changing Political Spectrum," *Report on Eastern Europe*, 31 January 1992, 2.

49. Information from Institute for Public Opinion Research, Prague, March 1992.

50. Institute for Public Opinion Research, Prague, *"Postoje čs. veřejnosti k základnim politickým institucím,"* March 1992.

51. From information from Institute for Public Opinion Research, Prague, June 1992.

52. Butorova *et al.* See also Wolchik, *Czechoslovakia in Transition*, especially Chaps. 2 and 3.

53. Association for Independent Social Analysis, *Výzkum politických postoiu*, 15–24 Dubna 1992 (Prague: ASIA, May 1992).

54. V. Krivý and J. Radičova, *Atmosféra dôvery a atmosféra nedôvery?" Socioloqické aktuality*, 1992, No. 2, 12–13.

55. See Joseph C. Brada, "The Mechanics of the Voucher Plan in Czechoslovakia," *RFE/RL Research Report*, Vol. 1 No. 17, 24 April, 1992, 42–45.

THE ROLE OF THE POLITICAL RIGHT IN POST-COMMUNIST CZECH-SLOVAKIA

Otto Ulc

After the swift bloodless demise of the communist regime in November 1989, the society that has been largely passive for two generations turned to politics with a voracious appetite. Within three months no less than 58 political parties and 334 associations obtained registration—the Royalist Party, the Czechoslovak Nonviolently Anticommunist Party, and the Party of the Friends of Beer included. Others such as the Czech Anarchist Alliance and the very visible Independent Erotic Initiative (*Nezávislá erotická iniciativa - NEI*) enriched the political landscape shortly thereafter.[1]

An extreme of a totalitarian uniformity gave way to extreme political fragmentation. A lack of experience with a give-and take reality of a democratic political process prompted great many people to view a compromise as a dishonorable surrender of principles, regardless of the eventual insignificance of the issue. On the political landscape, criss-crossed with ravines of sectarian intolerance, an ominous paradox emerged: the Communist Party, the former monopolist of all power, despite the defection of most of its members managed to retain a dues-paying membership base of 430,000, greater than the rest of the parties combined. Fortunately for the cause of democracy, in 1991 the Communist Party, too, started to experience the same kind of fragmentation, recently became known as "the Polish disease."

The injurious impact of the proportionate representation system is mitigated by the application of the German rule barring from parliamentary seats marginal parties that fail to obtain a least 5 percent of the total vote. As a result, in Czechoslovakia's first general election held in June 1990, of the numerous contestants only eight managed to get into the federal National Assembly.

Second, general elections were scheduled for June 1992. Small parties were forming temporary alliances in order to pass the legal hurdle. Public opinion surveys indicate considerable dissatisfaction of the electorate, especially with the state of the economy struggling to cope with the ongoing radical reform.

The analysts are in agreement on several points: First, the forth-coming electoral contest will radically change the composition of the federal parliament that had been dominated by the Civic Forum (*Ob-canské hnut i*), the victorious movement that swept away the old regime but has since fallen apart. Secondly, a return of the commu-nists to power in the Czech Republic remains outside the realm of the possible. Unlike the situation in the Slovak Republic, the Czech Communist Party is increasingly a preserve of senior citizens and un-able to find any coalition partners. Third, the Czechs who in the 1946 free election voted for the communist ticket in greater propor-tion (38 percent) than any other nation on earth, (and the several million citizens who subsequently passed through communist ranks) in the post-communist era of the 1990s judged the political Left out of favor. At the same time the political Right has become 'fashion-able.' In the Czech Republic the frontrunner in the polls, with the support of over 20 percent of the electorate, is an offshoot of the Civic Forum, known as Civic Democratic Party (*Občanská demokrat-ická strana - ODS*), created and led by Václav Klaus, the federal Minister of Finance, and the architect of the economic reform. This forceful personality characterizes the *ODS* as "the strongest and most promising rightist political party in all of post-communist Europe."[2]

No such equivalent party came into existence in Slovakia. Its political spectrum is dominated by nationalist, populist parties with little sympathy for federalism, liberalism, pluralistic democracy, and market economy. An increasing number of observers including re-sponsible public figures president Vaclav Havel included, characterize this dominating political preference as "national socialism." Con-sidering the substantial dichotomy of trends in the two republics, a viable workable federation is quite difficult to envisage.

Havel in his interview for Warsaw's *Gazeta Wyborcza*, conducted by its editor, the well-known intellectual Adam Michnik stated:

> Judging by what is beginning to appear in Czechoslovakia, the most menacing demons are anti-Semitism, ethnic intoler-ance, and xenophobia, which all can be observed in Slovakia and, in somewhat different forms, in the Czech regions. .

. . It is a combination of complexes, chauvinism, fascism, intolerance, and hatred toward everybody who is different. There is an element of "racial purity" in it. It is a return to the phenomenon of Czech fascism, which differed from the German only by being Czech. In Slovakia, there exists what the communists called "clerofascism": They want to relive the period from 1939 to 1945 and anti-Semitism is beginning to appear.[3]

As to the roots and appeal of radical rightist extremism after a long lasting rule of an officially revolutionary, leftist party, it is fitting to quote the astute political thinker Milan Simečka, that "Communism is not dead because . . . it never existed".[4] These words he wrote in September 1989, two months before the demise of the communist dinosaur. Simečka stressed that behind the facade of the Marx-Leninist jargon a reactionary populism was firmly imbedded, characterized by class egotism, primitive consumerism, nationalism, anti-intellectualism and anti-Semitism. After all the decades of an alleged striving for a communist utopia, nothing else was left but this debased populism, a perplexed wavering ideology of a status quo. The society that had emerged from this experience is impatient, frustrated, unprepared for the burden of making their own decisions as free citizens, and all too eager to distribute the blame to others for its own shortcomings. A tradition of plebeian egalitarianism begets envy—the *Leitmotiv* that survived in robust health the end of the communist era.

Almost every adult citizen has been tainted by collaboration with the former political system. Its permanence was not in doubt; a vast majority of the people criticized the system without any mental preparation for an alternative existence. "In 1989 we gained freedom but we did not get the instructions on how to use it," commented the multitalented artist Jiñi Suchy.[5] Intoxication with suddenly obtained freedom turned many of the beneficiaries into becoming contemptuous of this precious commodity. Three generations grew up with the ideology of class struggle, a search for an enemy. Now, an ideology thoroughly discredited continues to cast a long shadow: nationalistic, chauvinistic bigotry is ready to fill the void.

Agencies associated with Gallup International conducted a public opinion survey in all European countries in 1991. As to the question about the near future ("Will 1992 be better or worse than 1991?"), the Czechoslovak respondents were the most pessimistic on the continent, followed by the Russians, Estonians, Hungarians, and the Lithuanians.[6] Fear of the police state was replaced by a fear of the future, the looming economic uncertainty. The human products of an autocratic experience are now looking for new autocrats to provide direction, purpose, identity.

In view of all these democracy-unfriendly indices it may come as a pleasant surprise, that in the Czech Republic only one extremist party attracts enough following (4 to 7 percent of the electorate) to have the chance of passing the 5 percent hurdle and gaining an entry into the parliament. This is a group with a somewhat redundant name, "Republican Party - Association for the Republic." Devoid of a comprehensive program it tries to exploit public discontent about various issues; the weakness and dilettantism of the government, disarray in the legislature, chaos in the economy, an alarming increase in criminality, etc. The role of the enemy is assigned to the foreigners, the Gypsies, the communists past and present. Prominent on the hate list is the government and president Havel in particular, accused of a multitude of personal vices, including his alleged complicity and conspiracy with the old communist power holders. Open letters with preposterous charges are addressed to the president, demanding his resignation.[7]

Aside from the message, the greatest weakness of this party is the fact that it is a creation of one man - Miloslav Sladek, a young, photogenic, skilled orator-demagogue, formerly a docile collaborator with the previous regime, employed as a communist censor. When Sladek appeared on the political scene with his ultraradical thunder, some suspicion arose as to his motives and his eventual role as a proxy for the Communist Party in the plan of destroying the young fragile democracy. However, this does not seem to be the case though not infrequently Sladek's extremist demands are echoed on the opposite end of the political spectrum by his allegedly mortal enemies. Sládek's megalomanic temperament has reduced his party to a one-man show. His lieutenants are largely invisible and several of them have already deserted this unsavory movement. Sládek resorts to calling for actions well out of order within acceptable democratic moves. One of these was his cry for tossing all the cabinet members in the Vltava river, and a suggestion to march to the state television station attempting by force to gain entry and secure free broadcasting time. Sládek finds support in the scandal sheets, notably the daily tabloid *Spigl* (unauthorized Czech phonetic spelling of the influential German weekly *Der Spiegel*), an enterprise with several former officers of the disbanded secret police in its editorial ranks. Irresponsible accusations lead to frequent law suits and punitive judgments. Sladek is supported by malcontents of different stripes, ranging from teenagers ill at ease with their excess hormones, to embittered senior citizens. Their ranks are invariably augmented by "professional demonstrators" led by individuals with sinister connections to the former *nomenklatura* and the secret police.[8] However, the overwhelming part of the electorate, frustrated and full of anxiety as to the economic future, are more likely to turn to the Social Democratic Party or the Communist Party promising the same undeliverable welfare state nirvana.

The configuration of the political forces and its underlying political culture in Slovakia is quite different as are its historical experience and the current economic problems. Czechs fascism was an episodic, marginal affair. Led by Radolo Gajda, a retired general and not a very skillful politician, the movement stressed autocratic rule and Czech nationalism not at the service of German Nazi interests. During the wartime years of 1939–1945, the Czech part of the dismembered republic was under German occupation, supported by a handful of local anti-Semitic collaborators and their publications, *Vlajka* ["Flag"] and *Arijský boj* ["Aryan Fight"]. No volunteer units to fight along the Germans were organized as was the case in some other parts of occupied Europe.

On the other hand, Slovak separatists contributed to the destruction of the democratic republic of Czechoslovakia. They were rewarded with Slovak statehood and sovereignty, though substantially restricted and tainted by their alliance with Berlin. An autocratic Catholic regime declared war on the Allies and sent some units to fight on the Eastern front. Looking more to Spain than to Germany as a model, its fascism developed "a somewhat operetta appearance."[9] In the neighborhood of apocalyptic destruction, Slovakia was a tranquil, harmonious oasis, and its non-Jewish population prospered.

The defeat of Germany ended the existence of the first independent Slovak state, still remembered with fondness by a great number of Slovak patriots. Had it not been for the generosity of the Allies, Slovakia, instead of being included on the victorious side under the common umbrella of a restored Czechoslovak Republic, would have had to share the punitive measures meted out to Hitler's other eastern satellites.

The Czechoslovak federation is the last remaining entity inhabited by more than one Slavic nation that has not yet fallen apart.* The twice as numerous, culturally and economically more advanced Czechs have developed a different political, cultural, and national identity. During World War II, the Czech lands were Hitler's victim, whereas the officially independent Slovakia was Hitler's ally. The Slovaks collaborated with the fascists, the Czechs after the war failed to resists the lure of Stalinism. After the subsequent bitter experience, it was the Prague—not Bratislava—Spring of 1968, the "heresy" of "socialism with a human face" that prompted the Soviet tanks rolling. In 1977, the human rights manifesto, Charter 77, was signed by some 1,700 individuals among whom only four were Slovaks. Much more numerous were Slovaks, who considered this prodemocracy movement as one aimed at discrediting President Husak because he was a Slovak. As in 1968, the upheaval in 1989 that ended the communist era, was a Czech affair. Anticommunism has never fully reached Slovakia.

The introduction of a market economy begot unemployment, a dreaded novelty in the country. Productivity in Slovakia in general, has been lower, the energy consumption has been higher, and the prospects of doing business as usual is dimmer. The current decline in production is greater than it was during the Great Depression of the 1930s. The plan by the Federal government of converting the armament industry to the production of goods of non-lethal nature is widely resented and interpreted as an insidious plot to stab the Slovaks in their back—allegedly the greatest catastrophe to be endured since the Turkish invasion in the seventeenth century.[10] Social discontent is markedly higher in Slovakia than in the Czech lands: over 80 percent of the Slovak public is opposed to the prospects of the introduction of a market economy and expressed preferences for what is increasingly termed as "national socialism." In the March 1991 survey, 89 percent of respondents in Slovakia identified socio-economic security as the most fundamental, desirable value. Less than one-half considered democracy a priority. The lower the level of education, the greater is the preference for an autocratic rule.[11]

Public Against Violence (*Verejnost oroti násiliu - VPN*) in Slovakia, the sister organization of the Civic Forum and the main force of Slovak democracy—with Alexander Dubček as the Speaker of the federal National Assembly and Marian Calfa as the Premier of the fed-

---

* Even that statement appears incorrect today.

eral cabinet in its ranks—in less than two years almost reached the point of its extinction. According to a survey conducted in February 1992, its electoral support stands at a mere 2.2 percent to guarantee its demise from future participation in the legislative and executive branches of the government.

Unlike the people of the Czech Republic with their strong conservative, anti-socialist preference for a pluralistic democracy and a market economy, in Slovakia a full four-fifths of the electorate support the nationalist, pro-socialist orientation. "Nationalism thus represents the last chance of a new mutation of communism," as it was acknowledged by Pavel Kanis, the head of the by now defunct federal structure of the Communist Party, a lifelong ardent internationalist reborn as a no less ardent nationalist. Whereas the majority of the Czechs are inclined to view nationalism as the last stage of communism and as an expression of a "collective inferiority complex," the majority of Slovaks cherish it as a prime value to which other considerations must be subordinated. The party with the largest following (over 38 percent of the electorate) is the Movement for Democratic Slovakia (*Hnutie za demokratické Slovensko - HZDS*), created by the former Premier Vladimir Mečiar, a former communist official, a rather vulgar personality with a strong populist appeal.

Three other parties enjoy a roughly even support (14–15 percent) of the Slovak public:

1. The former Communist Party, renamed as the Party of the Democratic Left (*Strana demokratické lavice - SDL*), led by the capable young Peter Weiss;
2. The Slovak National Party (*Slovenská národná strana - SNS*) led by the vehemently anti-Czech, yet Czech-born Jozef Prokeš;
3. The Christian Democratic Movement (*Krestianské demokratické hnutie - KDH*) led by Ján Čarnogursky, a former imprisoned dissident and the current Slovak Premier.

None of these four political formations support the preservation of the Czechoslovak federation in its present form. Prokes calls for an immediate secession and declaration of Slovak independence whereas Mečiar and Weiss seem to prefer a variant of a confederative arrangement. Čarnogursky's KDH is split, espousing notions of a loose federation, confederation or sovereignty one moment, only to repudiate it several hours thereafter. Čarnogursky's Christian Democrats advocate unabashedly antiliberal values. Their opposition to the so-called "Pragocentrism" is motivated by their rejection of secular values espoused by the Czechs. Havel, honored abroad, is spat upon in Bratislava with the advice "You swinish Jew, go back to Prague."[12] Čarnogursky delivered an eulogy at the funeral of his former jailer, Husák, and found words of sympathy for those who remembered the wartime Slovak independent state with fondness. The Slovak cabinet declined to comment on the republication of the "Protocols of the Elders of Zion" but initiated a prompt criminal action against a novelist for having written a short, allegedly blasphemous story concerning Jesus. In the communist days, the prime villains were Washington and Bonn. Their places are now taken by Prague and Budapest. The Ukraine is being considered as the potentially prime ally of Slovakia.[13]

The separatists characterize "Czechoslovakism"—i.e., a concept of a common unitary state—as "a monstrous fascist, genocidal theory aimed at the extermination of the Slovak nation," and the humanist Havel as "the most evil personality of the twentieth century, second only to Lenin."[14] The fear of radical economic transformation is a significant but not the sole factor behind such vehement verbal overkill. In Prague it is being recognized that Slovakia has not yet had the opportunity to fulfill its national aspirations—and it is generally accepted, that "everyone has the right to live in his nineteenth century." This craving for national identity largely unrecognized by the outside world, at times resembles an encounter with the absurd. According to the historian Milan Stanislav —Durica (now living in Italy), Slovakia is the oldest nation in Central Europe, with a record of its own oldest statehood.[15] Such extravagant claims then prompt a response among the Czechs that "Adam and Eve, too, were Slovaks."

The profascist tendencies are to a considerable extent fomented and supported by the circles from among the defeated communist regime. The former *nomenklatura,* individuals compromised by their secret police connection and service to Soviet interests, now use extremist nationalist sentiments to undermine the young democracy that deprived them of their power. In this effort they are aided by strange bedfellows, namely, the exiles with a war criminal record who found refuge in Canada. However, the influence of the organization, called the World Congress of the Slovaks, (*Svetouý konqres Slaváov*) funded by the billionaire Stefan Roman (now deceased), is subsiding. So is the vision of a largesse to finance a Slovak version of a Japanese economic miracle.

In 1991, Stanislav Panis, a former nightclub musician, founded an openly fascist party called Slovak National Unity (*Slovenská národná jednota*) with a program of immediate declaration of Slovak independence and stringent measures such as the adoption of a law "to punish those who offend the religious feeling of the Slovaks."[16]

Ominously, the mass media in Slovakia almost without an exception follow a nationalistic, highly intolerant line. The profederal Slovaks—the allegedly silent majority—is both totally silent and invisible. Occasional writers of letters to the Czech press are identified merely by their initials, with the explanation of a need to protect them from possible harm. The threat of violence comes not only from sinister anonymous sources but also from public figures holding high offices. Jan Slota, Mayor of Zilina, a major town, issued a threat of public lynching to those Slovaks supporting the preservation of the Czechoslovak federation. Slota violated the Criminal Code with impunity and he continues to keep his seat in the federal National Assembly. Josef Bakšay, the federal minister of foreign trade and one high on Slata's hit list, responded: "I survived communism and I will also survive fascism."[17] However, other targets of proposed vengeance take the threats more seriously. Fedor Gál, the former prominent official of the VPN, after receiving numerous menacing letters, he and his family were forced to seek police protection and leave Slovakia. The profederation Slovaks threatened him with lynching and accused him of "not speaking Slovak but Hebrew."[18] "Gál's talmudic gang!" (*Talmudistická Gálova kamarila*) fumed the periodical *Navý Slovák*, further on defining Talmud as "that diabolic teaching asserting that it is permissible to cheat the Aryans."[19]

Whereas 5 percent of the Czechs feel that the Jews exercise an unduly great influence in society, in Slovakia, 25 percent of the respondents feel this way.[20] Slovak anti-Semitism has a long and sordid tradition. Starting in 1939, the "independent" state with its president, Roman Catholic Monsignor Jozef Tiso, passed anti-Jewish laws exceeding in severity their German model, as it was proudly emphasized. The mass deportation of the victims to destruction followed. No other country sanctified such actions by law. Only one parliamentarian cast a dissenting vote, the Hungarian aristocrat János Esterházy, subsequently persecuted by the Gestapo (after the war he was arrested by the Soviet secret police and, in 1947, sentenced by a Slovak court to death *in absentia*).[21]

March 15th—the day of the declaration of the first fascist Slovak state—is now celebrated in Slovakia. A memorial plaque honoring the executed war criminal Tiso, whose government sent tens of thousands of Jews to the gas chambers, was unveiled in October 1990, the very day of the Israeli president's state visit to Czechoslovakia. The record of prewar Czechoslovakia is rejected *in toto* and the acts of wartime genocide are simply glossed over by the public. Jewish cemeteries are regularly vandalized, pamphlets and books are published against this "eternal enemy," and Jews are accused of causing Slovakia's current suffering. The Slovak authorities have yet to initiate the first criminal proceeding against such anti-Semites.

Václav Havel in his interview with Michnik pointed out that national allegiance got imbedded in people more profoundly than class allegiance. One of the communist's utopian goals was the imposition of uniformity—from Prague to Vladivostok. Society, thus, lived in imposed seclusion. But then suddenly the high walls were torn down, "strange people" emerged in the midst of changes. The residents of communist states, long unaccustomed to strangers, as they were unfamiliar with personal freedom, suffered a shock. Havel added:

> It is similar to coming out of prison: When you are inside, you yearn for the moment when they will release you, but when it happens, you are suddenly helpless. . . . This is why it [society] looks for an enemy on whom it can blame everything. It is easy to make an enemy out of the one who at first glance is different from the rest.[22]

A cross-national survey was conducted in Hungary, Poland, and Czechoslovakia to identify ethnic preferences.[23] T he Hungarians gravitate with their sympathies in the first place toward Germany, Poland and Czechoslovakia choose the United States of America. The Hungarians appear to be less distrustful of other ethnic groups than the two Slavic nations in this study. In the case of Czechoslovakia, xenophobia is stronger among the Slovaks than the Czechs. The three most resented groups of strangers are the Africans, the Arabs, and the Gypsies. They would be unwelcome to live in their neighborhood by 70 to 90 percent of the respondents.

In the previous forty years, the vast majority of the population had no opportunity to travel abroad and become at least visually acquainted with people of different ethnicity. Dark skinned strangers in Czechoslovakia were few, mainly foreign students from Third World countries. They were resented because of their privileged status (access to hard currency stores, preferential treatment by the school authorities with regard to accommodation and academic standards), and because of their presumed pro-communist sympathies. With the end of the communist era and the opening of the borders, the envious populace, having become well aware of its impoverishment in comparison to the outside world, vented its frustrations in a manner impossible under the conditions of the previous police state. They often resorted to demonstrations of hostility that not infrequently turned into physical violence. These are condemned by the authorities. However, they lack sufficient capacity or, at times the will to prevent them. The only political party not reluctant to sympathize with the racists is the extremist Republican Party of the demagogue Sladek, occasionally dubbed as the Czech Le Pen. In Děčín, a North Bohemian town, a Czech version of the Ku Klux Klan sprung up but the Ministry of Interior refused to register it as a legitimate organization.

Karel Kovanda, a U.S. educated prominent official of the Ministry of Foreign Affairs, described his experience in an article entitled "The Fascists."

> Two fascists attacked a Gypsy only because he was a Gypsy.
> . . . At the Wenceslav Square in front of the Ambassador hotel a group of perhaps one hundred fascists bloodied an Egyptian and some bystanders applauded. The Japanese embassy is issuing a warning to Japanese tourists not to wear jeans so that they will not be taken for Vietnamese who are also a favorite target of the fascists.[24]

The press reports incidents, violent and nonviolent, with a daily regularity. Acts of racially motivated brutality is credited to the movement of the skinheads: the term is adopted in the Czech language as skini. These are mainly working class adolescents, frequently the products of broken homes, who seek security in paramilitary bands and ultranationalistic slogans. They carry banners with a swastika or an American Confederate flag.

The sudden novelty of the democratic freedom of expression also encourages some substantially undemocratic sentiments. For example, on the May First holiday, in 1990, in the very center of Prague, some two hundred skinheads marched, attacking bystanders of darker skin, and shouting an increasingly popular slogan *CIKANI DO PLYNU* ("Gypsies be gassed!"). Under the spell of a heavy metal concert, some enthusiasts made an (unsuccessful) effort to lynch some

Gypsies. In the city of Plzeň, a Turkish citizen lost his life in a racially motivated killing, mistakenly taken for a Gypsy. The Gypsies reciprocate with their share of violent acts.

The Gypsies are Czechoslovakia's fastest growing minority. They were singled out by the Nazis, together with the Jews for genocide. Unlike the Jewish survivors, many of whom emigrated, the Gypsies, with no homeland of their own, stayed and multiplied. According to the 1980 census, their number reached almost 300,000. They were, however, under-reported and at the present time, it is estimated to be between 700,000 and 800,000 in a country of less than 16 million. Whereas the population ratio between the Czech and the Slovak Republic is 2:1, the ratio of the Gypsies is reversed and twice as many now live in Slovakia. Their concentration is largest in the Eastern province. In 1980, half of the residents of the town of Rimavaka Sobota were Gypsies. The city of Kosice now contains the largest settlement of Gypsies in the country and probably in all Europe. Under the headline "Population Explosion of the Gypsies" the widely read tabloid, *Express*, warned the public that Gypsy fertility may mean a tragedy, that within a century the country may well have to be renamed the Gypsy Republic (*Romská republika*).[25] Old stereotypes are being applied to all members of this minority regardless of individual lifestyle and degree of integration. The Gypsies are allegedly all primitive, antisocial, parasitic, and crime oriented. They supposedly breed too much, and extract from the state a host of undeserved benefits. The Gypsies' level of education, and their socio-economic advancement is indeed low, and their criminality is disproportionately, alarmingly high. The end of the communist era, the collapse of the police state structure and the subsequent evaporation of fear of authority triggered a huge rise of criminal behavior. Overall criminality tripled, robberies rose sixfold. The share of the Gypsy culprits in acts of violence is enormous: the Prague police directorate alone reported their 90 percent share of responsibility for crimes committed in the area.[26] Gypsies engage in thievery and robberies, a knife is their favorite weapon. They managed to turn once civilized neighborhoods into a wasteland resembling the South Bronx of New York City. Furthermore, the racism of the Czechs and Slovaks is being met with what is termed "Gypsy racism," violent acts against the skinheads.[27]

The undermanned police force, insecure of its stature under the rules of new democratic conditions, frequently abdicates its responsibility and the streets are left to the skinhead vigilantes to enforce order—through violence. Their actions are then met with sympathy by perhaps the major part of the population.

This situation is not likely to be short-term. Its resolution will depend on several factors, notably on economic improvement, stabilization of democratic roots, and the preservation or dissolution of the Czechoslovak federation. Currently, a major exodus of the Gypsies from Slovakia is reported, a move encouraged by Slovak authorities.

The June 1992 general election in which close to 90 percent of the electorate participated ended the era of the dissidents. In the Czech republic they were replaced by the technocrats., led by Václav Klaus, and in Slovakia by the nationalistic sympathizers with the old socialist ways, led by Vladimir Mečiar. This polarized result in the two republics produced a situation dubbed *as kočkopes (kočka - "cat"; "dog.")* an unworkable hybrid in which one part is pulled toward a "national socialist solution" while the other goes full speed ahead toward a pluralistic democracy and a market economy.

In the Czech republic every fifth vote went to the foes of pluralistic democracy—14 percent to the Communist-led Left Bloc, and 6 percent to Sládek's "Republicans" who thus managed to pass the 5 percent hurdle and gain an entry in the parliament. Sládek's message was exeedingly simple: blame all hardships on identifiable forces—the government, the Communists, the foreigners. Given the paucity of Jews in the country, the Gypsies filled the requirement. The higher the Gypsy concentration, the higher Sládek's electoral support. In Usti, the center of the ecologically devastated region Northern Bohemia, Sládek's party received 17.5 percent of the vote. Despite their militantly anti-Communist rhetoric, the political activities of these protofascists are very hard to distinguish from those of their allegedly mortal enemies. As a rule, both groups find common ground in condemning the policies of the government.

Following the electinn, Klaus and Mečiar, the two new premiers, after difficult but altogether civil negotiation agreed on the demise of the federation by the end of 1992. On January 1, 1993 two new sovereign states were born. In the meantime, Havel resigned the presidency and the parliament rallied to elect a successor.

In Slovakia, steps were already taken, familiar from past experience: purges in the state apparatus, de facto censorship, an introduction of what is termed "national socialism," along with a vow that freedom of expression will be guaranteed to all those who respect national interests defined by Mečiar. The process of further privatization has been stopped and steps are undertaken toward the re-establishment of the controlling role of the state over the economy.

In the Czech republic the government's priority on building a market econnmy has not weakened. The inflation rate is low and unemployment is almost non-existent. In contrast to the successes in the economic sphere, the machinery of the state show signs of serious malfunctioning. This is particularly the case of the judiciary, understaffed and demoralized. Crimes remain undetected and criminals unpunished. In the word of Lukáš Mašin, mayor of Ustñ: "In some localities the situation reached the point which deserves to be termed as a collapse of a civilized society."[28] The problems with the Gypsy minority is getting increasingly acute, their criminality disproportionately high in comparison to the society at large. The office of the prosecutor general submitted to the Czech legislature a bill called "Extraordinary Measures to Ensure Public Order" aimed mainly at curbing the Gypsy violators. Though decried as an initiative characteristic of a police state, it has the support of the overwhelming majority of the population. The "Gypsy Question" is becoming a prominently explosive issue, to be further exploited by the radical political right.

NOTES

1. At the NEI conferences, congresses, and symposia topless waitresses serve the needs of the participants. The biweekly *NEI REPORT* has a record circulation (380,000) in the country, second only to a television guide. *Lidové noviny*, December 30, 1991.

2. *Reportér*, December 5, 1991.

3. *World Press Review*, March 1992.

4. *Listy*, No. 2, 1990, pp. 50 51.

5. *Lidové noviny*, September 30, 1991.

6. *Lidové noviny*, December 28, 1991. The greatest optimists, in the descending order, were the Icelanders, the Danes, and the Swedes.

7. *Republika*, a biweekly sheet, July 15, 1991.

8. *Lidové noviny*, June 19, 1991.

9. Milan *Simečka in Listy*, No. 4, July 15, 1991.

10. *Forum*, April 10, 1991; *Lidové noviny*, November 22, 1991.

11. *Op. cit.*, May 8 and 16, June 13, 1991; *Zpravodaj* (Switzerland), No. 5, 1991.

12. *Reportér*, April 11, 1991.

13. This position of Čarnogursky was confirmed by Čalfa in *Lidové noviny*, December 6, 1991.

14. So stated at the meeting of the separatists in Bratislava. *Op. cit.*, May 31, 1991; *Forum*, April 10, 1991.

15. *Slovenský národ*, October 13, 1990.

16. *Lidové noviny*, January 7, 1992.

17. Interview in *op. cit.*, November 2, 1991. Cf. his interview for *Mlady svět*, same date.

18. *Verejnost*, October 8, 1990.

19. *Lidové noviny*, April 19, 1991.

20. *Op. cit.*, May 24, 1991.

21. Ibid.

22. *World Press Review, op. cit.*

23. *Lidové noviny*, May 24. 1991.

24. *Op. cit.*, January 25. 1992.

25. *Express*, July 2, 1990.

26. *Lidové noviny*, December 13. 1991.

27. *Reportér*, December 1991.

28. *Respekt*, January 11, 1993.

29. Ibid.

JOBBRA ÁT! [RIGHT FACE!]
RIGHT-WING TRENDS IN POST-COMMUNIST HUNGARY

Ivan T. Berend

Something About the Term: Political Right

In a dramatically changing environment and in a new world system in the making, it is rather difficult to define the exact meaning of the political Right and Left. Though history did not end or loose its meaning, historical terms did. They became rather amorphous and unstable. In the given situation one might accept Karl Popper's suggestion to "give up the naive belief that any definite set of historical records can ever be interpreted in one way only."

In its original meaning Left and Right represented the different sides of parliament. This term, however, gained a political content from the ideas and political goals of the groupings or parties that sat on a given side. In the last two centuries different sorts of Right and Left political trends confronted and struggled against each other or monopolized power. What is now the historical demarcation line between them? What are the characteristics of the Right in our changing times? Certain elements are easily recognizable, especially those that were notoriously emblematic and manifested extremism. Among them one should mention nationalist exclusiveness, or (using Hannah Arendt's term) tribal nationalism with its xenophobia, anti-Semitism, anti-Gypsy or, in a more general way, oppressive antiminority politics and hostility against other, often neighboring, peoples. One can name conservative political Catholicism (or religious fundamentalism). History, of course, produced different kinds of despotisms, and the differentiation between Right-wing and Left-wing despotism is more of a question of terminology than real content: dictatorial left-wing power could also be interpreted as a right-wing deformation of a genuinely left-wing trend.

The historical Right and Left in certain periods represented aristocratic or bourgeois interests, but then the Left became an exponent of the lower layers of society and represented social responsiveness, while the Right, in most cases, expressed the interests of the social elite or simply the rich. However, one has to stress that history produced Right-wing populism and even Fascism which often used Left-wing rhetoric and borrowed certain ideas that previously characterized the Left.

Regarding the changing content of traditional terms, it pays to note the transformed role of "free market ideology," which definitely belonged to the Left in the struggle against feudal bondage and for a national market. As Arthur Lewis rightly remarked, the idea of free market had to collapse because of the "Great Depressions" (or the Kuznets' cycles) of the last third of the nineteenth and first third of the twentieth centuries. A victorious Keynesism became an organic part of a Left-wing approach toward economic issues, which was rather similar to the social democratic idea of "organized Capitalism." As "free market ideology" collapsed because of the series of Great Depressions, Keynesism could not survive the uniquely long golden years of post-war prosperity. In recent decades Friedmanite free marketism has been an organic element of the Right's philosophy and practice.

What is the case in Eastern Europe? In my interpretation, the unlimited "free market ideology," with its lack of sensitivity toward social issues and its naive belief that market automatism would in due time (or better to say in the long run) solve all the social problems, is also Right-wing. This "economic Right," however, often characterizes otherwise Center-Left political parties, because of their conviction that State-Socialist bondage (as in the period of early Capitalism) would not be able to bring about freedom, democracy and would not, thus, in the long run, serve the genuine interests of society.

According to the measure of extreme or moderate representations of these ideas and politics, one may speak about extreme or mid-Right trends.

Just as in economics, there is a kind of cyclical development in political history as well. Like the 25–30 years of cyclical economic ups and downs, politics seems to have its own Left and Right long-term trends. The Left-wing resurgence of post World War II Europe, combining the half century domination of the "Keynesian revolution," and European social democracy together with the "lefty" 1960s re-

naissance of Marx, and the student revolutions of 1968 from Paris
to Berkeley, was then followed by a Right-wing "downturn." The
1970–80s witnessed a dramatic turn toward the Right: a conservative
reaction to 1968 was accompanied by the failure of Keynesism that
had simply stopped to work after the oil crisis. The role of the state in
the economy was discredited. Instead of the visible hand of the state,
the Smithian invisible hand of an almighty market had become the
idol once again. An almost religious belief in market automatism was
manifested in a decade of Reaganism and Thatcherism in the 1980s.
Postwar nationalization was followed by privatization in Western Europe. Around the end of the decade most of the European Social
Democratic parties were defeated, even in Sweden where its domination had been the most impressive and long lasting. This trend was
crowned by the spectacular collapse of East European state-socialism,
followed by the splitting up of the Soviet Union, which had ceased to
exist at the very end of the decade.

If we are going to speak about right-wing trends in post-Communist Hungary, we have to begin with the international success of the
political Right in the greater part of the late twentieth century world.

The trend is evidently strong in Eastern Europe. The pendulum
swings to the Right after almost half a century of Left-wing extremism; it is the well known "action generates reaction" law of physics.
This is definitely the case with nationalism, which had been swept under the rug for a half a century. The expansionist Soviet super-power,
dressed in the toga of internationalist Marxist ideology, precluded any
kind of small power national consciousness. With the collapse of state-
socialism and Soviet domination, a previously dethroned nationalism,
the leading political trend of the nineteenth century and inter-war
Eastern Europe, immediately filled the ideological-political vacuum
and gained back its primary role. Even if it is a natural reaction
and a manifestation of the right of self-determination of peoples, one
should not forget two important points. First, the nice-sounding right
of self-determination in the "belt of mixed population" is a dangerous
ideology. As Karl Popper formulated in his famous *Open Society and
its Enemies*:

> How anybody who had the slightest knowledge of European
> history, of the shifting and mixing of all kinds of tribes, of
> the countless waves of peoples who had come forth from
> their original Asian habitat and split up and mingled when
> reaching the maze of peninsulas called European continent,

how anybody who knew this could ever have put forward such an inapplicable principle, is hard to understand.

Second, nationalism, as it was explained by Robert Kann, had lost its clear, unmuddled progressive content in the region already by around the mid-nineteenth century. International solidarity and friendship of free peoples, which characterized the early national movements, turned toward (or at least mixed with) national exclusiveness, national hatred and antagonism. Indeed, the first half of the twentieth century became the witch's Sabbath of unleashed hyper-nationalism, with the wild forces of tribalism arising throughout the region. All this is evident again today: the unwritten "threshold principles," which had, as Eric Hobsbawm remarked, a certain validity even in Versailles, has now collapsed, and a further Balkanization of the already Balkanized Balkans as well as the entire region is in the making. Just as after World War I, when countries that never existed before, such as great-Romania, Czechoslovakia and Yugoslavia, were founded, we are witnessing for the first time the birth of the new independent countries of Slovenia, Belarus, Ukraine and others, under the banner of the right of self-determination. As a consequence, minorities are already frightened, in some cases even suppressed: borders are already being challenged and civil wars have begun. The new trends of East-Central Europe are pregnant with nationalist skirmishes, endless struggles, border debates, civil wars and local warfare.

Is this historical trend entirely irrational in the age of European unification? Though it certainly seems to be, it still has its rationale. The existing multinational states and empires in the region cannot, while their nation-building process is incomplete, possibly join in a unification process. In other words, disintegration seems to be unavoidable as a pre-condition of integration. An attempt to accomplish these unfinished historical processes caused a historical asyncronity which unleashed trends that are moving against the stream of the development of the European Core. The rebirth of an East European nationalism is thus understandable and certainly unavoidable. But though clearly being the rational and logic of the history of the periphery it still may very well be counterproductive and suicidal.

The same is true with the Right-wing trends that were bottled up for half a century and violently reappeared in the vacuum of values which was left after communism. Recycled ideologies, revitalized populism, violent xenophobia, anti-Semitism, physical violence against gypsies, and nostalgia for decayed and long disappeared authoritarian-dictatorial Christian-national regimes—this variety of old ideological garbage was rediscovered and came to the surface.

Right-wing trends and authoritarian rule, though nowadays often connected with the area, do not represent some unique "Hungarian fate" or "East European characteristic." It certainly belongs to the failure of the peripheries and embodies their bitter, wild reaction and revolt against it. It is both a reaction to the previous decades as well as a consequence of the disappointment of such a bumpy and painful transformation. Certain elements of Right-wing tendencies, however, are closely connected with some successful Western trends, such as a re-born free market ideology or a peripheral but visibly present skinhead neo-fascism. Right-wing trends, partly marginal as they are, might become dangerous if the East European transformation does not produce an impressive and visible improvement, an increasing prosperity in the coming decade.

All these trends created the framework for the advance of the political Right in post-Communist Hungary.

In the Spring of 1990 free parliamentary elections gave a clear-cut victory to the newly emerging Center-Right parties in Hungary. Left-wing parties were all defeated. The Hungarian Socialist Workers party (*MSzMP*), the traditional communist wing of the former ruling party, and, much more surprisingly, the reorganized Social Democratic party (*MSzDP*), could not even gain the minimum votes to get deputies into Parliament. The Socialist party (*MSzP*) was formed by the reform wing of the former ruling party in October 1989. Although it deserved credit for previous reforms and liberalization and in preparing the peaceful transition, it paradoxically received the worst electoral result among the former, now reshaped Communist parties throughout Eastern Europe with only 10 percent of the votes. Carrying the burden of the past, the Socialists have now a rather limited role in Hungarian politics.

The governing coalition was formed by Center-Right parties and led by the Hungarian Democratic Forum (MDF), the senior partner of the coalition (with 42 percent of the votes). The coalition and the MDF—itself a coalition of three trends—is not a solidly structured political formation, but rather a sort of amalgamation of populist (including Right-wing populist), East-European-type Christian-democratic and liberal trends. The coalition government and the MDF leadership, however, never drew the line between the Center-Right and the extreme-Right, led by István Csurka, and carefully avoided distancing itself from the latter; it thus deliberately wanted to be a reservoir of the Right. In order to appear amenable to the European democratic community, however, the multi-faceted coalition and MDF made an effort to show a liberal face to the world in the first year of their rule. In an internal study, prepared for a confidential debate of an MDF conference in the Fall of 1991, (but leaked and published by one of the dailies, *Magyar Hírlap*), Imre Kónya, majority leader of the Parliament, declared that after having consolidated their power, it will not be necessary to maintain this liberal facade anymore. He advocated the establishment of a monopoly of power by seizing control over the media and eliminating the "dangerous" opposition. The right-wing hard core of the MDF, represented by Kónya and the populist members of the party, headed by vice-president István Csurka, who led the attacks against "liberal-communism, " thus, challenged the more moderate party line. This is a trend of authoritarianism, strident nationalism and anti-Semitism, which was clearly formulated in a study of István Csurka in August 20, 1992. The party's more moderate center, led by prime minister József Antall, competing with its radical Right wing, though successfully maneuvered and hindered the breakthrough of the Csurka-wing during the January 1993 national convention of the party, itself was gradually shifted toward the Right by realizing some of its requests.

The more "gradualist" economic strategy of the MDF, however, does not require an immediate "voucher privatization," nor is it in any hurry to effect "de-statization." The strategy has kept state ownership longer and state interventionism stronger than its liberal, moderate Left opposition desires, and represents a more moderate Center-Left practice of economic policy. Whether this is a consequence of a better understanding and a more pragmatic approach to economic affairs, or of second thoughts of maintaining major power positions and trying, in part, to use them to build an effective system of clients, is an altogether different question.

The parliamentary opposition (including the *MSzP*) represents different shades of a moderate Left political trend, according to most of the basic "parameters" which divide Right and Left. The second biggest party of the parliament and the strongest opposition party, the Free Democratic Alliance (*SzDSz*) and the increasingly popular Young democrats (*Fidesz*) are clearly against xenophobe populism, nationalism and conservative political Catholicism. They share the ideal of democracy and are struggling against the attempt of the

MDF to monopolize power. The majority of the opposition (except the *MSzP* and some independent representatives), however, is less pragmatic than the MDF and more ideological in their "Thatcherite" line regarding a "free market ideology." Unlike most of the European Left, they believe in the market mechanism and subordinate social questions to it. For instance, János Kiss, former founding president of the *SzDSz*, blamed the Government in January 1992 because of its caution regarding unemployment in the process of privatization. Center-Right trends, thus, are strongly present in the politics of the opposition parties as well.

The dominance of Center-Right parties, and the confused Center-Left and Center-Right tendencies in the opposition, are not only reactions to the previous rule of the monolithic communist regime. They are also a continuation of an interrupted historical trend in the country. Even if the Smallholder and Christian Democratic parties have some direct continuity, practically all of these parties are representing trends which existed in Hungary before 1948. Moreover, most of these parties are expressing European political streams and representing certain political goals of the middle class. Hence, their existence and participation in the political life of the country is basically a positive expression of a properly developing political structure. Hungary with its more structured political scene has an advantage compared to her neighbors, who initially replaced communist monolithic regimes by the monolithic rule of the former opposition. (Splitting, however, began after the electorial victory in Poland and Czechoslovakia and, in the Polish case, led to another extreme of dozens of competing small, scattered parties.)

Some of the existing parties, mostly outside parliament, or certain wings of different parliamentary, and even government, parties represent the continuity of dangerous and wild political tendencies of twentieth century Eastern Europe. Right-wing populism, which is equally present in both the MDF and the Smallholder Party, has an infamous history in the whole region from the late nineteenth century on, as becoming a source of Fascism. Besides tradition, it also has a social basis in the desperate and disappointed lower middle class and in certain blue collar layers. Populist xenophobia, anti-Semitism, anti-Westernism, and extreme nationalism combined with excessive anti-communism might be attractive for certain groups, especially after the spiritual and political breakdown of Marxism.

The dominance of Center-Right tendencies, thus, represents mixed and ambivalent possibilities: European and anti-European trends, ("modernizer" and "anti-modernizer" nationalisms, as Péter Hanák suggests) conservative democratic and conservative anti-democratic alternatives as well. For the time being, a part of these differences is hidden behind a common anti-communism and a common aim of reintroducing Capitalism.

The Dominance of a Reaganite "Free Market Ideology"

The Center-Right coalition and its opposition share the view (or at least the slogans) of *laissez faire* liberalism, which led them to the idea of an all round "privatization of state properties." As in other East European countries the government does not want to consider the continued existence of a state sector (such as in France, Italy or Austria). Hungary, though following a gradual privatization policy (unlike Poland and Czechoslovakia, where a great part of the shares are planned to be distributed among the population either free of charge or for a nominal fee), has made no effort to transform and stabilize a state owned sector. This sector operates and acts side by side and in accordance with market rules.

Moreover, the state no longer promotes and subsidizes certain spheres of the economy. The most outrageous *laissez faire* extremism is the ending of agricultural subsidies. This decision endangered and sent shock waves through the previously most successful branch of the Hungarian economy. The strongly ideological approach to agricultural subsidies, encouraged by international financial institutions, is especially curious in the international environment of a highly and increasingly protectionist agricultural policy in the most advanced Western world. President Bush, in one of his campaign speeches in Kansas city, accused the European Community of "hiding behind its own iron curtain of protectionism" and vowed he would not scrap American farm subsidies until the Europeans end their own broad subsidy program—reported the *Los Angeles Times* in mid-January 1992. Hungary, along with the other Eastern European countries, is running with a neophyte's enthusiasm in abolishing state interventions and involvement in the economy, going faster and further than the "ideal" *laissez faire*" countries, let alone traditionally etatist Japan and other successful Asian countries.

The 'economic Right' which dominates Hungarian (and East-Central European) politics remained blind of the shortcomings and mistakes of the negative consequences of the free market and anti-state ideology applied in practice. It did not realize, what Frank Hahn of the University of Cambridge emphasized in his lecture at the British Academy in February 1992: there are "special economic problems which are the consequences of the incomplete markets" and these are not curable by nonexisting free market automatism. Keynes, he stressed

> has been declared out of date and wrong by the very simple device of ignoring and assuming away all of the difficulties which he thought to be important. When, as now appears to be the case . . . economists will again become more circumspect in their judgement of market economies . . . [Keynes] will again be seen as pointing to the right questions.

Indeed, outstanding Western expert such as Richard Portes and Domenico Nuti convincingly argue that the dramatic and unforeseen decline of output and national product during the transition years was a consequence of policy mistakes, most of all, as Nuti stated in the *Newsletter* of the World Bank in January 1993, "the failure in government management of the state sector." From ideological considerations, even the gradually privatizing Hungarian government had written off a still determinant state sector and generated a more than unavoidable decline. Right-wing conservatism rejects "social partnership" through a compromise between the government and the trade unions. Instead, almost the entire parliament was united in trying to destroy the "Red" unions (*MSzOSz*) in the summer of 1991. A renewal of membership was ordered with the hope that the old unions will lose their members. But it did not happen: more than a million members renewed their membership, while the newly emerging competing "Christian," "free" and other unions had only a few tens of thousands of members.

The "Thatcherite" hostility against the unions is going hand in hand with a governmental passivity regarding social policy issues. The old social safety net which in the state-socialist systems was built into economic policies (such as subsidized prices, rents, transportation fees, services etc.), or provided as "free" health care and education, has been gradually eroded. It will mostly be destroyed by the introduction of the private-market economy and market prices. The need of a new social safety net, which was the focus of debates in the first period of transition, almost disappeared from public political interest. According to a typical right-wing, conservative way of thinking, the new political and entrepreneurial elite both share the view that somebody has to pay the bill of transformation. But they do not hesitate to point to the lower layers of the population—the wage earners and retired people.

When György Csepeli, a sociologist, publicly challenged this position and urged a new social policy orientation at the end of 1991, the head of *Fidesz*, Viktor Orbán, rejected this approach by announcing that the matter was presently not on the agenda. This neophyte rush to copy Reaganite and Thatcherite policy, as the only possible course in re-establishing classical capitalism, has paradoxically occurred in Hungary and in other East European countries when such a policy is already being strongly questioned in one of its 'homelands,' the United States.

The Right-wing ideological approach toward social questions is partly a reaction of sorts to the other extreme, state socialism. That system sacrificed efficiency and necessary measures for a quasi-egalitarian social order. The previous "religious" socialist egalitarianism and anti-elitism, promoted the interests of the lower layers of society at the cost of the upper layers. It inhibited risk-taking and abolished entrepreneurial incentives. All interest in high quality and responsible work was rejected. What we are seeing now is social responsibility shifting more and more from the state to the individual. One cannot avoid drawing parallels with the changing concepts and attitudes of early capitalism (brilliantly analyzed by the medievalist historian Bronislaw Geremek) toward the poor and poverty in general. Attitudes shifted from a Christian-religious basis to an economic one. Unlike in the previous period, poverty did not generate sympathy and succor but rather blame. Poverty became a sort of crime, a consequence of personal irresponsibility, deleterious habits and inadequacy. Is the newly emerging East European capitalism, which unavoidably manifests quite a few of the characteristics of early Capitalism, about to reintroduce a similar change of values and attitudes? Is a "religious" socialist attitude toward poverty and the poor about to be replaced by economic "rationality" and negligence?

Attempts to Monopolize Power: The Danger of a New Authoritarianism

It is probably too early to speak about a potential danger in a period when the process of institutionalization of democracy is in its early stages. There has never been such a free and untampered election in Hungarian history than that in 1990. Currently, parliament is engaged in very intensive legislative work, and there is a constitutional court deciding contested issues whose decisions decisively contribute to the learning process of democracy. The constitutional changes that established the Hungarian Republic with its democratic legal basis occurred before the elections. They were part of the preparation for a peaceful transformation, and the new constitution is still lacking the separation of legislative and executive power and the guarantee of the independence of the courts. In other words, the creation of a democracy based on the classical principles of Montesquieu have already been realized.

The reason for the historian to speak about a potential danger to democracy is partly a consequence of previous historical experiences. From the nineteenth century on there was a traditional "dualism" between Western type democratic, constitutional, legal systems and their real application in everyday life in Eastern Europe, including Hungary. In some cases Western legal systems were copied. Yet, in reality, authoritarianism characterized political practice. In some way it was a continuous practice in the whole region. In the fragile new parliamentary system the same might happen again.

It would be rather unjustified to warn of this danger on a mere historical basis, since there is no evidence that history will repeat itself. However, there are certain signs and actions which make this danger more realistic and current. Parallel with the creation of a Western type democratic legal-institutional framework, there is also a trend to monopolize power and generate fear. Montesquieu is right in stating that the essence of despotism is fear. Certain Right-wing groups of the MDF and the coalition are deliberately trying to generate fear in the country. One of the apparent and available weapons is anti-communism, that is often equated with democracy.

In order to create a long-lasting democratic system the country has to rid itself of the political legacy of state-socialism. An anti-communist witch-hunt, however, might serve other goals as well. It is being manipulated by the coalition and its parliamentary majority. An important element of the witch-hunt is a new interpretation of recent history. Government spokesmen do not differentiate between the worst years of Stalinism, the rule of Mátyás Rákosi in the fifties, and the reform-oriented and relatively liberal era of the second half of the Kádár-regime, thus equating terrorist Stalinism with Hungarian reform-communism. (At the time it was praised and admired worldwide). In late 1991 an MDF initiative led to the enactment of a law which retroactively modified statutory limitations on murder and high treason if such acts were not punished because of political considerations after 1945. The liberal-democratic opposition voted against the proposition. President Göncz expressed his doubts about the constitutional validity of the law and sent it to the supreme constitutional court. The liberal-democratic opposition maintained that the introduction of democracy and proper legality should not start with a retroactive modification of law. Liberals argued that crime is punishable according to the law which was valid at the time when it was committed. Even political murder cases (such as the suppression of the 1956 revolution or the execution of some of the victims of the Imre Nagy trial) would be difficult to reexamine after a third of a century, especially since most of the culprits are no longer alive. "High treason," itself an amorphous category cannot be judged retroactively. Members of Hungarian trade delegations who signed Soviet or Comecon agreements might be considered to have committed this crime. In the early Spring of 1992 the supreme constitutional court unanimously declared the law unconstitutional. The MDF leaders announced that they will find another way to realize their aim, and some of their representatives harshly accused the constitutional court "of making decisions against the will of the people."

The secret list of former police informers and the much broader concept of "collaborators" offer an excellent possibility for use and abuse. Everything depends on definitions and the most violently populist politicians are conspicuously attempting to appropriate the right to decide who was or who was not a collaborator. (As *SzDSz* representative Miklós Haraszti wittily put it: The MDF maintains that "who is not 'our communist' is communist.") Whoever is ready to serve the MDF, and is a loyal and obedient neophyte, even if he was a communist party secretary or the leading "Middle-East expert" of the TV, who subserviently assisted and propagated "anti-imperialist" and "anti-Zionist" Soviet Middle-East policy, is more than accepted and nominated or appointed to leading positions. On the other hand, talented technocrats whose "collaboration" was nothing more than good and successful work in their field of expertise are from time to time accused of collaboration and dismissed.

The anti-communist campaign as promoted by the populist wing of the MDF is seeking to create a real revolution. István Csurka and Sándor Csoóri often complained of the lack of a genuine revolution in Hungary. This belated anti-communist "revolution" from above, with its extremely flexible enemy-categories is an excellent weapon to generate uncertainty and fear. It should be added, that a strongly emotional anti-communism of the liberal, Center-Left opposition, whose leading elite suffered the most as former "dissidents," sometimes inadvertently helps the coalition's campaign. István Eörsi, an uncompromised former 'dissident' writer and one of the most Left-wing, even openly socialist founders of *SzDSz*, flatly stated in his article "*Undor*" [Disgust] in *Népszabadság* in late 1991, that practically the whole intelligentsia and the bulk of the population "collaborated" with the Kádár regime.

The heart of the matter, of course, is not an intellectual debate. Anti-communist nationalism is able to mobilize extremist groups. Certain Right-wing politicians are ready to turn to the mobs. An open (and televised) discussion in the fall of 1991 in Budapest between majority leader Imre Kónya (MDF) and minority leader Iván Petö (*SzDSz*) with the participation of hundreds of MDF sympathizers, became, as some commentators called it, the "first Fascist meeting." The mob actually threatened Petö, questioning his "Hungarianness" ("are you Magyar at all?"), and called for his lynching. One of the parliamentary deputies urged lynchings even during a debate of parliament. A witch-hunt atmosphere is a good environment for authoaritarian rule, for discrediting the opposition, for dismissing "disloyal" or independent-minded intellectuals and promoting party loyalists. This trend, therefore, is strongly connected with a new-old paternalism and an emerging clientelism. Party appointees, for example, undermine the legal, democratic separation of different branches of power and may create an informal network of power. An outstanding example of the introduction of a Latin-American type of clientelism was the scandalous case of György Surányi, president of the National Bank, an independent-minded, excellent young economist, who was appointed by the new government after the election, and who became one of the most successful bank presidents in the whole region. Serving the policy of transition and the government for one and a half years, he was suddenly dismissed by Prime Minister Antall at the end of November 1991. The official explanation caused a heated debate, because the quality and work of Mr. Surányi was not questioned at all, and the only accusation was that he participated in the signing of a so called "Democratic Charter," initiated by the well-known former "dissident" writer and now president of the International Pen Club, György Konrád, also one of the founders of *SzDSz*.

The Charter argued that democracy in Hungary is in danger and is running into a dead-end, and urged broad cooperation among different democratic forces. Konrád was declared to be "disloyal" to the government. Whoever urges democracy in a democratic country is either hostile or insane, added the prime minister.

Surányi's dismissal and its explanation generated a vehement debate. The case became a symbol of distorted values: absolute preference of party loyalty as opposed to expertise and effectiveness. There are, no doubt, aspects of the case that illustrates this practice. The real meaning, however, is even worse than that. Surányi was dismissed at the end of November. The National Bank, which in monolithic state-socialism was under the control of the government became independent from the government from December 1, 1991, as part of democratic institution building and separation of powers. The formal separation of powers, in this case, was practically annulled by the dismissal of an independent-minded bank president and the appointment of Péter Ákos Bod, a former Planning Office official and the minister of industry in the new government. He is not a banking expert at all, and his real and only strength was his absolute loyalty to the MDF. His appointment was an assurance to stabilize party dominance in the banking area and to rule the National Bank, which, by law, supposed to become independent from the government. Here again was the kind of dualism between a correct legal-constitutional system, and autocratic practice that characterized Hungarian (and Eastern European) practices since modern Western institutions were adopted in the region in the mid-nineteenth century.

In addition to this rather telling episode, it is equally characteristic of the situation that the introduction of absolute freedom of the press also irritates the right-wing monopolist forces of the coalition. The prime promoter of the populist Right in the MDF leadership, vice-president Csurka, has led a ruthless crusade against the critical, hence "communist," "cosmopolitan," "non-national minded" media since 1990. The issue of control over the National Radio (recently declared to be a "communist fortress"), the TV and the newspapers caused the most heated debates and drastic state interventions. The government pushed out a liberal Scandinavian group from the privatization of one of the leading dailies, *Magyar Nemzet*, and promoted a conservative, right-wing French group. The daily harsh attacks against the critical attitude of the press and the rather frequent accusations of "treason," "traitors to the nation" and "rootless cosmopolitanism" (a well known code word for Jews), effectively serve to frighten the press. On October 26, 1991 a mass meeting, organized by the MDF, mobilized the mob to send a message. The lynch atmosphere which characterized the meeting further escalated the intimidation of the media. "Why are you afraid of their publications" cried one of the participants, "I will bring ten thousand men, any time you want. (Ovation in the auditorium.) We thought we should go to the TV and throw somebody out the window on the third floor, then somebody else on the second floor. (Laughter and applause),", reported the *Népszabadság* on October 28, 1991.

The threat was almost realized on March 15, 1992 when the mob indeed was mobilized for a violent demonstration, disturbing the celebration of the national holiday. "Lynch atmosphere before the TV headquarters," "Journalists were insulted by demonstrators in the Szabadság square," reported the *Magyar Hírlap* on March 16, 1992. The crowd of about five thousand people attacked the building. It was saved by a strong police force. One of the organizers, András Márton, addressed the crowd: ". . . we do not have arms yet, but if needed we shall get them in minutes!" Groups, however, armed with chains and clubs physically insulted journalists. Even György Konrád, the well known former dissident and opposition leader hardly escaped from the agitated mob.

The incident was part of an organized campaign. One should recall the founding meeting of a new Association of Hungarian Journalists (*MUK*) which was held a day before and initiated by the *MDF* against the existing old Association (*MUOSZ*). As *Magyar Hírlap* reported on March 16, 1992, István Benedek, an old psychologist and writer, freshly decorated by the government with the prestigious Széchényi-award, chaired the meeting and declared:

> The homeland is in danger..we are surrounded by external and internal enemies . . . the external ones are directing the internals.. We do not want the freedom of the press, because it leads to an intolerable revilement, we do not want the freedom of speech because it becomes revilement. We demand honesty of the press and honesty of speech. Nobody would get the possibility to denounce the government, to be a liar; nobody would have the right to hate our development.

Closing his speech the chairman proclaimed: "As we are creating our new association we hopefully will be able to shut the old association up." (It pays to note that the sentence, a quip in Hungarian, had a double meaning: the 'new association', (*új szövetség*, in Hungarian) means both the new association of journalists and the "new testament," and "old association' (*ó szövetség*, in Hungarian) means both the old association of journalists and the 'old testament'. One of the speakers, Gábor Balla did not hesitate to speak about "[There are] at least four Jewish dailies," while "there is no one newspaper where citizens can publish without any trouble.") As these quotes indicate, the constitutional, legal freedom of the media, is already being assaulted through informal denunciations and moral terror. The dualism between democratic legal framework and its real (autocratic) content is in the making.

Clientelism, paternalism and the change of guard based on political loyalty is a method of creating authoritarian power. One of the leading politicians of the ruling coalition, *Géza Zsiros* [Smallholder Party], declared in an interview at the end of 1991:

> We gained the votes of the citizens on the basis of our promises before the election. We are going to realize what we promised. We are doing it on behalf and instead of the citizens!

"Even against them?" interrupted the reporter. "This is a rather difficult question," answered Zsiros "You know, when a kitten achieves the age when he is not nursed anymore, do you know what his master does? He pushes his nose into a cup of milk. Could you imagine that he does not start to lap." The forces of a new right-wing authoritarianism are biding their time.

Rising Nationalism

There are also much more explicit phenomena of Right-wing trends in evidence in Hungary. A rising nationalism of various ethnic groups mutually generating each other in the whole region, is a leading trend. It is a dominant trend in the ranks of the newly formed Hungarian political elite. On the other hand, the population has been,up to now , much less inclined to follow national extremism and shows little interest in nationalist slogans. Though the populist wing of the ruling party and other populist groupings are using often profane nationalist rhetoric, and members of the government occasionally join them, the government policy is, for the time being, much more moderate. The exalted nationalism of the "*Vatra Romaneasca*" of Romania, Serb, Croat and Slovak nationalism certainly exceed official Hungarian national trends.

The danger, however, is immense because the sacrosanct stability of post-war borders are more than questionable. All the peace treaties that were mutually guaranteed by all of the great powers and all of the countries involved in the Helsinki-process in the mid-seventies are now no longer valid. This may open a new chapter in East European history. The disintegration of Yugoslavia and the former Soviet Union, the Czech and Slovak separation, the reappearance of the Moldavian question and a possibility of a further enlargement of Romania, all contribute to the revival of Hungarian nationalism. The minority question (on the agenda of Hungarian populism for a long time), border disputes brought about by the Trianon-treaty, all long-lasting taboos, are reappearing in an economically disturbed and depressed period. They offer an excellent opportunity for political demagogues to exploit popular dissatisfaction in the hope that the nationalist wind will blow into their own sails. The presence of what is not yet a determinant, and partly hidden, nationalism in the Hungarian political arena may be strengthened by rival Eastern European nationalisms.

The Csurka-wing of the MDF leadership (nearly one-third of the presidium of the party, elected in January 1993), which founded the *Magyar Ut* [Hungarian Road] movement, became the pioneer of a militant political nationalism. "This fall is our last opportunity," declared Csurka in his article in *Magyar Fórum* on August 20, 1992, advocating a radical nationalist program:

> There is no other sacrosanct value but national interest. . . . In 1995 the Yalta agreement expires [*sic!*]. . . . The new century and situation opens new possibilities . . . for the Hungarians. The key question is whether a new generation . . . will be able to exploit these opportunities to assure a new Hungarian living-space.

(The Hungarian term he used was the exact equivalent and translation of the notorious Nazi term of *Lebensraum*.) A frightening *déjà vu* of inter-war hostility is with us once again, the possibility of sharpened national hostilities and national conflicts are *ante portas*.

The newly emerging Hungarian nationalism, however, might not be the same as its inter-war predecessor because the internal social structure changed and so did the international political environment. Nationalism might not be linked with Fascism as an official political trend as it happened in the thirties. The historical trap to turn toward the national question instead of a methodical work of building a modern economy and civil society, is open again. The old reflexes and the new difficulties together create real dangers. One should not forget that it is always easier to play out the national card than to solve burning economic and social problems. The temptation, in the nationalistic East European environment is, thus, quite strong.

Right-wing populism and Center-Right conservativism are both inclined to be markedly national, and even nationalist. There are some clear signs of this trend. In his first statement, after being appointed prime minister, József Antall emphasized that he "wanted to be the premier of 15 million Hungarians." This "spiritual" revision of the existing borders (only about 10 million Hungarians live in Hungary proper) and the proposal to represent all the Hungarians in Hungary, in neighboring Romania, Czechoslovakia and Yugoslavia, and indeed, all over the world, caused quite a stir in neighboring countries and also among important groups of the Hungarian minorities there. More recently (in February 1992) Lajos Für, minister of defense and chief executive of the MDF, stated at Miskolc:

> The concept of the Hungarian nation in the Carpathian Basin is not limited to the citizens of the Hungarian Republic. The notion of the Hungarian nation in Europe means a Hungarian-speaking united nation. One-third of it, as a consequence of the Trianon Treaty is living a minority life. To defend national security in the Carpathian Basin is inseparable from the defence of the whole Hungarian nation. The parliament and government have to do their best to stop the endangering of the Hungarian minorities outside the Hungarian borders.

It should be added, that minister and party leader Für, in another lecture in the Budapest headquarters of the MDF that same month, spoke for the first time since the early forties about a "three thousand year long (!) Hungarian history" which was "deliberately falsified since the late forties." Since Hungarian history is hardly longer than one thousand years, this was the first time in post-communist Hungary that a leading politician entered into the grotesque and childish race with Romanian nationalists, the latter of whom always maintained the existence of a more than two thousand year-old Rumanian history, (to "prove" their Roman origins and their earlier presence in the region than any other ethnic groups, and especially in Transylvania.)

A more drastic challenge to the border question was an initiative to restore the so-called "Irredenta statue" which was erected in the first years of the Horthy regime and symbolized the territories detached by the Trianon Treaty. In the Summer of 1990 a committee was founded, headed by Ernö Raffay, member of the MDF and the government (he was then under-secretary of defense), to prepare the rebuilding of the statue, which had been destroyed after World War II. As the proponents stated it', the goal was only the "cultivation of traditions." Under this banner they planned to restore even the citation from Mussolini (written on the foundation of the statue) about the correctness and justification of Hungarian territorial revisionism. When the plan was vehemently attacked by the liberal-democratic opposition, the minister of defense, the same Lajos Für cited above, openly defended his deputy's action. However, because of very heavy criticism the plan was dropped. It is hardly surprising that the mob expressed these sentiments in a much more brutal and direct way: in December 1990 posters appeared in the Northern Hungarian city of Salgótarján, declaring the rejection of the Treaty of Trianon (a leading slogan of the Horthy regime) and the reclamation of the territories detached from Hungary. The police removed the posters but the coalition parties did not deem the incident worthy of condemnation.

All these trends are understandably linked with an attempt to rehabilitate the Horthy regime. While the openly fascist periodicals, such as the *Hunnia Füzetek* and the *Szent Korona*, published articles urging this rehabilitation, there is also a much more indirect preparation going on. An organization has recently proposed to return the remains of Miklós Horthy from his grave in Portugal back to Hungary for a reburial. The daughter-in-law of the former regent spoke about a "family burial" in the former family estate in Gödöllő, but she did not propose the exclusion of the public from "expressing esteem or saluting him." The minister of the interior openly broached the idea of Horthy's rehabilitation in an interview. He stated that there is no need for formal rehabilitation because admiral Horthy was never formally sentenced by the Allies as a war criminal. One of the most extreme attempts of historical rehabilitation of the Horthy regime was a speech in Parliament by former general Kálmán Kéri, a representative of the MDF, who stated in the summer of 1990 that Horthy-Hungary's participation in the anti-Soviet war (in alliance with Hitler) was a just effort: "If we had won against the Soviet Union, we would have saved mankind from communism," he said. The statement could be considered to have been an irresponsible remark by an old man, (he was 80 at the time) a former high-ranking officer of Horthy's army. However, in the angry debate that followed the speech, the minister of defense Lajos Für and prime minister Antall defended General Kéri.

In early 1992, at a celebration of the 50th anniversary of the battle of the Don, where the Second Hungarian Army, in alliance with Hitler's *Wehrmacht*, participated in the attack on Stalingrad and was partly annihilated, premier Antall himself praised the heroic struggle of the Hungarian army. *Hunnia Füzetek*, in November 1990, called anti-fascist communists who were killed by the Horthy administration or by the Nazis "traitors, who spied on Hungary for money on behalf of the hostile Soviet Union."

Verbal, political nationalism was transformed into action when the government secretly sold Kalashnikov sub-machine guns to Croatia. When the scandal exploded, the government persistently denied the sale in the Fall of 1990. Prime minister Antall defended his ministers who were involved in the secret action, and resisted the opposition's demand for their resignation. The connection between the arms sale and the policy of the government against Yugoslavia became, however, rather clear when the prime minister announced that the *Vajdaság* (Vojvodina) a territory was given by the Trianon Treaty to Yugoslavia, not to Serbia. The implicit meaning of this statement was the first challenge of the existing borders: if Yugoslavia disintegrated the legal status of Vojvodina will no longer be valid.

The nationalist trend is strongly linked with a Christian ideology. The marriage of nationalism and religion is a traditional historical phenomenon in Eastern Europe. In some cases a religion other than that of the dominant, oppressing nation—Serb and Bulgarian Orthodoxy fighting against Muslim Ottoman oppression, Polish Roman Catholicism struggling against Russian Orthodoxy and German Protestantism, Croat Catholicism against Serb Orthodoxy—became a major instrument of national self-identification, with the autonomous Church becoming a substitution for national autonomy. In the sixteenth century the Hungarian national struggle against Habsburg domination was closely linked with the Reformation. The Habsburgs, having fought against the Hungarian rebels, also fought against and attempted to annihilate Protestantism. On this historical background Catholicism or Christianity gained a new additional meaning in the twentieth century. Horthy 's "Christian-national course" from 1919 on was a rejection of both atheist communism and Jewry. In post-World War II Eastern Europe, religion was an unambiguous antithesis of Communist ideology and a clear expression of an anti-Soviet stand. In post-1989 Eastern Europe, when a lack of traditional values led to new-old substitutions, nationalism is clearly merging with the Christian religion once again. Consequently, it is not surprising that the oft-used rhetoric of the current ruling coalition in Hungary is highly reminiscent of the "Christian-national course" of the early Horthy regime. As that time "Christian and national" represented national and political exclusiveness. It was and often is a negation of non-Hungarian and non-Christian elements, often equated with atheists, communists, Jews, liberals, "rootless cosmopolitans" and non-Magyar neighboring peoples, especially the ones whose governments ruled over Hungarian minorities. As Géza Jeszenszky, minister of foreign affairs announced:

> Europeanism . . . in national commitment, social sensitivity
> . . . democracy and the man-centered morality represented
> by the cross . . . in their entirety are accepted only by
> MDF, *FKgP, KDNP* [the coalition parties] and those who
> voted for them.

Answering to an interpellation in parliament, he added: "the Hungarian or Christian ideals should not be the property of the party of atheists and Marxists."

The church, especially the Catholic Church, has gained a special advantage regarding its old possessions. Even if reprivatization (giving back previously nationalized property to former owners) was not on the agenda in Hungary and only compensation was to be paid, the Church, as an exception, was to get back its former real estate (except the landed estates), schools etc. The minister of education, Bertalan Andrásfalvy (MDF) initiated the introduction of compulsory religious education in schools. The program of the Smallholder party, a member of the governing coalition, stated: "The teaching of religion or ethics has to be included in the curriculum of every elementary and secondary school." Subsequently the government dropped this program and religious education became optional. However, it was integrated into the school system, and religion classes are held during the day in most schools and not before or after classes. A newly created subject, "ethics," offered the possibility of smuggling religious education and clergy into the public schools in the 1991–92 school-year. On February 19, 1992 *Népszabadság* reported the introduction of daily prayer in the kindergartens of remote Erdőkertes.

The coupling of national and Christian ideas is a deliberate attempt in developing a rightist ideology. In the September 1991 issue of *Hitel*, a semi-official periodical of the MDF, Zsigmond Oláh linked national and Christian as opposed to liberal and anti-national. The latter terms, it should be added, are synonyms of 'Jewish' in a coded language which became rather popular in the vocabulary of the Right wing of the Right, i.e. the populist wing of MDF.

It should be added, however, that Right-wing populism also exists outside the ruling coalition. The tiny People's Party, was founded by Gyula Fekete, one of the founders of the MDF. He left the party before the elections after suffering an early defeat because of his uncompromising populist "third road" anti-Westernism. He could not gain enough votes to enter parliament. Fekete and his party are only marginal, and his often repeated denunciations of "Western cultural dirt" and his harsh attacks against the low birth rate and one-child families have no practical importance. Yet, he has to be acknowledged as a factor in Right-wing politics.

It is interesting to note that Left-wing populism, aiming at combining social sensitivity with a healthy national consciousness recently attempted to organize itself. Zoltán T. Biró, a Left-wing populist and a founder and first executive president of MDF, left the party because of its shift to the right. Biró revived the well-known populist idea of a third-road of "neither socialism nor capitalism." He formed a new centrum movement (party) with his friend and former leading reform-communist Imre Pozsgay who left the *MSzP*.

Open Anti-Semitism

Some of the Right-wing trends and radical nationalism are, in a quite traditional way, closely linked with anti-Semitism. Anti-Semitism has deep roots in several East European countries, including Hungary. Anti-Jewish legislation against Jewish "over-representation" in universities was introduced in Hungary as early as 1920, and the government enacted strong anti-Jewish laws from 1938 on, preparing the ground for the eventual murder of much of Hungarian Jews in the Holocaust.

History also proved, especially in the decades following World War II, that there is in Eastern Europe at least a rather loose connection between existing Jewish communities (the number of Jews) and anti-Semitism. "Anti-Semitism without Jews," using the title of a book by Paul Lendvai, appeared in Poland, and anti-Semitism gained a more complex content in several other countries as well. The meaning of the terms "Jewish" or "Judaized" now connote an attitude, a strongly urban, cosmopolitan (markedly non-nationalist) and liberal tendency. If certain social groups or individuals espouse these trends, their "Hungarianness" is immediately questioned. Those who adhere to these concepts must have some of their ancestors, at least one grandparent Jewish, in the popular mind. A "Judaized" politician must have a Jewish wife or husband, or at least adopted "Jewish manners," as the popular saying goes. In other words, some "Jewish blood" or "Jewish influence" has to be behind such "alien" attitudes. (In the 1930s the Hungarian Right used the term "Jewish agent.") Anti-Semitism, therefore, is not only directed against a certain ethnic or religious group but, in a much more complex way, also against Westernizing modernization and European integration trends which, in this view, endanger traditional Hungarian consciousness, national values or "Hungarianness."

These tendencies already appeared in the earliest stage of "refolution" using the excellent term invented by Timothy Garton Ash before the elections. Open anti-Semitism was immediately connected with the revival of populism. Sándor Püski, a publisher who lived in emigration and returned to fund a publishing house in Hungary to promote populist ideas, aired the accusation of a shameful late nineteenth century, anti-Semitic religious, ritual murder trial at Tiszaeszlár in response to an attack on him by a rival publisher, Cserépfalvy. In the press debate which followed, he stated in *Magyar Hírlap* in December 1988, that the Horthy regime entered World War II because it wanted to save the Hungarian Jews (!). According to him, this was the reason why Hungary could not end the alliance with Hitler: it wanted to save a few hundred thousands Jew, but "did not care about the interests of 14 million Hungarians." This incredible statement concerning the Horthy regime, a government that initiated Nazi-type anti Jewish legislation, entered the war against the Allies to gain back territories with the help of Hitler, and assisted in the deportation and murder of more than half of Hungarian Jewry, provoked a heated debate. The biweekly *Hitel* (of the MDF) rushed to defend Püski, its chief editor-of-honor. The executive president of the MDF contended "we do not have any reason to distance ourself from Sándor Püski."

"Intellectual anti-Semitism" became frightening and violent rather quickly. In 1989 a demonstration was organized by the then opposition MDF against Károly Grósz, at that time secretary general of the leading "state-party," the *MSzMP*, who visited Borsod county. The demonstration, against the will of its organizers, was transformed into a lynch mob. "Dirty Jews, rotten communists, you will be hanged," cried the mob according to the reports on the demonstration. There were some attacks against the synagogues of Debrecen and Budapest, whose chief rabbi (and very many others) received anonymous death threats. (The chief rabbi, Alfred Schöner, soon emigrated.) Some "letters to the editor," published by leading Budapest dailies or local newspapers in the countryside, rediscovered the well-known Nazi concept of "Judeo-bolshevism" and described the previous decades of state-socialism as "43 years of Jewish revenge." Even the very liberal abortion law of Hungary (unlike in some other hardline communist countries) and the broadcasting of Western criminal movies on Hungarian TV was interpreted as a Jewish conspiracy against the Hungarians. In November 1989, in his long article, "Letter from Budapest," David Shipler cited István Csurka, who stated to him in an interview:

> It cannot be denied that there was a special group of communist party leaders, represented by György Aczél. As a Jew, he collected around himself Jewish people in the leadership in the Kádár era..They are still in power in the press, television, radio.

Csurka became one of the most open, though, tactful advocate and champion of nationalist anti-communist anti-Semitism. "If this government remains in place." declared Csurka in *Magyar Fórum* in March 1991,

> it will lead the country out of the crisis and then the game is up, forever, for Bolshevism, cosmopolitanism, foreigners dressed in liberal clothing and the humiliation of the nation. Then, it will finally be the Christian middle stratum who creates the European Hungary, and if this is so, Hungary then remains the property of the Hungarians.

In an earlier radio program in January 1990, two months before the free election, Csurka launched an infamous coded anti-Semitic attack:

> As long as it is possible to make life for Hungarians of *völkisch*-national character impossible in Hungary . . . while what is *völkisch* is suspicious, while a small minority can make their truth the truth, and get the whole society to accept it . . . as long as the radical-liberal tendency today is nourished from the same Marxist, Left-wing, Lukacsist roots as during the Kádár-Aczél regime, the large *völkisch* masses of Hungarians cannot feel at home in their own country. Wake up Hungarians!

The code, however, was deliberately made to be easily decipherable; cosmopolitans, foreigners who dressed in liberal clothing, the small minority who humiliates the nation—these are terms traditionally used (already in the inter-war years) as synonyms for Jews. To be even clearer, Csurka linked Marxism with its famous Jewish representative, György Lukács, and instead of speaking about Kádár's regime he associated it with the only Jewish top leader of the period, György Aczél. Additionally, the closing slogan, "Wake up Hungarians!" was borrowed from an infamous extreme nationalist-anti-Semitic, Jew-bashing organization of the Horthy regime, the Awakening Hungarians, led by former Prime Minister Gyula Gömbös, of the 1920s and 1930s.

One of the founders and ideologues of *MDF*, the populist writer Sándor Csoóri, in one of his articles in *Hitel* in September 1990, openly expressed the view that the Jews were alienated from the Hungarian nation since 1919. "The last moment when the Jews could identify themselves with the national problems of Hungary was the pre-World War I period; but today," continued Csoóri, "reversed tendencies of assimilation are appearing in the country. Liberal Hungarian Jewry is trying to 'assimilate' the Hungarians in their style and thinking. For this they have even fabricated a parliamentary springboard for themselves." (Csoóri, a representative of so called "intellectual anti-Semitism" an ideology whose advocates do not propose the repression of the Jews but struggle against their spiritual influence of alleged "denationalization" (*elnemzetietlenités*), joined those who denounced the rival *SZDSZ* as a "Jewish party." The remark on the "parliamentary springboard" is a clear expression of that.)

The gates that were closed for so long are now opened. If even the word Jew was a taboo for decades after the war, anti-Jewish sentiments have now gained open forums. Half a century after the tragic Holocaust of 4 million East-Central European Jews, including Hungarian Jews, one cannot marginalize the importance of a renewed anti-Semitism.

Though the openly anti-Semitic politicians, with the exception of Csoóri, are marginal and unimportant, they are still contributing to the creation of an atmosphere of hostility. The lessons of the 1920s and 1930s are rather telling and instructive. In April 1990 György V. Domokos published a long article in *Népszabadság*. He joined those who spoke about "Jewish revenge" and dictatorship, Jewish "over-representation" in several fields of public and intellectual life. Domokos stated:

> If I had been humiliated . . . regarding the Jewish am-
> bitions in post-World War II Hungary, I would have done
> everything to rise above others, in order to avoid being hu-
> miliated again. Since I am forced to acquire power to sur-
> vive, I would also abuse (power.) For example, I would not
> allow people to seek an explanation of the high number of
> Jews in Hungarian—and not only Hungarian-communism.
> . . . I would cry anti-Semitism because this would be the
> only way to avoid the recognition of the fact that . . . we
> indeed unite, indeed seek power. . . . As with the Jews,
> the non-Jews have a limit of tolerance. . . . This is why
> the Jews should be understanding and limit their ambitions
> to acquire power. . . . I think it is desirable to take into
> account numcrical proportions. . . . Anti-Semitism is a
> reaction to something. The dictatorship of the minority can
> exist.

This traditional interpretation of anti-Semitism, namely, that it is generated by Jews (and not by anti-Semites) and the desire for "nu-merical proportion," the inspiration of the first anti-Jewish laws in Hungary in 1938, do not need comment.

In one of the September issues of *Hitel*, István Benedek went even further:

> Hungarian-Jewish relations were poisoned not by Nazism,
> but by Bolshevism. I understand the angry revenge of the
> first years [after the War]. They were grave reprisals for
> grave personal injuries, unjust and inhuman in the same

way. . . . The Hungarians are truly ashamed for what had
been forced on them . . . . some of the Jews, however, are
proud of having been able to be just as vile as the fascists,
and then became so accustomed to depredation that they
could not stop. Now they silently strive after judeocracy
and loudly cry anti-Semitism against everyone who tries to
turn against their tyranny. In their fear they talk about
Christian regimes and try to discredit the government.

The falsification of history and the equating of murderers with victims, the equating of the murder of hundreds of thousands of Jews
with the so-called Jewish (?) "revenge" in the execution of less than
two hundred war criminals, and the attempt to "explain" on this basis the "Judeo-Bolshevik" tyranny, is a good example of unrestrained
anti-Semitism.

Certain radical, extreme Right-wing, quite openly fascist groupings and publications are also present (in an isolated way and without
real importance) in the Hungarian political arena. *Hunnia Füzetek*
and *Szent Korona*, the two radical-Right papers publish together
about 5,000 copies. They declare that Jews are "preparing to take
over," argue for a Hungary that is "free of aliens," and demand that
those who opposed Hungarian nationalism "could leave and be glad
that they were allowed to." They "unmasked" Cardinal Páskai as
Jewish, they accused film director Miklós Jancsó to be half-Romanian.
Their views on the democratic opposition and on the media is not very
much different from Csurka's opinion: The liberalism of the Jewish
(!) *SzDSz* is "anti-Hungarian" and they "want to defend Hungarian
spirit against the liberal-fascist (!) press."

Besides attempting to create a hostile atmosphere, the so called
'intellectual anti-Semitism' which remained 'theoretical' and 'spiritual', was coupled with a same endeavor on the top political level.
Although anti-Semitic trends and atrocities are present in several
countries of Europe, Hungary is in a way unique in incorporating
this trend into the government party. In his already cited August 20,
1992 study, István Csurka, that time vice president of the Hungarian Democratic Forum, attacked president Arpád Göncz maintaining
that he resisted the demands of the MDF "because he was ordered
to do so by the communist, reform communist, liberal and radical
nomenklatura and the connecting middle men of Paris, New York
and Tel-Aviv."

The concept that an international, communist-Jewish-American

conspiracy attacks Hungarian national interests was even more drastically expressed by Gyula Zacsek, member of the presidium of the
MDF in the newspaper of the government party, *Magyar Fórum* in
September 3, 1992. The article, titled "Termites are devouring the
nation," launched a Nazi-type attack against the Jewish-cosmopolitan
conspiracy led by George Soros, the Jewish-Hungarian born American
multi-millionaire and philanthropist who helped the "cosmopolitan,"
(meaning Jewish) communists to preserve their power by giving it
over to the "cosmopolitan" dissidents. "The Soros Foundation was
the vital tool and resource in laying the groundwork for this transition."

At the end of 1992 and early 1993, József Antall distanced himself
and his government from their own Right-wing extremists for the
first time. This was a response to a debate in the Congress of the
United States that sent a strong message to Hungary. Antall had
to act in any case, because the extremists openly attacked him and
his moderate policy line, urging him to use authoritarian methods.
They also suggested to replace Antall as both party and government
leader. The convention of the Hungarian Democratic Forum, held in
January 1993, however, preferred to maintain a unified party. The
fact is that István Csurka and his convictions enjoy the recognition
and the backing of nearly two-thirds of the party members. This is
not the case among the population at large.

Hungary shared in the awful experience with other East European and Western countries in the anti-Semitic incidents and xenophobic atrocities committed by skin-head organizations. In January
1992, after a murderous fight between black African students and
young Hungarians, an innocent Hungarian bystander was stabbed to
death at the tramway station in Köbánya. Police report one, sometimes two dozen attacks on African students. In the west Hungarian
city of Györ a neo-Nazi organization was established. In early 1993,
a seventeen-year old Jewish girl was stabbed, and a "Jewish looking"
man was beaten by skin-heads wearing arm bands with Swastikas.

The extreme Right, however, is still marginal and does not determine government policies in Hungary. There are strong political
forces resisting such developments. Though Right-wing populism did
penetrate the ruling coalition and attempts to push it to the Right,
the moderating role of the European environment, the country's need
of foreign assistance, and a strong liberal democratic opposition and
the generally liberal public opinion have been successful in counter-

balancing its efforts. Counterdemonstrations also proved this to be the case. The decline in the economy and living standards, increasing poverty and sharp social differentiation might be a hotbed of extremism. Counterbalancing unions and the various Center-Left socialist trends (social democracy) are weak and always on the defensive because even the term "socialist" is discredited and unavoidably carries the burden of the past. They are defenseless against demagogy. The reemerging "early" capitalism with its limited boom and flourishing speculation can promote the well-being of only a small layer of society, while an unfortunate majority, confused and powerless, can find no real, effective representation. They might serve as a basis for political apathy. Huge masses are withdrawn from political activity because, as Iván Szelényi explained in his sociological analysis, they do not feel represented and have not found a proper channel for political expression and articulation of their interests. This may explain the unprecedented apathy expressed in the very sparse participation of voters in elections. After the parliamentary elections in the spring of 1990, the local elections in the fall of the same year already became a disaster of low participation. Since then, most of the parliamentary by-elections failed due to 7–8 percent participation of the voters. Apathy on the one side, however, might easily be exploited by extremism on the other.

Giovanni Sartori pointed out the difficulties of economic transition. He noted in the summer of 1991 the threat of its declining into "sheer populism, into sheer demagogic rhetoric" in East-Central Europe. Karl Popper formulated already a half a century ago that "Fascism grown, partly out of the spiritual and political breakdown of Marxism . . ."

The vicious circle of one extremism generating the other in Hungarian history from 1919 to 1991, should be ended by balanced politics of social partnership and political tolerance based on a generally rising prosperity. The positive results and accomplishments of the peaceful Hungarian transformation in its most difficult early years, and the possibility of being able to join the European Community, may prevent an extreme Right-wing breakthrough. Hungary, together with some other countries of the Western rim of Eastern Europe has a chance of participating in European integration. The Right-wing extremism of today may remain an ugly but marginal episode in the history of transition to a democratic society in Hungary's stormy history in the twentieth century.

This essay is based on publications of Hungarian dailies, weeklies, by-weeklies and periodicals, inciuding *Népszabadság, Magyar Hírlap, Magyar Fórum, Hitel, Heti Világ Gazadaság,* and others, representing the entire political spectrum of Hungarian parliamentary and extra-parliamentary politics. The material was partly collected by Nora Berend.

BUILDING CIVIL SOCIETY IN POST-COMMUNIST HUNGARY

Joseph Held

Perhaps one should modify the term, "civil society" in relation to East Europe in general and Hungary in particular to "civil(ized) society." This would express better the needs of the region and provide a more focused treatment of the subject. Of the many definitions of such a society, John Keane's provides probably the best basis. According to him, "it is the self-organization of society, relatively autonomous from the state . . ." Keane also lists elements strengthening civil(ized) society, arguing that these elements include the state of social development reached, the amount of social and economic authority available for the respective local governments, and the availability of all sorts of political and social organizations for citizens to join voluntarily if they so wish.[1]

I would like to expand this definition by saying that public discussions should be civil and restrained, and the respect of opinions different from those supported by the majority of citizens should be among the shared values of society.

A civil(ized) society usually does not exist in an authoritarian system. Democracy and the existence of democratic institutions are a *sine qua non* of such a society. In turn, this presupposes the functioning of an internally legitimate government. This concept was advanced first by Guglielmo Ferrero in the early 1940s.[2] arguing that legitimate governments usually come into existence through generally accepted means and rule in a predictable way, that is, through laws not the whims of individuals. Such a government is not feared by the people and is not afraid of the population. Most people will voluntarily cooperate with such a government and this provides the basis of social and economic progress.[3] Without such cooperation there is no possibility for civil(ized) society to come into being.

In the last decade of the twentieth century all this sounds like common sense. Yet, we are all certainly aware of the fact that common sense is not always the guiding principle in human affairs. As a consequence, most of us have become suspicious of common sense; after all, it tells us that the sun rises each day in the east and goes down in the west at dusk. It is, however, obvious that it is the earth that turns causing the phenomenon. The communist system had left such a mess as its legacy in almost all spheres of social existence in Eastern Europe and the Soviet Union, that a common sense-approach to its solution does not appear to be sufficient to restart the stalled development of societies.

Although the current Hungarian government does not really have a social basis,[4] and consequently it does not represent specific economic or social interests, it is unquestionably legitimate. It had come into existence through free elections and it continues to receive voluntary cooperation from most of the population. It governs through parliament by laws with minimum coercion. Much of the population believes that it is working for the "public good." Yet, at the same time, the government is developing into the representative of an increasingly powerful and relatively isolated elite. This elite is not entirely convinced that political pluralism, one of the characteristics of a democratic society, is suitable for Hungary. According to some spokesmen of this elite, pluralism places too many obstacles in the way of efforts to achieve the "public good." Furthermore, in a pluralistic political system power regularly changes hands, according to the wishes of the electorate. The governing elite in Hungary, however, is convinced that the opposition is the enemy of the nation and is, therefore, loath to see the possibility of the opposition emerge victorious in the next round of elections slated for 1994.

There are signs that certain groups in the governing elite, led by István Csurka, would like to move towards the establishment of a new authoritarian system.[5] There is sufficient social pressure to obstruct such a move at the present time. However, it has become clear during the last few months that the renewal of trust, a hallmark of democracies in the West, existing between the political elites and society at large, has ground to a halt in Hungary. A corollary of this process is the government's efforts in strengthening discipline among its parliamentary deputies and allies, as well as within the Hungarian Democratic Forum which is increasingly loosing the "democratic" from its name. This is not to say that Jozsef Antall wants to be a dictator. Yet, he has gradually moved towards supporting the authoritarian wing of the Forum. Since Iván T. Berend has already discussed the inherent dangers permeating the current Hungarian situation in the previous essay, I would like to focus instead on the emergence of elements of civil(ized) society that, in the long run, could prevent the restoration of an authoritarian system in Hungary. It is true, as Hanna Arendt has so correctly pointed out in her famous work on totalitarianism,[6] that the more autonomous or semi-autonomous groups exist in society, the better defenses it has against authoritarianism. All these groups are certainly part of civil(ized) society.

At the present time the lack of an organic social basis means that there are no outside pressures acting on the Hungarian government. This is clear from the fact that its ministries have not yet come up with a comprehensive plan to get the country out of the deep economic crisis left behind by the communists. The lack of a social basis was shown during the election campaign as well; during the process the political parties vied with each other mostly over who could condemn communism in more vehement terms. In the heat of the campaign they all seemed to forget that it was the reformist wing of the Communist Party that made the peaceful transformation to the present government possible. The Hungarian Democratic Forum and its coalition partners won the elections not because of their plans for the development of Hungary (besides a few vague slogans such as the need to create a market economy), but because they won the contest for the most strident denunciation of communism. Not surprisingly, the current leaders are desperately trying to build a new social stratum that could eventually become the missing social basis. The struggle over privatization intended to create a new middle class that would presumably support the current governing elite, is part of this effort. For this very reason it has generated tremendous controversies in and out of parliament.[7] Similar controversies were created by the efforts of the Prime Minister to gain government control over the national television and radio stations. Surprisingly, the Antall government argued for state control over these important means of communications on the basis of a law enacted by the Kádár-government in 1974! The purpose is clear; Antall and his supporters want to disseminate their own political views over the airwaves during the coming elections without hindrance.[8]

The spokesmen for the governing elite argue that the stabilization of the economy, the elimination of the system of industrial subsidies that continued until very recently to prop up inefficient enterprises, the necessity of establishing a new foreign policy-orientation, all require decisions that are, by their very nature, unpopular. Reaching a broad consensus over these matters is almost impossible. But such arguments are contradictory; if anything, they certainly discourage the emergence of civil(ized) society. Furthermore, the tone of the arguments used by the elite as well as by its opposition is vehement and unrestrained. Not surprisingly, each side considers the other as an enemy not a political opponent that should be, at best, excluded from political life altogether.

Let us now turn to the issue of the development of municipal governments as a major component of civil(ized) society.

In part, such a society certainly consists of many disparate elements. There are institutions that are independent of the government, others cannot be and should not be completely free of government supervision. Among the former we can find circles of friends, informal associations of football fans, beer drinkers, cultural circles, local theater groups, library associations, and miriads of other civic groups. These have been multiplying rapidly in Hungary during the last two years.[9] They all have a role to play in strengthening a sense of civic pride and providing support for individuals in time of need. Municipal governments, however, belong to another category. They could be effective not only in providing roadblocks for centralization and authoritarianism, but could be schools for developing democratic ways of thinking among the population.

Municipal governments between 1948 and 1988 simply served as the local representatives of the central communist authorities. Their leaders were usually members of the Communist party, or in rare cases when they were not, were trusted fellow-travellers. The chairman of a municipal government and the membership of the institution were chosen through rigged elections. Their task consisted, first and foremost, in the reinforcement of communist control over society. Each village, district, and county, as well as towns and urban centers had their municipal councils. Their chairmen were subordinated to the corresponding party secretary who, in his turn, reported to higher party organs. There were few municipal officers indeed who represented their constituencies. The activities of the councils were conducted on the basis of "democratic centralism," an oximoron if there has ever been one. This was a rigid, unbending system that seldom considered its task the promotion of local initiatives, unless they were in line with the ever-changing party line. Since the activities and functions of municipal governing institutions were strictly curtailed, "individual initiatives" often led to petty—and, sometimes, not so petty—pilfering, nepotism and outright corruption. This was the way the situation developed especially after 1956.

Even in localities where "private" initiatives were possible, where a local council chairman or a chairman of a successful collective farm had high connections, the outcome was usually the establishment of a "petty kingdom," so to speak, with personal rule by the chairman. A perfect illustration of this system existed in the town—later city—of Tiszakécske in eastern Hungary.

The chairman of the local council was an Istvan Miskó, a physically robust, hail-fellow-well-met type. He was chairman for more than ten years and gradually established his semi-dictatorial control over the power structure in his town. He placed his friends and supporters in control in every institution, including the local Gymnasium (High School), the state vegetable collecting station, and other administrative centers. The local party secretary was his close friend. These friends were rewarded for their loyalty to the chairman. They received, among other privileges, choice pieces of building lots on the banks of the Tisza river for minimal compensation. The municipal authorities, under Miskó's direction, built first-class swimming and fishing facilities there. They also built cabins for the use of visiting dignitaries from Budapest, including the president of the Republic, comrade Losonczy, a personal friend of the chairman. Bribery, illegal land transactions, and other illegal activities were overlooked by the higher authorities, since they, too, benefitted from the chairman's generosity.

Miskó finally failed over his attempt to dictate the grading of students in the Gymnasium. He "suggested" to one of the tough Hungarian Language and Literature instructors, to loosen up her standards and give good grades to the son of the local party secretary and two other students who were taking entrance examinations for advanced study. He made his "suggestions" in the presence of the assistant principal of the Gymnasium, another personal friend whom he placed in his job. The teacher accepted the "suggestions," but she also made the whole sordid business known by announcing it in her class to the students and by inviting a reporter from a local paper to bring the affair to public attention.

Eventually, the national media took hold of the scandal and it became a *cause celebré*. By then, the calendar said "1988," and the communist system was on the verge of collapse in Hungary. Nevertheless, the scandal became a painful reminder of the general corruption that permeated every level of Hungarian society. As the result of all the publicity and open condemnation, Miskó committed suicide by shooting himself in the head.[10]

Many other episodes of official corruption were uncovered in the following months by a suddenly free media. They had all shown a similar pattern followed by municipal governments in the country. But the scandals were not restricted to the rural sphere; other scandals reached into the highest levels of society, including the Ministry of Defense and the office of the president of the Republic. It turned out that the communist system, rigidly controlled by the central authorities, was never subjected to proper supervision. Since the local constituencies had little say in the way municipal officials were elected, they had no chance to limit their authority and the party-center was in "far away Budapest." One observer of the scene noted in anguish,

> What can one do in a situation in which values had been degraded? When people are no longer paying any attention to (high) ideals because they were used for purposes of corruption?[11]

This was, indeed, the fundamental question.

Tiszakécske was, therefore, not a singular episode of a man gone astray, but it was the pattern by which municipal governments in every region in Hungary functioned during the communist era. One could argue, of course, that the citizens took communist slogans at their face value and did not make distinctions between public and private property, thereby reaching the highest stage of communism. Stealing was, therefore, no longer being considered a matter of dishonesty, but rather the appropriation of goods which, by right, belonged to those of the people who needed them. The Hungarian pattern was also typical for the entire Soviet bloc. Instead of the rule of law, the system was based on rule by petty despots who copied the dishonest behavior of their superiors. In fact, when the misdeeds of local municipal officials were discovered, they were usually treated with leniency, since, as the saying went, "they were the puppies of our own dog." This is a legacy of communism which is, at the same time, a major obstacle in the way of the emergence of a civil(ized) society.

Urban municipal governments did not differ greatly from their rural counterparts. The closer they were physically located to the center of power, the more pervasive the control exerted over them by the party leaders, and the less opportunity for individual citizens to make their words count. Elections for city councils were rigged everywhere, and the general hypocrisy permeating the entire system included urban institutions of government. How could one expect that the new post-communist municipal governments would become, almost overnight, the promoters of the development of civil(ized) society in their localities, burdened with such a legacy? Yet exactly this was what happened in Hungary during the last two years.

With the collapse of the communist order municipal governments in Hungary came to a momentary halt. Their officials, not receiving instructions from the center, were at a loss as to what to do. In addition, they were being intimidated by the local and national media, freed of the heavy handed censors, which continued to uncover local misdeeds one case after another. They publicized wholesale corruption, nepotism and other criminal activity.

The new coalition government that came into being in June 1990 was confronted by the prospects of impending chaos in urban and rural communities. It was obvious that new laws regulating the functioning of municipal governments would have to be enacted, and quickly. Yet, parliament bogged down over this issue, each party seeking advantages, and took a relatively long time and acrimonious debates to come up with necessary legislation. Finally the law which regulated local elections was enacted. It also provided certain restrictions on the authority of municipal officials. At the same time, local governments were made responsible for the maintenance of schools— the right to determine the content of local school curricula was to be decided later—and they were given control over real property formerly housing party-and mass-organizations. But legislation did not stop there. Another law, compensating former corporations and individuals, including the churches, for properties confiscated by the communists was also enacted. This law created a great deal of confusion because the confiscated buildings were mostly used by party- and mass-organizations and the municipal governments did not know which law to obey. The conflict has not yet been resolved at the time of this writing. Parliament was still not satisfied. It enacted into law the establishment of the office of Republican Overseers, individuals responsible for the smooth, lawful operations of municipal governments in each county. These overseers are theoretically independent of the government, but their salaries are paid from the national budget. Although the law stipulated that the role of overseers would be restricted to insure that municipal governments acted strictly within the laws, there is no guarantee that they will not become arbitrators of local decisions. One of the overseers, Dr. Sándor Skultéty, already noted that there is an increasing tendency to politicize local decisions. This trend is encouraged by the political parties whose parliamentary deputies visit rural districts with increasing frequency, chiding the local governments for decisions not favoring their political stance.[13] All this points to a rather fluid situation that needs time for stabilization in the interest of local autonomy and, incidentally, for the development of civil(ized) society.

When the first municipal elections were held they provided surprising results. Not only were large numbers of former municipal council chairmen, many running as independents, reelected, but the majority of local constituencies chose their municipal officials from the membership of the Free Democratic Alliance, the largest opposition party in parliament.

There were several reasons for the results. First of all, during four decades of communist rule the authority of local council chairmen were unchallenged and unchallengeable. Many of them succeeded not only in eliminating all contestants for power, but preventing the emergence of possible successors to their authority. Second, the population, especially those living in rural districts, had become so much accustomed to the system, that they found little objection to its previous functioning. They preferred known faces, regardless of their past, to unknown personalities. Third, and perhaps most importantly, during the last decade of the Kádár-regime the party coopted a great many members of the intelligentsia, including engineers, scientists, historians and the like, since the system no longer worked on the basis of the old Stalinist affirmative action principles.[14] These were people not easily swayed by empty rhetoric. They were businesslike administrators determined to make the system work. Most of them were not tainted by the general hypocrisy and corruption of the system; although they were *apparatchiks*, their livelihood did not depend solely on the whims of party officials, since they could always return to their earlier occupations. In the mid-1980s they represented the core of the reform-communist movement who swept out the old guard and made the peaceful transition to the democratic system possible. Thus, during the municipal elections of 1990, they represented an alternative to the candidates of the governing coalition. Consequently, the population was often quite willing to elect them to head municipal governments.

Nevertheless, the current situation points to an important flaw in the emerging democratic system in Hungary. Most Hungarians, especially the rural population, have not yet been able to adjust to the fact that, in a democratic society, local government officials would be responsible for their actions to the local electorate, and that if they want to stay in office, they must respond to local needs. The people have not yet become accustomed to a situation in which direct orders do not come from Budapest, but from the local government which, in its turn, needs their voluntary cooperation. It is also clear that few people are familiar with the often confusing—and contradictory—set of laws and regulations relating to the functions of municipal governments and the duties and obligations of elected officials as well as ordinary citizens. Thus, ignorance of the laws is one of the major obstacles in the way of asserting popular control over locally elected officials. It has become quite clear that free elections alone are not sufficient to insure the emergence and functioning of institutions of civil(ized) society that will function according to the spirit of democracy. Unless the population is educated in these matters—and soon—municipal governments could revert to their earlier pattern of functioning. In that case civil(ized) society will not emerge in Hungary very soon.

One can hardly emphasize strongly enough the importance of another element in the development of civil(ized) society, namely, the tone of public discourse in politics but also in everyday communications. This tone is directly related to the level of tolerance existing in society. Since the parliamentary elections, the tone of discourse has become so vituperative in Hungary that it is reminiscent of the early days of communist rule. Scores of articles in the newspapers of various hues excoriate and berate individuals and groups if their actions do not meet the expectations of the writers. If Hungarians today discern a tendency of deterioration in the civility of public discourse, which many of them do, it does not mean that they have a way to check the process. For instance, an article published in the daily newspaper, *Pesti Hirlap*, that is supportive of the government and the Hungarian Democratic Forum, was typical of the vulgarity characterizing discussions today. The author, Ferenc Kubinyi, wrote:

In the Spring of 1990, the last testament of the dictatorship, born in the bundle of seventh hell and dishonorably dead

45 years later, was opened. Onto the table of this small country an unimaginable flow of slime is being dumped ever since. Cheating, forgery, embezzlement and murder, the putrid smell of the chamberpots of jails, the nose-wrenching smells of the sweat of death, the smack of males kissing right on the mouth, the Bolshevik faith of generals shining with decorations which was simply prostitution, the cloud of lies reaching higher than the peaks of the Kékes mountain, the horselaughs of pickpockets sponsored by the regime, the belted, soft-stockinged whores wearing soft boots who were masters of eavesdropping by telephone, the salivating libels in personal files, the whirring of the storm-warnings of early morning doorbells, the full-mouthed rhythmic yelling and hand-clapping, the goon who forced one to drink urine from a canteen, the unHungarian belching of the Marxist philosopher, a traitor to his country, the heroic cantata produced with the accompaniment of a brass-band, the whispering of the provocateur pushing the innocent in front of the barrel of the pistol, the prayer breaking forth from the bloody mouth of the monk tied up in the hallway of the prison, "Lord, forgive them their sins." This hellish testament is still covering the table of the nation and its putrid smells continue to pollute not only the environment of Hungary, but it also ruins the people's trust in God's eternal and human justice.

The writer then added to his "stream of consciousness":

He who knows even vaguely of Hungarian history [not that written by Elek Karsay, György Ránki, Iván T. Berend, and their ilk] knows well that all our national revolutions miscarried, they were betrayed. Why should not this 'noble tradition' be repeated in 1990s.[15]

István Csurka, one of the vice presidents of the Hungarian Democratic Forum, usually writes in a similar manner. His brazen attacks on Hungarian-American philanthropist, George Soros, who spent millions of dollars in support of the opponents of the communist regime, are well documented. Soros is Jewish; this fact in itself disqualifies him in the eyes of this champion of "Hungarianess" from participating in current national life. What Csurka conveniently "forgot" was that he himself enjoyed financial support from Soros during the mid-1980s, as he was sponsored by the Soros Foundation during his trip to the United States.[16] Csurka went so far as to "positively state" that Soros was actually part of a Jewish conspiracy of over one hundred years to dominate Hungarian culture and politics and that his current activities were really but a camouflage of his real intentions.[17]

István Benedek, a professor at Eötvös Lóránt University in Budapest, proclaimed at a meeting of a newly established union of newspaper writers created to oppose the long-established journalists' union,

> The fact is that we do not want the freedom of the press. Because freedom of the press quickly turns into freedom for mud-slinging to an unbearable extent. We do not want freedom of speech either, because freedom of speech quickly turns into rancor. What we want is the decency of the media, the decency of speech . . .

and then the good professor who, in another article proclaimed that the United States was a country without culture and the center of human misery, added,

> What we want is to make it impossible for anyone to stand up and scream, his saliva dripping, that the government is lying, that the prime minister is a liar; that no one should be able to put down without punishment, to belittle or to hate all our developments that are taking place. Because there is development, there is liberation from the Soviet army! It is not true that the country is impoverished, that it is on the way down and out! All this is asserted by the internal enemy; it is what they write, whisper and spread. And when you form the new association, then perhaps we will be able to throttle their association.[18]

As another example of this sort of "public discourse," György D. Varga stated in a particularly offensive article,

> With us, neither the strictness of the laws of the Old Testament, nor the forgiving justice of the New Testament are the guiding principles. Our true guiding principle appears to be: power, power above everything else![19]

As the few examples quoted above illustrate, the demagogues, the peddlers of vulgarization of political ideas, have had ample opportunity to come forward during the last two years. However, we must also point out that their shrill voices, usually raised on behalf of some program sponsored by the Antall government, are often counterbalanced by saner comments. One of these was an exchange between Sándor Csoóri, the leading Hungarian novelist/poet today, who had written that the Jews in Hungary cannot assume solidarity with Hungarians because they had done too many injuries to the Hungarian nation,[20] and Péter Hanák, one of the best known historians in Hungary today, (one who barely missed Kubinyi's list). Hanák responded in a moving article, stating that Jews came in as many convictions as there existed among other peoples, and that they came back to Hungary after Auschwitz simply because they wanted to come home.[21]

Two contrasting events must be mentioned in this connection to illustrate further both the possibilities and obstacles to the development of civil(ized) society in Hungary in the 1990s. One of these was the taxi-drivers' blockade in the fall of September 1991, and the other a demonstration in front of the building of the national TV on March 15, 1992.

The taxi drivers' blockade paralyzed transportation in Hungary for more than three days. It was a well-organized affair. The drivers blocked the main highways leading in and out of urban centers, preventing the flow of normal civilian and military traffic. There was a tremendous congestion at the railroad stations and airports as a consequence. However, they permitted food deliveries to enter the cities and towns. The strike was orderly and effective. It elicited all sorts of comments but also a great deal of public support. The reason for the blockade was that the government suddenly, without notice, nearly doubled the price of gasoline, endangering the livelihood of nearly everyone depending on the use of motor transportation. This was an obviously intolerable situation not only for the taxi drivers but also for the drivers of power rigs as well as the automobile-owning public. The strike was eventually resolved peacefully; the government backed down and halved the price increase and the taxi drivers lifted the blockade.

This event brought forth a number of interesting personalities. The head of the National Association of Businessmen, János Palotás, negotiated on behalf of the drivers with the government. He turned out to be a smart, pleasant fellow who outshone the government negotiators on national TV. He immediately became an important political figure in Hungary despite his disclaimer that he wished no political career. He is still being considered by public opinion as a "favorite son." On the other hand, the government, especially its minister of the interior, Balázs Horváth, lost face during the strike. József Antall, the prime minister, was in the hospital at that time, being operated on for brain tumors. Thus, Horváth who substituted for him, came through as an authoritarian, truculent character, who first wanted to move the blockading vehicles out of the way by the fire departments then by the army. He was prevented from doing the latter by Árpad Göncz, the president of the republic, who simply used his post as commander-in-chief of the armed forces to veto the idea. But the affair highlighted the poverty of ideas of the Antall government and its ineffectiveness in dealing with public protests. It was reported, although strongly denied by Horváth, that the minister of the interior wanted the police forces deployed and, if needed be, fire on the striking taxi drivers!

The strike pointed to several surprising developments. First of all, the striking taxi drivers were not condemned by the public which was inconvenienced by their action indeed. Outside of a narrow group of extremist government supporters, the public considered the government as a collection of bunglers who did not gauge public sentiments correctly, and acted in an arrogant, inconsiderate manner. The first spontaneous public action by a group of people belonging to civil(ized) society proved that they could force changes on a reluctant political elite. This is an important lesson that is not being forgotten in Hungary . Some aftereffects of the strike are still lingering on. István Eörsi, a parliamentary deputy of the Free Democratic Alliance, openly charged the former minister of the interior, Balázs Horváth with the intention of giving police the order to fire on the taxi drivers. This was not only vehemently denied by Horváth who is now minister without a portfolio in the Antall government, but he went so far as to sue Eörsi for libel. Horváth is a personal friend of Antall and, although the prime minister considered it prudent to remove him from heading the ministry of the interior, he remained a member of the prime minister's cabinet. The lawsuit is still pending.

The other event I want to discuss occurred on March 15, 1992. It was a demonstration organized by several Right-wing groups in front of the national TV building. The day marks an important event in Hungarian history. On that day in 1848 university students and young revolutionaries in Pest and Buda ushered in the revolution against Habsburg domination. The famous poem, "National Song" written by the young poet of the revolution, Sándor Petöfi, was read to a crowd of excited people on the steps of the national museum. This poem has been recited every year since, except during the darkest days of revenge after the suppression of the revolution in 1849 by the armies of the friend of the Habsburgs, Russia's Tsar Nicholas I. During the communist regime, the celebration of March 15 was discouraged. It provided too many painful reminders of freedom and of the oppressive nature of Russia's government. The days celebrated by the regime included the day of "liberation" of April 4, international workers' day of May 1, the holiday of the "new bread" on August 20 (originally the day of King St. Stephen of Hungary) and, of course, November 7 in honor of the Russian Bolshevik revolution. During the last years of the Kádár-regime attempts at celebrating March 15 in public were prohibited. Secret police thugs attacked demonstrators on those days in several years running, beating and arresting them. With the collapse of the communist system, March 15 once again became a national holiday. Speeches were delivered from the steps of the national museum in Budapest and the day was observed in every village, town, and city. The celebrations in 1992, however took an ugly turn in Budapest. There was an official celebration at the national museum at which György Szabad, the president of parliament spoke to a large crowd of people. But another "celebration" was organized by the "Association of 1956." Its leaders, include Gergely Pongrátz, an embittered demagogue, who was, in 1956, the commander of Corvin-köz, a small alley in Budapest, that resisted the Russians from beginning to end, Attila Geréb, Pál Esztergár, Jenő Fónay, András Márton and János Roik. They were all fighters during the revolution of 1956.

The meeting started early in the morning at Petöfi's statue. The speakers made every effort to incite the crowd that soon was joined by the Hungarian version of skin-heads. Then they moved on to the museum with the openly declared intention to disrupt Szabad's speech. But the crowd at the museum blocked all entrances to the garden and the demonstrators could not enter.

By then, they numbered about 1,500 people, whipped into a frenzy of hatred for all those who, in their judgment, prevented the compensation of the victims of the Kádár-regime, and for those who did not immediately "take care" of the former communist leaders after the collapse. The crowd then moved to the national TV building on Szabadság-square.

The building's entrance was blocked by a police cordon, three deep, and there were soldiers stationed inside to make sure the demonstrators did not enter. The crazed crowd surged against the police lines and almost broke through but was eventually repulsed. Their leaders took portable microphones to address them. András Márton said, "They say we are only a mob; let us show them otherwise . . ." Fónay then took the speaker and attacked the government for not having rehabilitated the victims of communist terror. While he spoke, several fights broke out in the crowd. Skinheads especially attacked radio and TV reporters, breaking cameras and physically abusing their holders. Punches were thrown, kicks were delivered. By then, members of the "Association for Historical Justice" joined the demonstration. This group was founded in 1988 by Miklós Vásárhelyi and others, decent democrats, who were members of the entourage of Imre Nagy, the communist prime minster of Hungary, who was over-thrown by the Russian troops in November 1956. But the group split, Vásárhelyi and his friends leaving the organization that has become radically Rightist. Those who endorsed the extremists were now in the crowd with skinheads and other Right-wing elements and joined in the denunciation not only of the government but of the democratic system itself.

During the demonstration demands were voiced for the dismissal of the directing personnel of the national TV and radio stations, be-cause, as the speakers proclaimed, they were of the old regime. The crowd swelled to about 5,000 people. After some more speech-making, they eventually dispersed.[22]

The two events discussed here, the taxi-drivers' strike and the demonstration before the TV building, vividly demonstrate the con-trasting attitudes to the development of modern society in post-communist Hungary. Together with the new role of municipal gov-ernments and the deteriorating tone of public discussions they show a society that has not yet found a sure way to establish a stable democratic system. Yet, despite the danger signals, this writer is optimistic that society as a whole will not permit the extremists to impose their will on the population. The upcoming elections in 1994 will probably end with the reduction of the influence of the Hun-garian Democratic Forum and the creation of a new Left of Center government coalition. Until that happens, however, we must keep our collective fingers crossed.

NOTES

1. John Keane, *Civil Society and the State* (London, 1988).
2. *Principles of Power* (New York, 1942). Also the evaluation of

Ferrero's ideas in Robert A. Kann, *The Problem of Restoration. A Study in Political History* (Berekeley, CA, 1968), pp. 46–54.

3. Ferrero, Ibid.

4. There is a very informative discussion of this subject in a short essay by Ervin Csizmadia, "Ki uralkodik? Ki kormányoz? A posztkádárista átmenet társadalmi bázisa" [Who Rules? The Social Basis of the Post-Kádár Transformation] *Magyar Nemzet* February 27, 1991, 25–26.

5. See the instructive article by C. N. L., "Fennáll a tekintélyelv üség veszélye" [The Danger of Authoritarianiam is Present] *Magyar Hírlap* March 13, 1991, 46; and "Privát társadalom nélkül nincs demokrácia" [There is no Democracy without Private Society] *Kritika* No. 8, 1992, 27–32.

István Csurka who, as one of the vice presidents of the Hungarian Democratic Forum, carries a certain weight in politics, has recently published an essay in which he proposes a new course for his party and government. The essay is an openly fasctistoid work. It is permeated with a conspiratorial interpretation of history, charging that a Jewish conspiracy has been keeping Hungarian politics in bondage ever since the mid-ninteenth century. He also equates the opposition with this conspiracy. He proposes a policy of the iron fist, using the police to suppress opposition to the government. As might be expected, there was a series of condemnations of Csurka's proposals. Among these the strongest was by József Debreczeni, another leader of the Forum and others. The discussions continue but it is decidedly taking an anti-Csurka tone. See "Néhány gondolat a rendszerváltozás két esztendeje és az MDF új programja kapcsán," [A few thoughts concerning two years of the change of systems and the New Program of the Hugnarian Democratic Forum] *Magyar Fórum*, August 20, 1992, 3–18; József Debreczeni, "Nyilt levél Csurka Istvánnak," [Open Letter to I. Cs.] *Népszabadság*, August 27, 1992, 19–20; János L. László, "Az MDF távolodik Liberálisaitól?" [Is the MDF Distancing Itself from Its Liberals?] *Magyar Hírlap*, August 28, 1992, 23–25; István Elek, "Csurkának meg kell tagadnia szörnyszülöttét," [Csurka Must Deny His Bastard] *Magyar Hírlap*, August 28, 1992, 23–24; Sz. ? Sz., "Folyamatos kompromisszumok," [Continuous Compromises] *Népszabadság*, August 28, 1992, 27–28; Gusztáv Molnár, "Mitöl félünk?" [What Is It We Are Afraid Of?]; *Magyar Hírlap*, August 28, 1992, etc.

6. Hannah Arendt, *The Origins of Totalitarianism* (New York,

1951), "Postscript." See also Carl J. Friedrich and Zbigniev Brzezhinski, *Totalitarian Dictatorship and Autocracy* (2nd ed., New York, 1968), pp. 279–342.

7. See, as an example, Melinda Kamasz, "Gyorsitani kell a privatizációt," [Privatization Must Be Speeded Up] *Magyar Hírlap*, July 23, 1992, 10; and Éva Voszka, "Tart a visszaállamositás" [The Re-Nationalization is on] *Figyelő*, August 6, 1992, 33–34.

8. András Bencsik, "Levélaria" [Aria or Letters] *Pesti Hírlap*, August 11, 1992, 24–26; and Sándor Révész, "Ultima ratio," *Beszélő*, February 8, 1992, 21–22.

9. See H. J., "Egyesületalapitási láz" [Feverish Establishment of Associations] *Magyar Hírlap*, March 13, 1992, 46.

10. For the episode see István Tamás, *Glasznoszty Tiszakécskén. Kik vagyunk mi, hogy igazat merünk modani?* [Who Are We to Have the Courage to Tell the Truth?], (Budapest, 1989).

11. Ibid., p. 169.

12. Imre Krajcár, "*Alattvaló vagy főispán?*" [Subject or Head Administrator?] July 30, 1992, 17–18. This is an interview with the Republican Overseer of three counties.

13. Ibid.

14. It is worth noting that affirmative action, Stalinist style, had many parallel characteristics with the American version and both of them have been rooted in feudal practices and ideals. Both are based (in fact if not in open discussions) on the feudal concept of the accident of birth, not on ability and hard work. In both the United States and the Soviet bloc justification for such a system was provided by alleged past injustices for which the new generation was made responsible retroactively. In the Soviet bloc this led to counterselection, the eventual denigration of ability and hard work. If a trustworthy comrade had ability and worked hard, that was all right but not absolutely necessary.

15. Ferenc Kubinyi, "Emlékmüavatás" [Dedication of a Memorial] *Pesti Hirlap*, June 27, 1992, 47–48.

16. István Csurka, "Vidéken" [In the Countryside] *Magyar Fórum* August 6, 1992, 35.

17. It is interesting to note that following Csurka's attack on Soros, the government cancelled the agreement with the Soros Foundation for the continuation of its activities in Hungary. A new agreement has been signed but it restricts the foundation's activities. See "Szerződés új feltételekkel. A soros Alapitvány jövöje" [Contract

with New Conditions. The Future of the Soros Foundation] *Uj Magvarország,* August 7, 1992, 25.

18. "Az értékek felszinre töréséért. Benedek István a magyarságról" [For the Emergence of Values. István Benedek about the Hungarians] *Magyar Fórum,* August 6, 1992, 33.

19. György D. Varga, "Össznépi Fridi-show" [All-Populist Fridi-show] *Pesti Hirlap,* June 29, 2992, 54.

20. Sándor Csoóri, "Nappali hold" [Moon at Daytime] *Hitel,* No. 18, 1990, 6-7.

21. See the moving response: Péter Hanák, "Hagyomány és jövökép," [Tradition and the View of the Future] *Népszabadság,* September 29, 1990, 3-4.

22. See Éva Ónody, "Veszélyben a szellemi haza" [The Spiritual Homeland is in Danger] *Uj Magyarország,* March 16, 1992, 15; János Bercsi, "Lincshangulat a Magyar Televizió elött [Lynch-mood in Front of Hungarian Television], *Magyar Hírlap,* March 16, 1992, 9-10, and by the same author, "Annak oka lehet, hogy az emberek demonstrációt tartanak" [There Must be a Reason for People to Demonstrate] Ibid., 10.

THE REVIVAL OF THE POLITICAL RIGHT IN POST-COMMUNIST ROMANIA

Michael Shafir

Visiting a newspaper vendor's stand in contemporary Bucharest can be very confusing for anyone searching for neat divisions alongside the classical "Left-Right" continuum. With the possible exception of *Socialistul,* a sporadic publication put out by the Socialist Party of Labor, the self-declared successor of the deceased Romanian Communist Party (RCP), hardly any other daily, weekly or monthly would be prepared to admit that it belonged to the "Left" of the present Romanian political spectrum. And yet, for some time after it was first issued in 1991, the editor-in-chief of *Socialistul* was none other than Radu Theodoru and among the members of its editorial board one can also find the name of Mircea Musat, a former prominent falsifier of Romanian historiography under Ceausescu. Both Theodoru and Musat, however, are Vice Presidents of the Greater Romania Party (GRP), a xenophobic, anti-Semitic and anti-Hungarian political formation set up in 1991 and led by two former Ceausescu hagiographers, the writers Corneliu Vadim Tudor (President) and Eugen Barbu (First Vice President), who also have an established record of collaboration with the former secret police, the *Securitate.* Theodoru and Musat are frequent contributors not only to the GRP's two official publications, the weeklies *Romania Mar* [Greater Romania] and *Politica,* but also to the weekly *Europa,* the political line of which is similar to that of the GRP, and which is suspected of being financed by Iosif Constantin Dragan, a former member of the Iron Guard and collaborationist of the Ceausescu regime, who returned to Romania after having amassed a fortune in the West. It turns out, then, that the title of Sarah Terry's inquisitive contribution to this volume ("What Is Left, What Is Right, and What Is Wrong in

Polish Politics?") applies to Romania as well, although within different parameters. For anyone who is only slightly familiar with the contents of *Romania mare, Politica* and *Europa* would not hesitate to place these publications at the "radical Right" end of Romania's post-Communist political spectrum.

At this point in the discussion, an elucidation of terminology might be warranted. In what follows, a distinction will be made between the "traditional" and the "radical" Right. This distinction is hardly new. It has been amply used in analyzing the difference between, on one hand, the "within system" negation of equalitarian or socialist values, and, on the other hand, the "system-destructive" negation of democratic values. The latter trend, also termed "revolutionary Right," served, first, the political discourse of fascist ideologies, and later the ideological credo of fascist or national-socialist regimes.[1] No reference will be made to the "aristocratic right" mentioned by Iván Völgyes in this volume, for the simple reason that in Romania that segment of the "Rightist" spectrum practically disappeared from the country's political map in the early 1920s when the Conservative Party (which mainly represented the interests of the owners of large *latifundia*) ceased to play any role in the country's politics.

In his seminal discussion of the radical Right, Zeev Sternhell defines it as characterized by a

> refusal of individualism, of capitalism, of liberalism, of Marxist determinism and of its Social-Democratic variety, of the 'democratic disorder' and of bourgeois mediocrity.

Above all, Sternhell mentions, members of the radical Right conceive the individual "as a social animal, as an integral part of an organic whole," which is the ethnic national state.[2] The "organic view of history," which necessarily excludes from the national community anyone who does not belong to the ethnic nation, is primarily entrenched in communitarian values, perceived to be shared by past, present and future generations. No wonder, then, that the radical Right is constantly in need of both "external" and "internal" enemies. While both vary according to geographical and historical circumstances, most radical Rightists share anti-Semitism as a common trait, for "the Jew" cannot possibly belong to this community of *Blut und Boden.*

In the context of post-communist transitional East European societies, the traditional Right can be defined in juxtaposition with Sternhell's analysis of the radical Right. The traditional Right advocates individualism and (unlike some shades of the radical Right, as it will be shown), it supports a quick transition to market reforms leading to capitalism. It views democracy and a "civil society" as a *sine qua non* condition of the only acceptable order of things in the polity and, consequently, it supports the respect of human rights. While rejecting Marxism as an ideology, and while occasionally advocating the disqualification from participation in the polity's political life of individuals who had been involved in the imposition of totalitarian communist values and persecutions, the traditional Right is an ideological adversary of Social-Democracy, but not its deadly enemy. Collaboration or compromise with parties of the moderate Left (or with "centrist" parties) is viewed as legitimate and, in some cases, even as warranted. In short, the traditional Right fits into what Hans Rogger describes as "classical conservatism," (which only adds to the terminological confusion associated with the discussions on the different shades of the "Right."). It is temperate, compromising, and opportunistic, dedicated to inherited [in this case, pre-communist] institutions and values, to privilege (or at least to social and economic stability), and fearful of mass politics and mass passions.[3]

The Traditional Right

Having been annihilated by the communist regime at the end of the 1940s, Romania's two "historical" parties, the National Liberal Party (NLP) and the National Peasant Party, re-emerged immediately after the ousting of the Ceausescu regime. The latter political formation added the title Christian and Democratic (NPP-CD) to its name not long after its revival.[4] Although individuals belonging to both these parties had exposed themselves politically towards the end of communist rule, neither the NLP nor the NPP-CD had worked out any real alternative political program before their re-emergence. The leaderships of the NLP and the NPP-CD were mostly made up of the few who had survived long terms of imprisonment and subsequent persecution and some émigrés who returned to Romania from exile. Some of these leaders, such as the NPP-CD President Corneliu Coposu, had displayed admirable courage in resisting past persecution; most of them were rather aged and, regardless of whether they had spent the bulk of the last forty-five years in Romania or abroad, they tended to be in many ways out of touch with the changed socio-political reality of the country. Viewed from this perspective, the two main parties of the traditional Right may be said to have constituted the country's "nostalgic opposition." The nostalgia rested in, first, an idealization of the country's interwar democratic traditions. They overlooked many of the weaknesses of the Romanian polity in the short period in which the country had been ruled under a system of democratic constitutional monarchy. The newly re-emerged parties of the traditional Right also overlooked the fact that in the inter-war period much of Romania's political life had been dominated by politicking rather than by policy-making.

Above all, however, the traditional Right chose to ignore the transformations that the Romanian polity experienced under com-munism, somehow naively expecting to quickly regain the dominant role they had played before the communist takeover. Yet, an en-trepreneurial stratum, of which the main electorate of the NLP should presumably consist, no longer existed, having been totally obliterated by the former regime. The same applies to the electorate of the NPP-CD, which, one assumes, should have mainly been based on the small and middle-sized landowners in the rural areas of the country.

The first elections in the post-communist period were held on 20 May 1990 and their outcome was more than disappointing for the parties of the traditional Right. Ion Iliescu, a former presidential candidate of the National Salvation Front (NSF), (a heterogenous "catch-all" party which included many former officials whose careers had been stopped by intra-RCP skirmishes and by the domination of the RCP by Nicolae Ceausescu's "extended family," some second and third-level members of the former *nomenklatura*; but also some *bona fide* technocrats, as well as members of other social strata), won easily. He received over 85 percent of the total vote, against the NLP candidate Radu Campeanu (10.6 percent) and the NPP-CD candidate Ion Ratiu (4.29 percent). The NSF victory in the elections for the two chambers of the parliament, which were held on the same day, was somewhat less spectacular, but nonetheless overwhelming. The NSF secured 66.31 percent of the votes for the Deputies' Assembly and 67.02 percent of the ballots cast for the Senate. The NLP garnered 6.41 percent of the vote for the former and 7.06 percent of the vote cast for the latter chamber. Finally, the NPP-CD was backed by 2.56 percent of the electorate in the ballot for the Deputies' Assembly and by 2.50 percent in the elections for the Senate.[5]

It is true that the elections of 1990 had been hardly an example in democratic procedure. Nevertheless, Iliescu's victory, as well as that of his party, was genuine, even if its proportions were unnecessarily inflated. The victory had several explanations. First, prior to the elections, the NSF had indulged in populist economic policies and its electoral propaganda emphasized job security and a mild and gradual reform of the economy, rather than the radical and socially painful solutions advocated by the traditional Right. The electorate's reaction to these differences was typical of a population in which "subject" orientations are dominant in the political culture. Electoral choice was made with an eye on the governmental "output" and with little consideration for civic "input." Anxiety in face of the possible impact of a belated modernization process, requiring personal sacrifice, producing personal insecurity in the form of unemployment and inability to cope with inflation were skillfully exploited in the NSF's propaganda. In addition, Campeanu and Ratiu, who had returned to Romania from exile, were presented to the electorate as "willing to sell out" Romania to foreign capital. "While we were suffering here under Ceausescu, they had coffee and croissant in Paris," was one of the NSF's favorite theme in the elections. The NSF thus became the first political formation encouraging xenophobia which, for the time being, was targeted at the West and those said to represent its individualist values. The formula apparently worked, for many workers and employees felt obviously safer under the unproductive collectivism of public ownership than under the individualistic privatization promoted by the opposition's electoral propaganda.

Unable to keep the impossible promise of combining social security with economic reform, the NSF government led by Prime Minister Petre Roman began implementing painful economic reforms in the latter part of 1990, accelerating them in 1991. These policies led, on one hand, to the dismissal of Roman as premier in September 1991,[6] in what was an ironical twist of history. Roman was dismissed following a protest by the miners from the Jiu valley, who descended on Bucharest, demanding the government's resignation; but on three previous occasions, the same miners had travelled to the capital at the instigation of the NSF, to punish those who were opposing its policies, rampaging, among other things, the party headquarters of the traditionalist Right.[7] On the other hand, the outcome of the acceleration of the economic reform was the splitting of the NSF into two main wings, one led by the former Prime Minister and the other (at least unofficially) by Iliescu with the latter wing advocating a continuation of the policies pursued in the earlier part of 1990.[8]

As a result of disappointment with the government's unkept promises and the intra-party struggles in the NSF, the ruling party lost about half of its support in the local elections held in February 1992. The two parties of the traditional Right ran in these elections on the joint lists of the Democratic Convention, which included several other major parties (the Hungarian Democratic Union of Romania - HDUR -, the Party of the Civic Alliance - PCA -, the Romanian Ecologist Party and the Social Democratic Party of Romania), as well as other parties, associations and organizations opposing the NSF. The Democratic Convention's performance in the elections was impressive; it garnered nearly as much support (33.3 percent) as did the NSF (34.0 percent).[9] However, not long after this near-victory, the NLP leader Radu Campeanu announced that in the forthcoming presidential and parliamentary elections (scheduled for the second half of 1992), the NLP intended to withdraw from the Democratic Convention. Apparently, traditional politicking was again gaining the upper hand. Campeanu obviously objected to having the leader of the PCA (a centrist party emulating movements such as the Czechoslovak Civic Forum), Nicolae Manolescu, who had announced his own candidacy for the presidency, get the backing of the unified opposition. Ironically enough, Campeanu, who had come in second in the 1990 presidential elections mainly due to the support of the HDUR, offered as one of the reasons for his position the HDUR's alleged support for Hungary's irredentist position towards the Transylvanian question.[10] In fact, Campeanu was thereby playing into the NSF's hand, for one of the main accusations which the NSF, alongside the parties of the extreme Right, had directed against the Democratic Convention, was that of being "traitors" to the cause of Romanian territorial integrity.[11] Beyond the politicking which may have caused Campeanu to adopt this stance, the possible disintegration of the Democratic Convention demonstrated that nationalism is an important factor in contemporary Romanian politics, and that the traditional Right is by no means immune to temptations of manipulating it to its own advantage.

The Parties of "Radical Continuity"

Viewed from the perspective of the last twenty-five years of communist rule in Romania, the presence of the radical Right on the country's political map following the collapse of communism is hardly surprising. The Ceausescu version of "national communism" was probably unmatched elsewhere in the region in its efforts to entrench the legitimacy of both the party and its ruler based on nationalist symbols and on a political discourse that, for all practical purposes, resurrected the inter-war political credo of the extreme Right. Party hagiographers had in fact hailed Ceausescu as one who had "restored the dignity of the nation" by allowing official historiography and other forms of "superstructural" activity to be manipulated into becoming the servile instruments of the regime in exchange for giving vent to the strong nationalistic imprint with which much of the inter-war Romanian intellectual-political sub-culture had been imbued. Originally welcomed by the bulk of the intelligentsia, which has had to suffer nearly two decades of de-nationalization and "cultural Sovietization," these policies eventually opened the door wide to opportunists who were eager to pose as the champions of both nation and party. In the course of this process, they proceeded to push aside personal and cultural rivals who might have blocked their way to the apex where "worldly goods" were distributed by political power.[12] Furthermore, the policies of "Romanianization," pursued by the regime in actual practice, and directed against *vis-à-vis* the national minorities (the Jews at an earlier stage, the Hungarians at a subsequent and much longer stage), were certainly not out of line with the basic political belief-structure of the inter-war radical Right.

Apart from the "nostalgic" traditional Right, the typology proposed here distinguishes between two main sub-categories of radical Right. The first sub-category, which shall be termed as one of "radical continuity," derives its main frame of political reference and activity from the preceding Ceausescu period. In addition, it is known to have occasionally been linked with the ruling NSF or with segments thereof. The second sub-category is that of "radical return." Unlike the former, it does not view any of the Ceausescu period as "accomplishments" with approval and sympathy. It is untainted by any significant measure of collaborationism with the former regime. It displays an overtly adverse attitude towards the NSF, and it strives to return to what could be called the genuine roots of Romanian Right wing activism and thought, bypassing the communist interlude.

The two main political formations belonging to the category of radical continuity are the Party of Romanian National Unity (PRNU) and the GRP- The PRNU is the Political arm of the extreme-nationalist anti-Hungarian organization *Vatra romaneasca* [Romanian Cradle], whose honorary president is Iosif Constantin Dragan. *Natiunea*, a publication owned by Dragan, eventually became the official voice of the Cradle. *Vatra* was set up soon after the ouster of Ceausescu, in response to demands by members of the Hungarian national minority for the restoration of cultural and other collective rights that had been forcibly taken away from them beginning with the year 1959. The PRRU's "natural electorate" are those Romanian ethnics who had moved into Transylvania as a result of Ceausescu's policies of "Romanianization" of the region, and who fear that acceptance of the Hungarian demands (such as separate universities and schools) affect their vested interests.[13] It is not a matter of accident that in the local elections of February 1992 in Cluj, for example, the *PRNU* did particularly well in those new parts of the town that had been settled by the "imported" Romanian ethnic element.[14]

This is not to say that remnants of "historical memories" left by Hungarian discrimination against Romanians when the region was ruled from Budapest do not play a role in *Vatra*'s and *PRNU*'s popularity among ethnic Romanians. However, it takes a special psychogenic personality (whose analysis is beyond the instruments available to the political scientist) to admit, as *PRNU* president, Senator Radu Ciontea openly did, that one's mistrust and hatred of the Hungarians has reached pathological proportions. In an interview printed in two issues of the weekly *Baricada* in late 1990 and early 1991, Ciontea recounted that he had been born in "a small hamlet in the Mures valley, which had suffered all possible evils at the hand of the Hungarians." His father, he said, was "the village butcher," while his mother "had only four years of schooling." "Since I was a child," he added, "I was taught by my father not to trust the Hungarians. He told me that 'every Hungarian walks with a rope in his pocket'," and that with this rope "they strangle Romanians." When he visits Bucharest to participate in parliamentary debates, Ciontea said, "I do not have the courage to eat . . . at the hotel's restaurant, because I fear that the Hungarians would poison me"; furthermore, his apartment in the Transylvanian town of Tirgu Mures is "guarded around the clock by two policemen, since I do not want my wife and daughter to be raped, then murdered."[15]

In the case of the PRNU one cannot possibly speak of a proper "ideology." Anti-Hungarianism occupies the first place in its value-system, which is therefore basically negative and defensive. This does not, one should add, make *Vatra* and its political arm into non-aggressive organizations. What remains unclear is whether their aggressive anti-Hungarianism is not manipulated by forces connected with the former regime in general, and with the *Securitate* in particular. It has been quite amply documented that the inter-ethnic Hungarian-Romanian clashes of March 1990 in Tirgu Mures and in which *Vatra* members provoked most incidents, has served the purposes of many who might otherwise have found themselves out of bread (and in particular, out of butter).[16] Apart from anti-Hungarian postures, the *PRNU* advocates "military governance" as a solution to Romania's present problems, just as the GRP does. And like the latter party, the *PRNU* is for a "presidential republic" rather than for the constitutional monarchy advocated by some formations belonging to the traditional Right, such as the NPPCD. The GRP is also an opponent of the monarchy, but, at least according to Ciontea, the *PRNU*'s position on this issue is slightly more malleable: in the above mentioned-interview, Ciontea said that his party was for an authoritarian form of government and that parliamentary government "does not interest us." The *PRNU*, he added, wanted "a president with very extensive powers, to govern with an iron-hand." But should it turn out that "the people want a monarchy," his party would not oppose it, provided that the king "was a Romanian [ethnic]." A return of the Hohenzollern dynasty was to be ruled out from the start.

The collaboration between *Vatra*, the *PRNU* and the NSF goes back to at least mid-1990. At the outset of its rule, the NSF had seemed sympathetic to the grievances of the Hungarian minority. However, since the core of its activists consists of supporters of the former regime who saw their vested interests endangered by the Hungarians' demands, the NSF gradually embraced positions reminiscent of the Ceausescu period. It refused to acknowledge the legitimacy of collective rights and began accusing neighboring Hungary of fomenting discord in Transylvania. Sympathizers of *Vatra* (many of them, however, suspected of being police dressed up in civilian clothes and acting on the orders of their superiors), hissed members of the opposition suspected of being "soft" on the Hungarians at a solemn meeting held in Alba Iulia on the occasion of Romania's national day, on 1 December 1990. Instead of calming the atmosphere, Prime Minister Roman acted as mob cheerleader, as could be plainly seen on Romanian television. In what was apparently, an urge to demonstrate that he was a "genuinely good Romanian," Roman (the grandson of a rabbi and the son of a Spanish Roman-Catholic mother), claimed that he was the "bone," that is the offspring, of a family with an ancient tradition of struggle for Romanian rights in Transylvania. "In me, I bear the idolatry [*sic*] for this part of the country, without which Romania could not exist," he said.[18] The same urge prompted Roman to publish in the daily of his party the photocopy of a certificate attesting to his having been baptized into the Romanian-Orthodox church, which is the church to which the bulk of Romania's population belongs.[19]

As already indicated, in the local elections held in February, the NSF played the tune of anti-Hungarianism. In several localities, among them in Cluj, it even run joint lists with the *PRNU* (and with the GRP) in the elections for the local councils, and supported *PRNU* candidates in the elections for mayor. In these elections, the *PRNU* considerably improved its performance compared to that of the general elections. In May 1990 the party (which then ran as the Romanian Unity Alliance) garnered 2.12 percent of the vote for the Deputies' Assembly.[20]

The *PRNU*'s anti-Hungarian postures are more than matched by those displayed by the GRP, whose weekly, *Romania mare*, proclaimed the year 1991 as the "International year of struggle against Hungarian terrorism." The GRP, however, is just as militantly anti-Semitic and occasionally also anti-Gypsy. In fact, both parties of "radical continuity" ideally link the Jews with the Hungarians into what emerges as the image of the stranger who is the enemy of the "organic" Romanian nation. For example, an article published in *Natiunea* in May 1991 carried an open letter addressed by a retired junior military officer, who demanded clarification concerning "the Hungarian-Jewish alliance," which was said to have become "extremely aggressive and even very dangerous for the Romanian state." In turn, *Romania mare* published a caricature in which the name of the HDUR (abbreviated in Romanian as *UDMR*), was spelled as "Jude-MR.[21] Both Hungarians and Jews, but particularly the latter, are often accused of having brought the catastrophe of communism on Romania, thereby reviving the myth of Judeo-Bolshevism, which was dominant among large strata of the Romanian population in the inter-war period. There is almost no issue of either *Romania mare* or *Europa* which does not bring up this subject. Particularly targeted are Chief Rabbi Moses Rosen, Silviu Brucan, the later-day dissident under Ceausescu and a former ideologue of the NSF, and, (particularly since his dismissal in September 1991), former premier Roman, whose father was a high communist official under Ceausescu, accusing him of furthering "Sovietization."[22] In order to exonerate the national community of any guilt, some former Communist officials are posthumously "Judaized." The most prominent of these is undoubtedly Elena Ceausescu, the former dictator's wife.[23] Using hardly veiled terminology reminiscent of the religious discourse typical of the extreme Right in the inter-war period, Corneliu Vadim Tudor wrote in February 1991 about the "Eskimos" who used to throw into prison hundreds of thousands of genuine Romanians, and who had brought communism to the country and "nailed it into our bones and flesh till they crucified us."[24] Yet, this does not hinder the GRP to hail the alleged achievements of the country under communist rule. Nor are what the GRP regards as its misfortunes to be attributed to communists alone but those guilty of these misfortunes allegedly share the same ethnic origins. Indeed, according to a letter published in the 1992 almanac of *Romania mare*, the real name of the former royal family was not Hohenzollern but Cohen-Zollern and a photography of the last Romanian monarch taken at the age of six months shows that the naked baby-king was clearly circumcised.[25]

Both *Romania mare* and *Europa* (which in 1992 began serializing the "protocols of the Elders of Zion"), reject any accusation of anti-Semitism. Instead, they accuse the "denigrators" of Romania's heroic past (for example Rosen, who spoke out against the rehabilitation of war-time leader Marshal Ion Antonescu or the leaders of the HDUR, who protest against discrimination) of "anti-Romanianism."[26] ("Romanianism" was, in fact, one of the key elements in the development of inter-war Right wing ideology, being rehabilitated under Ceausescu with the considerable contribution of Tudor, Barbu and their like.[27] Even before the emergence of the GRP as a political party, *Romania mare* announced in its first issue (which was launched on 8 June 1990) that it had established a foundation with a special commission entrusted with investigating "anti-Romanian activities." After the set up of the party, the GRP officially stated that in order to deal with those opposing what the party considered to be the aspirations of the Romanian nation, it proposes to set up a government-sponsored National Committee for the Investigation of Anti-Romanian Activities. The committee would "severely punish all acts of national treason, destabilization and sabotage committed by Romanian or foreign citizens."[28] More recently, *Europa* announced the foundation of a National Institute for Romanianism and Romanianology. The present "spring" for anti-Romanianism, according to this weekly, is no one else than Rabbi Rosen.[29]

Tudor's and Barbu's notoriety dates back to the days when Barbu had been editor-in-chief of the weekly *Saptamina Capitalei* and Tudor his right-hand man. After Ceausescu's overthrow, the survival of *Saptamina Capitalei* became impossible. Yet in early 1990 Tudor and Barbu applied for permission to publish a new weekly. The request was turned down by the former dissident Andrei Plesu, at the time Minister of Culture. Plesu's decision, however, was overruled by Prime Minister Petre Roman.[30] Roman's role in facilitating the comeback of the two journalists was eventually confirmed in an editorial published in *Romania mare* on 16 August 1991. The weekly became the forerunner of the future political formation bearing the same name and quickly gathered around itself all those who shared its obvious enmity towards Western democratic values. Skillfully exploiting the social and economic difficulties triggered by the early stages of the transition to a market economy, *Romania mare* promoted traditionalist authoritarian ideas and became the champion of "a Ceausescu nostalgia." This trend is based on the population's refusal to allow equal deprivation to be replaced by selective deprivation, its reluctance to see freedom of choice take the place of authoritarian paternalism, and its unhappiness at witnessing illusions of "nationalistic grandeur" being usurped by harsh internationalist realities. At the same time, *Romania mare* became one of the main supporters of the former collaborators of Ceausescu who had been sentenced or were being prosecuted, repeatedly demanding that they be pardoned and rehabilitated. When the sentences against the former members of the RCP's Political Executive Committee became final in April 1992, the GRP's Steering Committee protested and called Iliescu to grant a pardon to "all political prisoner." The committee also termed the suicide of one of the leaders sentenced, former Foreign Minister Ioan Totu, a "political assassination."[31] This, as well as the fact that *Romania mare* often publishes documents incriminating its adversaries which could only stem from the archives of the former secret police, seems to corroborate Brucan's statement that the weekly is not just the mouthpiece of the former *Securitate*, but "the *Securitate* itself."[32]

The GRP's ideology, as reflected in the party's main documents (above all its statutes and the party platform published in June 1991) and statements by its leadership focuses on a demand for a drive to bring about a more "balanced," and hence more positive evaluation of the former regime's "achievements." For Tudor and his friends the supreme entity is the nation, which they perceive as being under a historically uninterrupted siege, having to fight against both foreign and internal machinations aimed at bringing about its destruction. To be able to resist this conspiracy, they argue, it is necessary to forge the "unity of all patriotic forces at home and abroad."[33] According to the party's platform, Romania has to cope with internal "occult forces," which are "supported and manipulated from abroad" with the purpose of bringing about "Romania's dismemberment." The international community is, for the GRP, the Western world that urges quicker democratization and the transition to a market economy. As Tudor put it in his address to the GRP's countrywide conference held in October 1991,[34] this community is intent on turning Romania into an impoverished and economically subdued nation. The GRP's drive to re-evaluate the communist regime's "achievements" is best reflected in those passages of its platform dealing with the economy.[35] Although the draft statutes claim that the GRP is a party of the "center-Left," a close examination of its recommendations proves that it opposes the establishment of any genuine form of a market economy and it advocates strong state interference in the economic realm. According to these statutes the country has to be freed from the *diktats* of such international bodies serving foreign interests as the International Monetary Fund. Only those who are deaf to "the voice of blood," and are therefore incapable of hearing the suffering of the nation (*Romania mare* wrote in the wake of Roman's dismissal) are ready to accept such *diktats*.[36] So much for gratitude to the man who made possible the weekly's appearance.

The GRP's blueprint for quick economic recovery provides for the immediate militarization of the national economy. A military government had been advocated by Tudor since December 1990. In the wake of the social unrest that brought about Roman's dismissal, the call intensified. According to the declaration issued by the party on this occasion, "the only solution for overcoming the crisis and safeguarding the nation is to set up a Romanian transitional, predominantly military government"[37] *Romania mare* often ridicules the parliament as superfluous and wasting the nation's money on empty talk. Like the PRNU, it opposed the financing of the local elections from the state budget, claiming in what was an obviously populist appeal that the resources should instead be allocated to the needy.

The GRP's weekly is also a persistent source of denigrations directed against those few Romanian dissidents who can claim a record of defending human rights under Ceausescu. What all this adds up to is a recipe for replacing Ceausescu's "national communism" with a "national socialism" in which the military would play a central role. As Tudor put it in his address to the GRP countrywide conference (after proudly listing many of Ceausescu's "white elephant" projects), "socialism had brought more good than bad to Romania."[38]

Despite their display of extreme nationalist postures, both the *GRP* and the *PRNU* have been very moderate in sustaining the Romanian cause in what used to be the Moldavian SSR and the former USSR and the setting up of CIS. This posture is strangely identical with the positions adopted by the NSF leadership and once more points to close links between this party and the parties of radical continuity. Fear that reunification between Moldova and Romania (which is supported by all three as a process to be "gradually" achieved) could open a Pandora's box on the Transylvanian issue probably plays a significant role in the adoption of these policies. At the same time, this position raises some questions concerning the genuineness of nationalism and its manipulated nature. This applies in particular to the *GRP*, whose very name ("Greater Romania") suggests an attachment to the country's borders of the inter-war period.

The *GRP*'s rather unimpressive performance in the first elections in which it competed, the local elections of February 1992, (in which it garnered only 1.6 percent of the votes) shows that the parties of "radical continuity" may be too tainted by past collaborationism to play a significant role in Romania's politics in the foreseeable future. The collaborationism is more blatant in the case of the GRP than in that of the *PRNU*; this (alongside regional factors, which make the PRNU mainly an ethnic Romanian Transylvanian party), explains why the *PRNU*'s performance in the local elections was considerably better than that of the *GRP*. In a possible future coalition with the Iliescu wing of the *NSF*, however, both parties could turn into influential partners. It is not insignificant that, following the split in the *NSF*, two former parliamentarians belonging to this party switched to *GRP*, which thus gained further influence in parliament.

The Radical Right: Return to Origins

Viewed from the perspective of past collaborationism with the communist regime, the other variant of the radical Right, which has been termed above as "radical return," may be at an advantage, being, like Ceasar's wife, "above suspicion," or nearly so. The party representing this sub-category of the radical Right is the Movement for Romania (MFR), which was officially set up by Marian Munteanu in December 1991. According to Munteanu (who was for a short time a leader in the communist student youth movement), one can in no way associate genuine nationalism with communism. Ceausescu's nationalism was but a "fake" nationalism; in fact, according to him, one cannot possibly be a Romanian and a communist at the same time.[39] Munteanu's models and heroes, as will be shown, are personalities that had forged the ideology *and* the praxis of the inter-war radical Right. What Romania needs, he stated in December 1991, was a "genuine Right," which "left no room for ambiguity."[40]

That Marian Munteanu should head a party of the radical Right is somewhat of a historical irony, for in June 1990 he had been turned into a symbol of the democratic opposition. At that time he was the leader of the Students' League in Romania and very active in the "marathon protest" held in Bucharest's University square against the NSF and "neo-communism." He was badly beaten by the miners who descended on Bucharest from the Jiu valley, was hospitalized, and subsequently arrested by the authorities. His cause was taken up by both the parties of the traditional Right, by independent movements of the democratic center and even Amnesty International.[41] When the Civic Alliance (which preceded the PCA) was set up as an organization of the extra-parliamentary opposition "from below" (in November 1990), Munteanu was even briefly elected as its temporary president. He held that office for a few hours only, however. His colleagues in the organizations' leadership "persuaded" him to resign. As one of the founding members of the alliance, the civil rights activist Gabriel Andreescu reminisced, there were several reasons for this move. In meetings preceding the setting up of the alliance, Munteanu had demonstrated no inclination to dialogue and little patience to listen to any other arguments but his own.[42] Munteanu himself admitted, in an interview with the students' weekly *Opinia studenteasca*, that he could not stand his former colleagues' "endless discussions." I like "order and clarity," he added. In another interview, he admitted that he admired his political adversaries, the communists and their heirs, "the NSF," for their "discipline." The ideal party to which he would like to belong, he added, would be one "with the best organization, the most rigorous discipline, and the most moral people."[43]

Whether by coincidence or not, the latter interview was published in an obscure paper printed in the Transylvanian town of Sibiu, which openly displays a pro-Iron Guard posture. In reply to a question concerning his attitude towards the Iron Guard, Munteanu claimed (as he did in several other interviews on later occasions) that he knew little about it, since he belonged to a generation that had not been given the opportunity to study the true history of Romania's inter-war fascist movement. He also stated in *Baricada* in March 1992, that he believed its history had been falsified by the communists.[44] If the belief of the Legion (as the Iron Guard had also been called) had survived, he said, this must be taken for an indication that these beliefs had reflected the "essence" of the Romanian nation.

> As far as I can understand the Legion phenomenon, it cannot be strictly resumed in its political aspects. One either belongs to it or one does not,... by one's very birth [into the nation].[45]

As to his views on the leader of the Iron Guard, Corneliu Zelea Codreanu, all he knew, Munteanu said, was that "together with four other friends, in 1927 he set up a political organization" that soon gained the adherence of those representing "the most important values of Romanian culture and science." And since these had willingly joined the movement in what was a free country, "it must mean" that the Legion had been "inherently Romanian." He reluctantly admitted that some members of the movement "may" have committed "deeds that cannot be approved of," but hastened to add that due to history's falsification by the Communists, one was unable to pass objective judgment on what happened at the time. "All I know," he said, is that Codreanu himself "was assassinated" and that he had managed to set up and organize an "anti-Bolshevik movement" at a time when "Bolshevism was being embraced" in many other countries. In itself, this was sufficient reason to "make one meditate" on Codreanu's merits. Furthermore, his followers "were killed, had to serve prison terms, have suffered, and still suffering calls for respect."[47] Munteanu chose to call the *MFR* a "movement," rather than a "party," as indeed Codreanu's organization had been called. The *MFR*'s official publication is also called *The Movement* [Miscarea]. Nor should one be surprised to learn that the editors of *Gezeta de Vest*, an independent weekly published in Timişoara, some time before Munteanu announced the setting up of the *MRP*, had been publishing eulogistic articles on Codreanu and his "legionnaires," and had joined the *MFR* *en bloc.*[48] *Gazeta de Vest*, according to the revelations of one of its former editors, is financed from abroad by Horia Sima, who had inherited Codreanu's mantle as leader of the Romanian fascists.[48] Nor does the "regimental" element lack in the *MFR*; if Codreanu's people were known for their green shirts, Munteanu's disciples have white shirts with badges carrying a variation of the symbol of the cross.

This attests to the religious fundamentalism that is one of the main components of the *MFR*, and which may be viewed as another link with inter-war Romanian fascism, the only fascist movement that was profoundly religious in character. Munteanu, who bears some resemblance to the classic depictions of Christ (a "Christ-like figure," according to Andreescu[49]) defines the doctrines of his political movement as "national democracy." a National Democratic party had already existed in Romania, being led by the historian Nicolae Iorga, one of the spiritual figures to which Munteanu traces his intellectual descent, and who was assassinated by the Iron Guard in what some historians regard as an act of "patricide." According to Munteanu, Iorga had lacked political talent, but the ideational "elements of national regeneration was an important part of Romanian national pride in the inter-war period." These young people (his examples are names such as Nae Ionescu, Mircea Eliade and Petre Tutea, all of whom had served as intellectual mentors of the radical Right[50]) represented "the spiritual peaks" of their times and "we try to make use of their experience." In this experience the religious element had played a central role. One must, Munteanu stated, always take into consideration "the national specificity"; and "Christianity" or rather the "Tradition of the Orthodox Church" had been a "fundamental and determinant part" of Romanian specificity.[51] Precisely this argument had been championed by Nae Ionescu, who is considered by many to have been one of the main spiritual fathers of the legionnaires. This might also explain why Munteanu's vocabulary is permeated with religious Iron-Guardist terminology, such as "purification," but also "dynamization."[52]

The latter term is used in reference to the young generation, whose leader Munteanu perceives himself to be. Like the Iron Guard, but also like many other fascist movements in the interwar period, the MFR is said to be above all a movement of the young and for the young generation. But at the same time, it intends to "forge a New

Generation [which], through its active and conscious forces, is duty-bound to take upon itself the responsibility of political action."[53] In practice, this will work out through the setting up of what Munteanu called a "Polycentric structure," made up of "groups" of 3-15 members imbuing the movement's values.[54] The GRP, with which Munteanu emphasizes that his movement has "nothing in common,"[55] has a similarly organized youth movement, and both resemble in more ways than one the original Iron Guard.[56]

The *MFR*, however, is different from the *GRP* as it is one of the most militant movements calling for the immediate unification of Romania with Moldova, indeed even attempting to monopolize that issue politically.[57] Although claiming that the *MFR* "respects the Constitution," that is to say the republican form of government, Munteanu (unlike the *GRP*) is prepared to recognize the historical merits of constitutional monarchy and of King Michael I personally.[58]

"Romanianism" is also part of the national-democratic doctrine, according to Munteanu. Its purpose is to forge "a powerful Romanian state," which, according to the *MFR* leader, must be achieved through "a Romanian *offensive* in the European and the international spheres." The Romanians must demonstrate to both foreigners and to themselves that they are "among the most superior people in Europe." There is, according to the *MFR* leader, no equivalent for the Romanians, who are a people that had managed to "set up a powerful state and to [continue to] exist in spite of its being the target of attacks from all sides."[59]

Unlike the GRP, the *MFR*'s program calls for the defense of private property,[60] and, at least in theory, Munteanu's movement claims to support democracy. This, he said, makes his party different from "the Legionary Movement, which did not believe in democracy and considered it inefficient."[61] His party did not compete in the local elections of 1992, but intends to participate in the general elections scheduled for the second half of the year. The *MFR* understands that it is following the course set by their fascist forerunners; their meetings usually begin with prayers said under the portraits of Codreanu, and that the *Iron Guardist Booklet for the Legionnaires (Carticica pentru legionari)* is freely distributed among members.[62] In his speeches delivered from the balcony of the Faculty for Architecture at the time of the "marathon-protest" of April-June 1990, Munteanu eagerly preached non-violence. Before taking his support for democracy at face value, one might be well advised to remember that Codreanu also claimed to be a partisan of nonviolence. He murdered one of his political adversaries and his movement liquidated other political foes—and Jews. But that, as they say, is mere history.

NOTES

1. See Zeev Sternhell, *La droite revolutionnaire: Les origines françaises due fascisme 1885-1914* (Paris: Editions du Seuil, 1978).

2. Zeev Sternhell, *Ni droite, ni gauche: L'ideologie fasciste en France*, (Paris: Editions Complexe, 1987), p. 60.

3. Hans Rogger, "Afterthoughts," in Hans Rogger and Eugene Webber, eds., *The European Right: A Historical Profile* (Berkeley: University of California Press, 1966), p. 576.

4. See Vladimir Socor, "Are the Old Political Parties Stirring in Romania,?" *Radio Free Europe Research*, Background Report No. 69 (Romania), 22 July Statement, ibid, Situation Report No. 12 (Romania), 6 November 1986, "National Peasant Group Silenced After Human Rights Initiative," ibid, Situation Report No.1 (Romania), 6 February 1987, "Dissent in Romania: The Diversity of Voices," ibid, Background Report No. 94, 5 June 1987, and "Ion Bratianu Dies," ibid, Situation Report No. 10, 21 September 1987.

5. *Rompres* (in English), 25 May 1990.

6. See Dan Ionescu, "Riots Topple Petre Roman's Cabinet," *Report on Eastern Europe*, Vol. 2, No. 42, 1991, 18–22.

7. The most devastating of these rampages was that of mid-June 1990. For details see Michael Shafir, "Government Encourages Vigilante Violence in Bucharest," ibid,. Vol. 1, No. 27, 6 July 1990, 32–38. See also Mihai Sturdza, "The President and the Miners: The End of a Privileged Relationship?," ibid., No. 39, 28 September 1990, 33–37, and "The Miners' Crackdown on the Opposition," ibid, Vol. 2, No. 2, 11 January 1991, 25–33. For details on the earlier descents see Michael Shafir, "The Provisional Council of National Unity: Is History Repeating Itself?," ibid., Vol. 1, No. 9, 2 March 1991, 18–24, and *The Independent*, 16 June 1990.

8. See Michael Shafir, " 'War of the Roses' in Romania's National Salvation Front," *RFE/RL Research Report*, Vol.1, No. 4, 24 January 1992, 9–15; Dan Ionescu, "Infighting Shakes Romania's Ruling Party," ibid., No. 14, 3 April 1992 24–28 and "Romania's Ruling Party Splits After Congress," ibid, No. 16, 17 April 1992, 8–12.

9. Ibid., Vol. 1, No. 11, 13 March 1992, 24–31.

10. See, for example, the pro-Iliescu NSF daily *Dimineata*, 5 February 1992 and the pro-Roman NSF daily *Azi*, 15 February 1992. On this issue, there was no difference between the two NSF factions.

11. See the interview with Campeanu in the independent daily *Romania libera*, 18 March 1992, in the independent weekly *Expres*, No. 14, 7–13 March 1992, and in the independent daily *Curierul National*, 13 April 1992.. For details on the NLP's decision to leave the Democratic Convention (in fact, calling for a new alliance which would mainly exclude the PCA and in which the NLP would probably be the dominant force) see ibid. 26 March 1992; the independent daily *Tiineretul liber* 26 March 1992; the NPP-CD daily *Dreptatea*, 26 March 1992; and Radio Bucharest, 11 April 1992, 8:00 p.m.

12. See Michael Shafir, "Political culture, Intellectual Dissent and Intellectual Consent: The Case of Romania," *Orbis*, Vol. 27, No. 2, 1983, 393–420 and "The Men of the Archangel Revisited: Antisemitic Formations Among Communist Romania's Intellectuals," *Studies in Comparative Communism*, Vol. 16, 1984, 222–243; and Katherine Verdery, *National Ideology Under Socialism: Identity and Cultural Politics in Ceausescu's Romania* (Berkeley: University of California Press, 1991).

13. See Dennis Deletant, "The Role of Vatra Romaneasca in Transylvania," *Report on Eastern Europe*, Vol. 2, No. 5, 1 February 1991, 28–37.

14. "Capital," *RFE/RL Research Report*, Vol. 1, No. 13, 27 March 1992, 23–30.

15. *Baricada*, 25 December 1990.

16. See Vladimir Socor, "Forces of Old Resurface in Romania: The Ethnic Clashes in Tirgu Mures," *Report on Eastern Europe*, Vol. 1, No. 15, 13 April 1990, 36–42; and Deletant, "The Role of *Vatra Romaneasca* . . ."

17. *Baricada*, 8 January 1991.

18. *Romania mare*, No. 28, 14 December 1990.

19. *Azi*, 13 September 1990.

20. See Shafir, "Romanian Local Elections," *op. cit.*

21. See the dispatch of the independent Romanian news agency AR Press, 13 May 1991 and *Romania mare*, 17 May 1991.

22. For details see Michael Shafir, "Anti-Semitism Without Jews in Romania," *Report on Eastern Europe*, Vol. 2, No. 26, 1991, 20–32, which covers a wide range discussion of the different aspects of anti-Semitism that cannot be discussed here in detail.

23. See *Europa*, No. 27, May 1991 and *Romania mare*, No. 89, 20 March 1992.

24. *Romania mare*, No. 34, 1 February 1991.

25. Ibid.

26. For example, see *Romania mare*, No. 90, 27 March 1992 and *Europa*, Nos. 66 and 67, March 1992.

27. For details see Leon Volovici, *Nationalist Ideology and Anti-Semitism: The case of Romanian Intellectuals in the 1930s* (Oxford: Pergamon Press), 1991, pp. 75–94 and *passim.*

28. See the GRP's party platform in *Romania mare*, No. 54, 21 June 1991 and ibid., No. 1, 8 June 1990.

29. *Europa*, No. 67, March 1992 and ibid., Nos. 66 through 70, March-April 1992.

30. See Gabriel Andreescu's article "'Who Is Guilty?'" in the Group for Social Dialogue's weekly 22, No. 30, 2-9 August 1991 and the independent weekly *Cuvintul*, No. 35, August-September 1991.

31. Radio Bucharest, 21 April 1992, 8:00 p.m.

32. Interview in the Romanian-language Israeli weekly *Minimum*, No. 51, June 1991.

33. See *Europa*, No. 47, October 1991.

34. *Romania mare*, No. 68, 18 October 1991.

35. Ibid.

36. Ibid.

37. Ibid, No. 28, 14 December 1990 and No. 63, 13 September 1991, respectively.

38. Ibid., No. 68, 18 October 1991.

39. See the interviews with him in the students' weekly *Opinia studenteasca*, No. 1, February 1992 and in the independent daily *Tineretual liber*, 28 March 1992.

40. See the report on the press conference held by Munteanu upon the setting up of the MFR in *Baricada*, 24 December 1991.

41. See Shafir, "Government Encourages Vigilante Violence" and Carmen Pompey, Dan Stancu, "Student Leader Under Arrest," *Report on Eastern Europe*, Vol. 1, No. 29, 20 July 1990, 35–38.

42. See Gabriel Andreescu, "History, Destinies," 22, Nos. 10 and 11, 13–20 March 1992 and 20–26 March 1992.

43. *Opinia studenteasca*, No. 1, February 1992 and *Puncte cardinale*, No. 4, 1992, respectively.

44. *Baricada*, 17–23 March 1992.

45. *Puncte cardinale*, No. 4, 1992.

46. Ibid.

47. *Cuvintul*, No. 13, March-April 1992.

48. See the independent weekly *Express*, No. 12, 24–30 March 1992.

49. Andreescu, "History, Destinies," 22, No. 10, *op. cit.*

50. See his interviews in *Ooinia studenteasca, op. cit, Baricada*, 17–23 March 1992 and in *Cotidianul*, 3 March 1992.

51. Interview in *Baricada*, 17–23 March 1992.

52. The report on Munteanu's press conference in the independent daily *Romania libera*, 13 September 1992.

53. *Baricada*, 17–23 March 1992.

54. Interview in *Cotidianul*, 3 March 1992.

55. *Baricada*, 17-23 March 1992.

56. See Michael Shafir, "The Greater Romania Party," *Report on Eastern Europe*, Vol. 2, No. 46, 1991, 28.

57. See *Baricada*, 31 March-6 April 1992.

58. See the interviews with him in *Ooinia studenteasca, op. cit.*

59. *Baricada*, 17–23 March 1992. Emphasis in original.

60. The program was published in *Cotidianul*, 3 March 1992.

61. Interview in ibid.

62. Andreescu, "History, Destinies," 22, No. 11, 20–26 March 1992.

STRENGTHENING OF THE RIGHT AND SOCIAL CHANGES IN CROATIA AND YUGOSLAVIA

Ivan Siber

A Brief Journey into the Past

There are geographic regions where different peoples, civilizations and religions mingle and confront each other; regions that play a key role in the course of history, in which peoples inhibiting them are victims of a sort of their own geopolitical positions. The Balkans is certainly one such region. From the eighth to the fourteenth century there emerged—and vanished—many small medieval states leaving behind mythical memories of greatness although in reality all were too weak to resist the non-Slavic peoples who conquered their territory. The conquerors included Hungarians from the north, Austrians from the west, Venetians from the south and Tartars and Turks from the east. Seen in the light of the history of the rest of medieval Europe there would be nothing special or unusual in this fact were it not for two events which took place at the time and which were to have a far-reaching and long lasting effect on the political processes in this region.

At the beginning of the thirteenth century the Christian world divided into the Eastern and Western churches, into the Orthodox and the Catholic faith. This division led the eastern section of the Balkans eventually to turn to Russia while the western section opened up to German and Italian influence. This different orientation of the Balkan peoples contributed to the formation of different cultural patterns in the eastern and in the western Balkans which then led to an increasing drift and differentiation and created the basis for potential conflicts between the two.

The penetration of the Ottoman Turks in the fourteenth century and their conquest resulted in the spread of Islam, on the one hand,

and in the creation of a powerful state whose internal structure, social system and entire cultural superstructure significantly differed from those of the European medieval states.

The Bogomil movement in the central part of the Balkans (the present day Bosnia) facilitated the spread of Islam. The penetration of the Turks into the west and the related flight of Serbian Orthodox population to the border between Hungary the Habsburg Empire and the Ottoman Empire (the so-called Vojna Krajina-Military Border Area) created an area characterized by a great mixture of different peoples and religions. In view of their different ethnic origin, historical development, popular mythology and certainly faith, two similar yet different peoples were formed: the Croats and the Serbs. Under the influence of Islam and owing to a special status enjoyed in the Ottoman Empire the Moslem Slavs developed an awareness of their own specific character.

The Serbs until the mid-nineteenth century and the Croats until the First World War were in a position of dependence on the great powers of the time. They also had their own legal constitutional tradition and a striving to establish their own states.

A centuries-long affiliation to a given civilization and a religious community necessarily led to different cultures, social mentality, and tradition. These, in turn, provided different preconditions for the establishment of an autonomous community.

There were also some common elements tying peoples of the Balkans together. First of all, they have had aspirations for establishing their own independent national states freeing themselves from the domination of the two great empires supreme in the region. They were also aware of their affinity with a broader Slavic community, intensified by great similarity of their languages. The mixing of Croatian, Serbian, and Moslem populations in Bosnia and in the Military Border Area made members of these peoples support each other in the common struggle for the realization of their aims.

The end of the First World War found different peoples in the Balkans in very different situations. The break-up of the Austro-Hungarian Empire made it possible for the Slovenes to realize the essence of their national character. This was preserved and shaped mainly in their culture and language. Croatia was torn between an aspiration to form its own state on the basis of its own legal constitutional tradition and a very strong movement for the union of the South Slavs in the spirit of the Illyrian Movement of the mid-nineteenth century. Serbia was on the rise as a victor in the war. It had already, after the Balkan Wars, established its domination on the territory of the traditional Serbian state including the territory of Macedonia which was referred to as "South Serbia." The Macedonians were denied the status of a separate nation. Montenegro lost its centuries-long state blending into "Serbianism." Moslems, having lost their privileges within the Ottoman Empire, did not manage to establish themselves as a separate national entity or even a political factor.

Two other elements are essential for the understanding of all the complexity of international relations in the Balkans both at the time of the formation of Yugoslavia after the First World War as well as at the time of its dissolution. The tradition of the bourgeois state did not (and still does not) exist on the territory of ex-Yugoslavia. Serfdom was abolished in Croatia in 1848, and the first towns emerged in Serbia as late as the end of the nineteenth century. Second, Yugoslavia was formed without prior economic links which could create the appropriate interest and social structure necessary for the functioning of the common state. In other words, Yugoslavia did not evolve as a result of a continued process of mutual interlinking of different territories, peoples, concrete economic and social interests, but was primarily a result of a political agreement and, to a certain extent, also of value orientation and emotion without realistic basis in the social, economic and cultural sphere.

Very soon it became evident that different nations entered the union with different expectations, and, above all, with different possibilities to realize their expectations. The initial idea about "one people with three tribes" (Croats, Serbs, and Slovenes) soon turned into a unitary, centralist state, with a pronounced domination of Serbia which, in addition to the Monarchy and the Parliamentary majority, also had a firm hold over the two main forces of repression—the police and the army. Enforced integration produced the reverse effect—a growing demand for secession on the part of the non-Serbian peoples while the "Piedmontese" role of Serbia turned into domination and became a constant source of conflict.

Since the Versailles Treaty of 1919 Yugoslavia did not manage to create mechanisms of integration that would respect national differences and aspirations. The aggression of the Axis powers in the Second World War not only succeeded in breaking all Yugoslav resistance in a very short time, but it found a fertile soil for the creation of little Quisling states which accepted the fundamental ideological tenets of Nazism. The Slovene national identity was completely denied. Serbia was dismembered and only a small part of it was made into a puppet state which accepted all the Nazi laws. Croatia yielded a large portion of its territory to Italy gaining Bosnia and Herzegovina in return. The traditional striving for the liberation of the Croats and for the establishment of an independent Croatian state was manipulated and abused, resulting in the creation of a Quisling State which made a concerted effort to create an ethnically "pure" territory. The crimes of the Balkan version of the SS units—*Ustashas* and *Chetniks*—inflamed mutual hatred. Even today it is hard to find a single family on the territory of ex-Yugoslavia which was not a victim of this mutual genocide.

At the same time it is important to stress that nowhere in Europe was the anti-fascist movement so strong and active as was the case in Yugoslavia. It had three basic aspects: liberational, national and social. It was during the Second World War that the foundations were laid for the solution of the national question in Yugoslavia based on the recognition of the national character not only of Serbs, Croats and Slovenes but also of Montenegrins and Macedonians. It was also decided that the future state would be a federation.

Yugoslavia after the Second World War - A Failure of a Model

The end of the Second World War meant at the same time the beginning of a new Yugoslavia, based on completely different foundations than the previous one. The federal model was to be the solution for the multinational character of the state, the nationalization of large-scale private property and agrarian reform were to resolve all possible social conflicts while the leading (and the exclusive) role of the Communist party (later League of Communists) was to be a guarantee that the aims set would be realized.

The people of Yugoslavia were tired of war. Under a strong influence of the triumphant Soviet Union the people easily accepted the grand dream, hoping that the new system would provide for fast development and a society of equality and prosperity. The initial successes were indeed great. Economic development for years placed Yugoslavia among the leading countries of the world. The resistance to the Soviet Union in 1948 and the foundation of the Non-Aligned Movement greatly contributed to Yugoslavia's good reputation and strengthened its influence in international relations. The introduction of workers' self-management was a social experiment that attracted great attention and was met with approval not only in scholarly and scientific circles of the world but in public opinion as well. It can be stated that regardless of the fact that Yugoslav society was not operating on the basis of a democratic constitution, it had internal legitimacy and enjoyed international support. The traumas of the Second World War, particularly in the relations between the members of different nations in Yugoslavia, were gradually suppressed. This was a period when Yugoslavia was considered a country that demonstrated that the establishment of a multinational community was feasible. Still, later events have shown that within the very structure of society processes were at work which were far more complex and generated more conflict than it seemed at the first glance. The inability of the communist state to ensure long-term economic development, the passing away of the charismatic figure of Josip Broz Tito in 1980, the collapse of communism in other countries of Eastern Europe, inevitably called into question the very ideological foundations of society.

Three main problems are at the core of the Yugoslav crisis and the crisis of the ex-Yugoslav union. I will try to present them here in the order I think is logical. The first problem concerns the absence of a market economy that resulted in three grave mutually related consequences: lag in the development of production, insufficient incentives to motivate workers, and the continuing importance of the state in the redistribution of profit. This third consequence seems to be the most important one and most directly related to the present processes on the Yugoslav political crisis. Since Yugoslavia consisted of 6 republics (also Serbia included two autonomous provinces) of very different levels of development (the differences in the development level of Slovenia in the north and the province of Kosovo in the south is 7 to 1). The redistribution of wealth by the state through economic measures necessarily caused latent and later increasingly manifest conflicts. The underdeveloped republics accused the developed ones of exploiting them through the single customs-system that protected the market, while the developed nations claimed that the economic measures of the federal administration robbed them of their income. This was a situation in which all considered themselves to be losers and, since some republics have mixed national populations, this created a fertile soil for the sharpening of ethnic conflicts.

The second problem was a complete absence of political plural-ism, a multiparty system and free democratic elections. In the period immediately after the Second World War the domination of the Com-munist Party was perhaps understandable. Its reputation and merits during the war, direct pressure from the Soviet Union, the loss of prestige of the pre-war parties because of their collaboration with the enemy, the necessity of reintegrating the country, were sufficient rea-sons for its rule. All these reasons gradually disappeared. Instead of a multiparty system, a system of "integral self-management," a sort of nonparty direct democracy was introduced. The system, how-ever, allowed the continued domination of politics by the League of Communists. The absence of a multiparty system, the increasing con-flict between the republics on economic matters, gradually led to the division of the League of Communists into six plus two communist parties. These splinter parties increasingly represented the interest of their republics or autonomous provinces. Perhaps it can be said that during that period (1980–1990) Yugoslavia may have had a version of a multiparty system on the federal level. In the process of decision-making, *ad hoc* coalitions were formed on given issues, while on the republic level the domination of only one organized political force re-mained: the respective republic's League of Communists. Already at that time one could observe the strengthening and integration of the nationalists within each republic. Leagues of Communists increas-ingly presented themselves as the protectors of the interests of "their own nation" that was allegedly threatened by "the interests of other nations."

The third problem concerned ethnic relations. It was not so much the normative solutions at the level of the Federation (one could hardly find objections to the Constitution of 1974 in that respect) that I have in mind, as the open treatment of ethnic relations by the media and general attitudes towards the manifestations of na-tional feelings and identity. In practice, it is possible to note three dominant problems: large and strong political emigrations primarily due to the problem of the national question in Yugoslavia. Emi-grants came from part of the population which, during the Second World War, collaborated with the enemy and which was later on pe-riodically reinforced by individuals and groups who left the country because of dissatisfaction with ethnic relations in Yugoslavia. Partic-ularly numerous were emigrants from Croatia after 1971. This was the year when the League of Communists of Croatia called into question republic-level relations within the Federation. The League was supported by a strong national movement that was eventually stifled by coercive measures, including persecutions and a number of political trials. Second, there was an effort for the systematic suppression of the importance of ethnic-national affiliations. This was the result of the fear of the possible recurrence of open ethnic conflicts that caused so much suffering during the Second World War. Thus, nationalism increasingly became regarded as a forbidden idea. National frustrations were not being resolved. They were rather gradually suppressed. Thus, nationalism became the nucleus and a center of the increasing social and political dissatisfactions. Third, manipulation of the national and political conflicts in Yugoslavia, at the moment when the system was not able to resolve open social, economic and developmental problems by the leading political force—the League of Communists—led to the eventual collapse of the federation.

The Crisis of the System - The Crisis of the Union

The long lasting crisis of society suppressed by ideological rationalizations and foreign credits in the second half of the 1980s, came into the open in 1989. The political processes in Serbia and Slovenia were the first indications that radical changes were essential and that the existing social system was not able to cope with the crisis. In Serbia there appeared a so-called "Serbian national program," the notorious Memorandum of the Serbian Academy of Sciences, that pointed out the obvious decay and backwardness of Serbia within Yugoslavia. The memorandum accused the League of Communists and Serbian leaders of "betraying the interests of the Serbian people" and "revealed" the "conspiracy, first of all of Croats and Slovenes, against Serbia."[1] Soon, the Slovenes respond with their own Slovene national program[2] offering the same conclusion—Slovenia is exploited within Yugoslavia and ought to turn to its own devices, including secession from the state.

There were certain reasons for these manifestations to occur first in Serbia and then in Slovenia.

Serbia, in a certain way, contains within itself all the conflicts characteristics of the Yugoslav state as a whole. It had a sort of a federal system with two autonomous provinces with a high degree of autonomy, multinational composition (close to 2 million Albanians in Kosovo, a large number of Hungarians, Croats, Romanians and others in Vojvodina) developed (Vojvodina) and underdeveloped (Kosovo) regions and a large number of the Serbian population living outside its territory (primarily in Bosnia and Herzegovina and Croatia). One also has to mention the conflict between the Piedmontese myth about the role of Serbia and the real centrifugal processes at work in Yugoslavia.

The Slovene national program had a somewhat different origin and was primarily concerned with economics. Economic needs were then rationalized in the realm of national interests. Since it was the most developed of all the six Yugoslav republics, Slovenia felt all the limitations of the existing economic system on its development of its own economic potential. Thus, it raised the question of the economic relations within the federation.

Both of these national programs were initiated by the intellectual opposition. They both contained fierce criticism of the existing political system and were markedly anti-communist. Yet the leaders of the Leagues of Communists in both republics soon accepted these programs. They are currently being realized in both former republics regardless of the difference in the configuration of the leading political party in power and the Leagues. In Serbia, former communists are now in power, and in Slovenia the united former opposition rules the republic.

The decision to hold free, democratic, and multiparty elections at the beginning of 1990 (first in Slovenia and Croatia and then also in other republics) resulted in the emergence of parties that expressed national programs. This marked the beginning of an end for Yugoslavia. On the one side were the republics (first of all Serbia). The Serbs rationalized their national interests in the form of the Yugoslav idea. They want a single, centralized state ruled by Serbs. On the other side were the two republics of Slovenia and Croatia that insisted on their own independent national states. The conflict resulted in open warfare with, at present, still unforeseeable consequences.[3]

Are We Going Back to the Past in Order to Move into the Future?

The processes that have been occurring in the former Yugoslav state show that the idea of national independence led to the destruction of the communist political system. It united members of the same nation and led to confrontations with other nations. Keeping in mind the historical development of the Yugoslav peoples it is easy to note that with the partial exception of Serbs and Montenegrins, they did not go through the phase of the establishment of their own national states. This was the phase that most European nations passed through during the mid-nineteenth century. In a way the present time is the moment for national banners, anthems and songs, the paraphernalia of an early phase of nationalism. It is hard to say whether it is essential for the development of every state to go through this phase, but it is a fact that at the present time, the nations of former Yugoslavia are going through just such a phase. Regardless of all the hardships and traumas currently experienced by the republics of former Yugoslavia, this is the process which will possibly lead to a new form of cooperation. If nothing else, the war will clear the air and will get rid of the burden of "unfinished dreams." On the other hand, possible future cooperation will certainly be burdened by the current drama taking place in the process of the establishment of the new national states.

The creation of new national states, whether that is the aim of the warring nations or if the process is to serve as a basis of different social relations after the destruction of the old system, is not the only "historical debt" to be paid on this Balkan territory. Being on the crossroads of two worlds, East and West, these lands never saw the development of capitalism and bourgeois society. Instead, a utopian system was superimposed on an underdeveloped economic basis which did not enable the natural process of development of the production forces to take place. In other words, another "historical debt" must be paid by the establishment of capitalist relations, at the level let us say of developments characteristic of the end of the nineteenth century. It is only then, after the real market economy is established and after the waving of national banners ceases to be all-important that the preconditions will be created for a truly pluralist society with a clear stratification of interest groups.[4]

Strengthening of the Right and Social Changes

The paradigm of Left-Right wings in the politics of the contemporary developed world today is questionable. The post-industrial society has actually destroyed the ideological divisions so clearly established in the past. Yet, the countries of post-communist Eastern Europe offer sufficient reasons for an analysis of the reemergence of the so-called Right-wing orientation in politics. First of all it should be stressed that notions of the political Left and Right were in everyday usage in these countries, very clearly and even rigidly describing

good and evil forces. The Left was considered to represent everything that was good, desirable, progressive, in short, that was *US*,
while the Right was the enemy, the threat, it was *THEM*. This distinction was an important component of political socialization, mass
media activity and political struggle.[5]

The change of the political system has brought also the change
in the evaluation of this dichotomy with a clearly expressed tendency
of political parties to present themselves as the so-called ideological
center. The notion of the Left began to be associated with the past
and with failure, while the notion of the Right was quickly losing its
negative connotations. This change in the concept of the Left-Right
relations is evident from three studies one of which was conducted in
1986, the second immediately before the first multiparty elections in
Croatia (both based on representative samples of the population of
Croatia) and the third at the end of January 1992, using a sample of
the inhabitants of the city of Zagreb. It should be pointed out that
the results of 1992 are only a rough comparison.

Table 1

Changes in Ideological Self-Identification 1986 - 1990 - 1992

	1986*	1990*	1992**
Left	29	16	7
Left center	30	21	10
Center	32	36	53
Right center	5	18	15
Right	4	9	15
Average:	4.01	5.16	5.92

Source: *Siber I. "Nacionalna, vrijednosna i ideologijska uvjetovanost
stranackog izbora," u: Grdesic, Kasapovic, Siber, Zakosek: "Hrvatska
u izborima 1990." Naprijed, Zagreb 1991.

**According to the *Danas* weekly magazine, 11 Feb. 1992.

The evident rejection of identification with the Left was followed
by the expression of election preferences as well as by the evaluation
of different political parties located on a Left-Right scale as is shown
by a recent research conducted by *Danas* magazine (4 February 1992).

Table 2

Perception of the Position of Different Parties along the Left-Right Scale

Party	1 Citizens' Assessment	2 Party Stand	3 % of 1990 Voters	4 Assessed 1992 Voter Orientation
SDP	3.57	Left center	27.52	10
SPC	4.06	Left center	6.23	1
SDPC	4.99	Left center		2
CSLP	5.32	Center		7
CPP	5.68	Center		20
CDU	6.30	Center	40.41	31
CCDP	6.35	Right center		1
CDP	6.65	Right	3.80	2
CPR	7.46	Right		6

Notes:
1. Citizens' assessment according to the *Danas* weekly magazine.
2. Party's views according to the statements of the party leaders.
3. Results of 1990 Elections.
4. The assessment is based on a number of public opinion studies published in the press in recent months. The difference to 100 percent is accounted for by the uncommitted voters. In the 1990 election a fair number of parties came out together in the so called "Coalition of Popular Agreement" and won less than 15 percent of the votes. A similar destiny was shared by a number of independent non-party candidates.

These results point to several interesting trends. The change of the political system has led to the "demonization" of the Left. The party which claims formal continuity with the Left tradition (SDP) identifies itself as the party of Left-center. On the Right such a problem does not exist and two parties are striving to take the place of the Right (in that context even the term "hot" right is used!). The dominant party in the 1990 elections - CDU (Croatian Democratic Union) is trying to present itself as a party of the center, but the voters still identify it with the Right. Generally, the center position is rather crowded and the coming elections will probably introduce greater clarity.

Studies of public opinion show that the electorate has, since the time of the last elections (1990), made a sharp turn to the "right." Causes for this are many, but I will mention here only three of them.

1. The great ambitions of the Left in the first elections collided against the different preferences of the voters. This resulted in great disappointment and apathy on the part of the electorate which favored Leftist options.

2. After the establishment of the new administration the public is systematically being fed information, presented through firmly controlled media, that blames the communist system, and the Left in general, for all the current troubles. This effectively destroyed and restructured the value-orientation followed by the earlier system.

3. The position of the Left claiming that the crisis of the Yugoslav union can be resolved through a democratic reconstitution of the federation, collided against the processes of dissolution and war.

The Essence of Right-wing Orientation

The discussion presented so far has been concerned with the general orientation of the electorate and its perceptions. What is also important, however, is the real empirical content of the revived Right-wing ideas. The concept of the Right, as used here, does not imply only aggressive, intolerant and totalitarian tendencies, but, instead, it connotes conservative and traditionalist views. Here, a general observation is in order. The failure of a model which was based on the ideas of social justice, equality, universal freedom and emancipation of man, inevitably leads to the other extreme. In the total absence of democratic traditions and a well-developed civil society, points of orientation and new meanings of life in the changed social relations are sought in traditional values. These provide a feeling of stability rooted in national affiliation and religion.

In this analysis I will not comment on each of the dichotomies, present in former Yugoslavia, but only on those which are dominant on the social and political stage.

Table 3

Some Fundamental Features of the Conservative and Liberal Mind[6]

Conservative Mind	Liberal Mind
Nationalism	Cosmopolitanism
Tradition and authority	Modernism and freedom
Past	Future
Custom	Law
Religion and obedience	Critical mind & independence
Religion and politics	Economics and science
Rural society	Industrial society
Romanticism	Realism
Limited civil rights	Unlimited civil rights
Community (*Gemeinschaft*)	Society (*Gesellschaft*)
Large family	Small family
Sexual restrictions	Sexual freedom

One of the essential elements in the ideology of the radical Right is a dominant ethnocentric attitude i.e. intolerance of all who are not *US*, based on racial, religious or national criteria. The importance of the multinational element for the Yugoslav crisis, and especially for the war in Croatia, has been already pointed out. The insistence on the creation of national states, preferably occupying the totality of the given historical and ethnic territory, is one of the most important features of the Right in all parts of former Yugoslavia. This demand is a part of the political program of the parties of the Right, and an important element of the crisis in Croatia, as well as an essential cause of the conflict in Bosnia and Herzegovina. National intolerance triggered by the crisis and inflamed by the war led to hatred and refusal of coexistence on the same territory. Mutual accusations of genocide further strengthened the influence of the extreme Right. The rights of the individual as a citizen and his value as a human being are thus suppressed. The right of the individual and his value as a member of the given nation becomes the central value.

One of the classic divisions between Left and Right-wing political parties is certainly the attitude towards private ownership and the role of the state in the economic sphere. In developed societies private ownership is not a central issue any longer. For the most part, private

ownership is realized through holding companies and the large owners are most often different funds (retirement fund, health fund and
the like), and professional management has the final say over policy
matters. Similarly, an important role is played by public enterprises
(especially in Europe) so that the ideology of liberal capitalism, typical of the end of the nineteenth century, has long become outdated.
At the same time, particularly, in western European countries, the
welfare state is increasingly at work. Through appropriate legislation
it ensures social security, retirement benefits, and health protection
for the vast majority of the population. Independently of politics and
ideology, there is a growing trend towards workers' participation and
involvement in decision-making. This is the result of the recognition
that such a process is important for the efficient operation of the
economy.

In Croatia (and not only there) the situation and trends are
moving in quite the opposite direction. The so-called transformation of social ownership is taking two directions. What is currently
happening is the increasing involvement of the state in the transfer
of ownership and the strengthening of the national economy. This
is an attempt for the national state to become the owner of its own
economy. On the other hand, more as a program-orientation, reprivatization is being planned. This will consist of a sale of shares without
consideration for the contribution of those who have invested their
labor in the respective enterprises. Yet, a growing number of people
are threatened by the lack of a safety-net. New laws on labor relations are being passed and these do not protect the workers. Instead,
they reduce the rights of the unemployed, the rights to health protection, retirement benefits. The individual is increasingly left to his
own (non) resources in dealing with issues of health, schooling and
old age. The values of earlier workers' movements that the countries
of Eastern Europe regarded as being in the center of their ideology
are rejected. The main argument of those who are attempting to
reevaluate the forces defeated in the Second World War is that these
forces were national movements. Their collaboration with the fascist
countries was allegedly a result of historical circumstances.

The creation of new states on the territory of the former Yugoslavia is an attempt, at the same time, to transform them from
an unsuccessful, utopian model into a civil society. This process is
taking place under difficult economic conditions, in a traditional (it
could be said parochial) political culture, during a time of aggravated

ethnic relations. These relations have been contaminated by traumatic historical experiences. All this has led to the strengthening of the political Right, including the reappearance of radical Right movements based primarily on the alleged historical interest of nations and hostility and concrete action against the members of other nations.

NOTES

1. Details on this see in: M. Kasapovic "Srpski nacionali zam i desni radikalizam," *Nase teme*, 1989, 1–2.

2. Contained in the special thematic issue of the journal *Nova revija*, No. 57, Ljubljana.

3. I do not enter here into the problem of who is to "blame" for the war since that is not the purpose of this paper. Still, the fact remains that the war is waged on the territory of Croatia and that it is the citizens of Croatia who are getting killed and that the war involves military intervention by the ex-Yugoslav army, and informally by Serbia.

4. In this context it is interesting to note how the problem of market is differently approached in bourgeois societies of the West and in the countries of the post-communist Eastern Europe. Said in a very simplified form, Eastern (Europe) approaches the market from the point of view of a precapitalist society, while the West, naturally, approaches the market from the point of view of a post-industrial society. It is in this that the reason for much of the misunderstanding in mutual communication between the East and West lies.

5. Here it is interesting to note that quite frequent were also political conflicts within the Left which by insisting on consistent ideological orientation criticized and thus also threatened those in power. From this comes a well known slogan about "the extreme left as the most dangerous right."

6. According to: Ivos, E.: "Americki neokonzervativizam," *Biblioteka Nase teme*, (Zagreb, 1989).

THE POLITICAL SPECTRUM IN POST-COMMUNIST BULGARIA

Luan Troxel

That a political "right" has emerged in Eastern Europe through the upheavals and elections of 1989–1991 is a fact. After all, when a system moves from a Communist Party-dominated one to a system with freedom of political association, nothing less should be expected. The political "right" in Eastern Europe has certainly been revived, then, in the sense that there is now space in the political arena for parties and politics of the "right." At the same time, however, we should not assume that the same "right-wing" politics which existed prior to Communist Party domination have necessarily returned. Such an assumption does seem to underlie a good deal of the concern about the revival of the "right" in Eastern Europe. Many observers have recently lamented the resurgence of the extreme "right" which, they argue, is found primarily in the guise of ethnic nationalism, exclusivism and general inter-ethnic hatred. Examples range from anti-Semitism most everywhere, divisions between Czechs and Slovaks in Czechoslovakia, the use of nationalist rhetoric by the Bulgarian Socialist Party, to the civil war wracking Yugoslavia.

Some elements of the prewar right have, indeed, re-emerged. Ethnic conflict is clearly on the rise and some prewar right-wing organizations have revived themselves. Nonetheless, these are examples of only one type of right-wing activity found in Eastern Europe today. This type does not exhaust the realm of the "right." Indeed, if we are to discuss the "right" in East European politics, we must work from a theoretically developed perspective of the "right." In this paper, then, I will discuss the meaning of "left" and "right" in politics, generally, and the possible uses of the term "right" for Bulgaria specifically.

This discussion will demonstrate that although there are many parties and organizations which can theoretically be categorized as "right" in Bulgaria, most have little support among the population. Second, even if a small "right" does exist in Bulgaria, it represents more of a "new right" than a revived one.

Which Right Is Right?

Political values in the West have traditionally been viewed as lying on a spectrum running from Left to Right. The Left was dominated by parties with values oriented toward social change in an egalitarian direction. The Right was dominated by more conservative parties which generally supported the status quo and, hence, maintenance of economic disparities. In short, politics was defined primarily by reference to economics.

Throughout the 1960s and 1970s, political cleavages changed drastically in the West. While support for social change and parties of the Left had traditionally come from the working class[1] more recent studies have concluded that support for social change throughout the course of the 1960s and 1970s began to come from a "post-materialist" base.[2] More specifically, those who had grown up under conditions of relative prosperity and physical security were more likely to support social change than they were previously and were more likely to support social change than was the working class.[3] Such a shift represents a fundamental change in traditional political cleavages in the West.

As the Left has come less and less to be identified with the working class, it has come to be more identified with new issues such as environmentalism, women's rights, and nuclear disarmament. To complicate the issue, many of those who had traditionally supported the Right became vocal advocates of the new leftist issues.

The changes which have taken place in Western politics over the last several decades demonstrate the difficulty of conceptualizing Left and Right and a left-right spectrum for contemporary politics. This difficulty is compounded when the conceptualization must be applied to Eastern Europe.

While the Left has traditionally been change-oriented and the Right has been associated with the status quo in the West, just the opposite identification was made in the former socialist bloc. Stalin, for instance, was on the Left and Bukharin on the Right. But Stalin represented the status quo at the time, and Bukharin opted for change. One might argue that the identification and confusion, in fact, make perfect sense because the Soviet Union had instituted a supposedly egalitarian economic system. One favoring egalitarianism (a leftist in the Western sense) would then be a leftist favoring the status quo. One favoring a market orientation would be on the Right and in favor of change.

The rise of "new" political issues has confounded the left-right spectrum in the West, suggesting that politics is rather more complicated than such a spectrum would allow. Specifically, these issues demonstrate that politics is multi-dimensional. This may be even more obvious in the East European case where many parties have recently arisen which do not have full ideological agendas, but which represent single issues—the environmental parties are perhaps the most prominent. It is not always clear how such parties can be placed on a left-right spectrum. To complicate the issue of identification, many of these single-issue parties are partners in umbrella coalitions which may include radical free-marketeers and social democrats.

Thus far, this discussion demonstrates that the political arena is complicated and that attaching labels to it, as social scientists are wont to do, may not always clarify the confusion. If this is true for the West where political developments in the last few years have been rather more static than in Eastern Europe, it is even more true for Eastern Europe where it is not clear whether the free-marketeers or the status quo-oriented are on the Right. New parties have also emerged in Eastern Europe which may be termed Left, but which may also be coalesced into movements, parties and associations along with the old politics of both the Left and the Right. Finally, the political situation has been very fluid over the last several years with nearly the entire political arena shifting to the Right (anti-Communist) immediately after the upheavals of 1989–1990.

Despite the confusion, it is possible to glean from the discussion at least three ways of categorizing the Right in East European politics. The Right may mean conservatism as in the desire to maintain the status quo. It may also be identified with a Thatcherist or Reagan-type free-market individualism. Finally, Right may mean reaction of a nationalist or neo-fascist variety. The last of these three Rights is most prominent in discussions of the revival of the Right in Eastern Europe. The other two, however, deserve discussion as well. Prior to this discussion, though, two caveats are in order. First, these three Rights are not necessarily mutually exclusive. Second, they do not necessarily encompass all types of "right-wing" activities.

Parties and Organizations on the Right in Bulgaria

Since Todor Zhivkov was removed as the head of the Bulgarian Communist Party in November 1989, the strongest proponents of the status quo have been the former communists, now calling themselves socialists. While it might seem odd to claim that the Bulgarian socialists are on the Right rather than on the Left, insofar as they have been conservative with respect to the status quo, they can be categorized as being on the political Right (while remaining on the economic Left). In fact, the Bulgarian Communist party (later the Bulgarian Socialist party–BSP) quite successfully utilized its "rightist" position to maintain support after the upheaval of late 1989.

In the election campaign of 1990, the BSP came out as the main supporter of the status quo in Bulgaria. Although it pledged its support to democratization, it maintained that radical economic changes would result in untold suffering for the Bulgarian populace. By focusing its campaign on the problems which would arise from a rapid transition—namely, unemployment and inflation—and on its own desire to minimize the effects of these problems, the BSP managed to win a majority of the seats in the first freely-elected parliament.

Support for the status quo did not end with the first post-Communist elections in Bulgaria. In fact, in the elections of October 1991, approximately 33 percent of the vote went to the BSP.

The most consistent and firm advocates of the market in Bulgaria have been the constituent members of the main opposition group, the Union of Democratic Forces (SDS). From its inception, the SDS has emphasized the mistakes of the past and focused on a rapid transformation to a capitalist, free-market economy as the only remedy for these mistakes. While just such a position proved successful for opposition groups elsewhere in Eastern Europe in the first free elections, it was something less than successful for the SDS which gained only 144 out of the total 400 seats in parliament in Bulgaria's first post-Communist elections.

Although electoral support for the party of the status quo remained substantial in 1991, free-marketeers managed to increase their power and support after the 1990 elections. The SDS picked up electoral support in the 1991 elections despite the departure of a number of its previous allies. It now dominates the parliament and controls the government. Most other parties which have since been formed, joined the SDS in calling for a radical transformation of the economy.

Even the BSP accepts the necessity of marketization, in principle. It simply refuses to accept the social consequences of marketization and, therefore, wants a controlled market system.

The final group on the Right is comprised of nationalists. The national problem in Bulgaria grew rather complex in 1992. However, prior to this time, it primarily centered around the sizable Turkish minority (approximately 10 percent of the population). While the Turks and the Bulgarians apparently lived together peacefully for much of the post Second World War period, tensions between them flared up in the winter of 1984–1985 when the Party initiated a campaign of "Bulgarizing" the Turks. Ethnic tensions appeared to die down somewhat between 1987 and 1988, but they reappeared with the mass exodus and forced expulsion of many Turks in 1989.

The removal of Zhivkov ushered in a period of reform for Bulgaria. Such reform extended to the "national question" as well. In January 1990, the Party announced plans to restore some of the Turkish minority's rights. Many Bulgarians did not respond kindly to this news. Having repeatedly been taught that the Turkish minority constituted not only a cultural, but ultimately, a political threat to Bulgaria's autonomy, ethnic Bulgarians came out in great numbers to protest the planned reforms.

From January of 1990 through the elections of 1991, the nationalist issue arose many times. Nevertheless, although there is a general popular sentiment against giving too much freedom to national and religious minorities, purely nationalist organizations garner little support from the population. Yet there are a number of purely nationalist parties and organizations on the Bulgarian political scene which have attempted to capitalize on the fears of ethnic Bulgarians (particularly those in ethnically mixed areas). Perhaps the most well-known of these are the National Committee for the Defense of the National Interest and the Fatherland Party of Labor. These are joined, however, by several smaller and, perhaps, less influential nationalist organizations: the Bulgarian National Radical Party, Bulgarian National Democratic Party, and the Union of Thracian Societies.

While some of these organizations certainly appear to have strong organizational structures, none of them command a great deal of support from the general population. Only the Fatherland Party of Labor had a representative independently elected to parliament in 1990. And, in the election of 1991, the combined total votes for the Bulgarian National Democratic Party and the Bulgarian National Radical

Party did not exceed 1.5 percent of the total votes cast.[4]

The lack of support for the purely nationalist parties appears to be out of proportion to the importance of the ethnic problem in Bulgaria. This is so because the BSP largely coopted the nationalist vote. This was true in the 1990 election as the BSP invoked the slogans "National Accord," and "Bulgaria above everything, above everyone," giving itself the image of a national party. It was even more true, however, in the 1991 election when the BSP ran a full-fledged national assault on the ethnic Turks and their party, the Movement for Rights and Freedoms (DPS). This assault included insisting on nationalist language in the constitution, protesting the registration of the DPS for the elections, and demanding a ban on the optional teaching of Turkish in some schools. When the BSP joined in a pre-election coalition with several of the nationalist parties (including the Fatherland Party of Labor), its nationalist position became perfectly clear.

That the BSP won about 33 percent of the vote in the 1991 election, however, cannot necessarily be attributed entirely to its nationalist stance. Certainly some Bulgarians voted for the BSP on the national issue, but others undoubtedly voted for the Party on the basis of its economic platform, and still others, perhaps, out of habit. So, the extent to which this 33 percent of the vote can be termed "right-wing nationalist" is questionable.

On a somewhat lower organizational scale, right-wing nationalism has also focused on the Gypsy minority. This group has received less attention than the Turks, perhaps partly because of its lower level of organization and partly because it has remained segregated from the mainstream of society. Nonetheless, attacks on this group have apparently increased since 1989.

Disputes between Bulgarians and Gypsies have taken on a particularly virulent character of late. In one case, sixteen houses were burned in a Gypsy quarter after an argument between Bulgarians and Gypsies.[5] In another case, several Bulgarians staged a hunger strike in protest to the "psychological and physical torture" that they claim to suffer at the hands of Gypsies in the community.[6]

The attacks on the Gypsies quite rightly fall into the category of right-wing nationalism. However, the differences between these attacks and those on the Turks are important. The attacks on Gypsies are not made primarily by nationalist parties and organizations. Rather, they are perpetrated primarily by individuals or unorganized groups. For this reason, the conflicts between the Gypsies and the Bulgarians are not as visible as those between the Bulgarians and the Turks. At the same time, however, because they originate at an individual level, they may be the most accurate indicators of widely-held, right-wing nationalist sentiments.

The categories discussed above offer a means of sorting out the "types" of Right existing in Bulgaria. They do not, however, speak to the resurgence of the Right in Bulgarian politics. The resurgence or revival of the Right suggests links between prewar and postwar politics in Bulgaria. Yet the parties and organizations categorized above have little connection to the prewar history of Bulgaria. The ethnic Turks, for instance, have not been singled out in interwar Bulgarian politics. While nationalism in Bulgaria today seems to look inward, nationalism prior to World War II was a different creature–focusing outward and on Bulgarian expansionism. This nationalism appears to have little support in Bulgaria, but it has indeed been revived in several stages.

In early 1990, at least two organizations emerged which seemed to be linked with the interwar Inter-Macedonian Revolutionary Organization (IMRO). These were a new IMRO and a group called *Ilinden*. These organizations seemed to have as their aim the reunification of Macedonia under purely Macedonian rule. As they were denied no official and apparently little popular legitimacy, these organizations faded rather quickly. Nonetheless, the Macedonian issue was not put to rest.

As Macedonia has become more prominent in the international arena with the intensification of the conflict in Yugoslavia, it has also become more prominent in the Bulgarian political arena. Bulgaria was the first state to recognize the legitimacy of Yugoslav Macedonia's independence. The Bulgarian National Radicals, for instance, aim directly not only to "chase out the Turkish population from Bulgarian soil," but also to "unite Bulgaria with Macedonia and Thrace."[7] These two factions are not necessarily linked, of course. The Bulgarian government recognized the independence of Yugoslav Macedonia, but it also overtly rejected the possibility of territorial annexation.

Nonetheless, the Macedonian question is not so simply dismissed by most Bulgarians. A Gallup poll, conducted in October of 1991, showed that 65 percent of the Bulgarian respondents considered Macedonians to be Bulgarian by nationality. While another 49 percent supported recognition of a sovereign Macedonia, only 31 percent felt that such recognition should lead to unification with Bulgaria.[8] Once again, though, it would be questionable to assert that this 31 percent wholly consists of "right-wing" nationalists. Indeed, many Bulgarians might like to see Macedonia united with Bulgaria, but just how many would condone the use of force in such an endeavor is unknown. Certainly those who would use force to unify Macedonia with Bulgaria would fall into the category of the extreme Right. But their number is likely to be as small as the election returns for the Bulgarian National Radicals (only 1.13 percent).[9]

Perhaps the most appropriate manifestation of a revival of the Right, everywhere in Eastern Europe, is in the form of monarchist parties and organizations. In Bulgaria, specifically, the issue of the monarchy has taken on rather important dimensions. By the fall of 1990, several monarchist organizations existed which called for the return of the monarch from Madrid and the reinstatement of a constitutional monarchy. These organizations reasoned that the monarchy had been illegally deposed and was, therefore, still legally in existence. They argued that as former Tsar Simeon is now an influential Western businessman, he would certainly use his skills and connections to pull Bulgaria out of its deepening economic crisis. Moreover, they viewed the Tsar as the single force which could unite the ethnic factions within Bulgaria and turn Bulgarian nationalism into the positive, outward-looking (if not expansionist) force that it had been. Under the rule of the Tsar, they reasoned, Bulgaria would become a place that Bulgarians everywhere would be able to call home.

Simeon, however, rejected calls for his return and frowned upon the monarchist organizations becoming formal parties. Later, however, he became somewhat more evasive about his position, saying that the time was not then right for his return, thereby suggesting that a right time might eventually come.

The monarchists believed that the time had come in the summer of 1991 when a date was set for a referendum on reinstating the monarchy. They felt assured that a majority of Bulgarians would vote in their favor and were sorely disappointed when the referendum was canceled. To countermand their loss, monarchists participated in the 1991 election under the auspices of the National Confederation of Tsarism. The confederation won a scant 1.84 percent of the votes cast. Apparently the monarchy is yet another vestige of the Right in Bulgaria which has yet to be revived with significant force.

The three parties (or coalitions) which are represented in parliament are the SDS, the BSP coalition, and the DPS. Given the descriptions employed above, only the DPS would fall outside the realm of the Right. Does this imply that only the ethnic Turks are not on the Right? Our answer depends on how Right is defined. However, this suggests once again that there are many ways of defining the Right and perhaps a more fruitful endeavor would not be to attempt to discuss Right and Left, but rather to discuss issues. This is true because Right and Left are terribly culture-bound. What is Right in the West may be Center in the former East bloc. And even what is Right in Bulgaria may be something less than Right in Poland, for instance. In this case, self-identification must be taken into account.

During the campaign of 1991, most Bulgarian newspapers, news commentators, politicians, and citizens agreed that the BSP was on the political Left, the SDS represented the political Right, and that a host of other smaller parties fell into the Center of the political spectrum. The major parties which dominated the Center were the United Democratic Forces, including the Liberal (SDS-L), the United Democratic Forces–Center (SDS-Ts), the Bulgarian Agrarian Union—United, and the Bulgarian Agrarian Union—Nikola Petkov. The SDS-L was made up of remnants of the Clubs for Democracy and the Greens. The SDS-Ts consisted of part of the Bulgarian Social Democratic Party and the Club Ecoglasnost.

Few of the parties identified as the Center in Bulgaria would be identified centrist parties in the West. At best, they might be Center-Left. All of the Center parties in Bulgaria called for social and economic fairness in their election programs. The BSDP (within SDS-Ts) went so far as to call for "fair" privatization wherein all citizens would receive stocks for ownership of enterprises, socialized health care, the right to housing and the eradication of unemployment. The parties all emphasized socialized medicine or a national health fund, social security for the unemployed or for the otherwise "socially weak."

Despite the seemingly leftist nature of these parties, no one in Bulgaria challenged their right to call themselves the Center. This might be the case because Bulgarians, themselves, are not, on average, what we might consider "centrist." In fact, when asked in October 1990 to identify their political attitudes as being on the "Left" or on the "Right," on a scale ranging from 1 to 10/Left to Right, 25 percent of the Bulgarian respondents labelled themselves as on the Left.[11] This is an exceedingly high number considering that it was precisely in the fall of 1990 that most new political formations and, seemingly, most citizens considered themselves anti-communist and, therefore, on the Right. After all, it was in the fall of 1990 that a nation-wide general strike was called to protest the BSP government of Prime Minister Andrei Lukanov, that mass protests pressured the parliament to call a vote of no-confidence (in which Lukanov dominated with 201 votes out of a possible 400), and that Lukanov did eventually resign in the face of tremendous public pressure. But the number of Bulgarians who describe themselves as leftist is also exceedingly high in comparison to the numbers of other East Europeans who considered themselves leftist at that time. Comparative figures ranged from 18 percent for Czechs and Slovaks to 8 percent for Poles.

This discussion, then, tells us two things. First, what is Right might not always be Right in all situations and in all places. Second, the Left is so broadly embraced in Bulgaria that it leaves little room for the Right. The latter contention, of course, would seem to contradict the earlier discussion which pointed out that there are many theoretically Rightist parties in Bulgaria and that, theoretically, almost all of the parties can fit into one or another category of the Right. I should reemphasize, here, that if we excluded the proponents of the status quo and the free-marketeers from the Right (since they both might equally be categorized as something more meaningful—namely old regime versus anti-communists), we are left with a very weak Right. Much as is made of the nationalist issue in Bulgaria, most Bulgarians do not appear to support a sort of neo-fascist nationalism. Rather, they now appear to be much more concerned with the pragmatic issues of economic well-being.

The future of the Right—regardless of how it is defined—is likely to be fleeting. The first category on the Right—proponents of the status quo—is likely to lose support over time. The BSP gained a majority of the seats in the first parliament by playing on the fear of the free market. Those fears have now become reality, however, and Bulgarians are finding that, however difficult it might be, they can cope. The BSP, then, will be unlikely to gain support on this issue in the future. It can, however, continue to play upon the fears of a "Turkish Yoke." This strategy is also likely to fail as Bulgarians continue year after year to see DPS deputies playing the parliamentary game. Under such circumstances, it seems unlikely that the BSP will be able to maintain such support indefinitely. Indeed, in the 1991 elections, it lost 14 percentage points of its 1990 vote.

The second category of Right—the free-marketeers—are also likely to lose some support. The SDS began to split apart in 1991 and the splintering of the movement is likely to continue as politics becomes somewhat more based on party programs. However, support for the unfettered market will continue to decline as well, if a strong program of social guarantees is not implemented. After all, in the 1991 elections, 33 percent of the electorate voted for the BSP and another 25 percent cast votes in favor of the Centrist parties, all of whom supported such guarantees. With a majority of the electorate in favor of a strong social welfare net, a welfare state certainly seems more likely than a system approaching the ideal, perfectly competitive, market economy.

The category of nationalists will also likely decline. As extreme nationalist groups have so far gained little support, there is no reason to assume that this situation will change. It could, of course, be influenced by the turmoil in Yugoslavia and the new rift in Greek-Yugoslav Macedonian relations. In that case the entire Balkan peninsula could become engulfed in yet another set of Balkan wars. Such a scenario seems unlikely at the present time. The Bulgarian government and Bulgarian people have more urgent concerns. These include the attainment of foreign aid and the stabilization of the economy. Neither of these would be forthcoming if Bulgaria thrusted itself into an international conflict. The Bulgarian government and President Zhelev are aware of this. It is at least partly for this reason that they have renounced any desires for territorial annexation. Once again, the concern with pragmatic issues may keep Bulgaria out of unwanted trouble.

NOTES

1. Alford, R. *Party and Society: The Anglo-American Democracies* (Chicago: Rand-McNally, 1963).

2. Inglehart, Ronald. *The Silent Revolution: Changing Values and Political Styles among Western Republics.* (Princeton: Princeton University Press, 1977).

3. Dalton, Russell, Scott C. Flanagan, and Paul Allen Beck. *Electoral Change in Advanced Industrial Democracies* (Princeton: Princeton University Press, 1984).

4. *Demokratsia*, October 22, 1991, p. 1.

5. Radio Free Europe/Radio Liberty Correspondent Report (Washington), July 16, 1991.

6. *Duma,* July 5, 1990.

7. *Demokratsia,* October 19, 1991, 1.

8. *Report on Eastern Europe,* October 4, 1991, p. 38.

9. For full details on the election results, see *Demokratsia,* October 22, 1991, 1.

10. These views were expressed in a private interview by the leader of one of the monarchist organizations.

11. Those considered to be on the Left chose 1, 2, or 3 on the scale.

12. All of the figures come from data collected by the Erasmus Foundation, 1990.

ALBANIA

Elez Biberaj

Albania's parliamentary elections in March 1992 marked a watershed in the democratization process of that tiny Balkan country by sweeping from power the communists who had exercised absolute power for more than forty-seven years. Their rule was characterized by violations of human and political rights. The Democratic Party, the first non-communist party to be formed after President Ramiz Alia was forced to sanction political pluralism in December 1990, won a landslide victory. But the post-communist government has inherited a country on the verge of an abyss. Albania lags far behind all East European countries in terms of political stability (with the exception of former Yougoslavia) and economic development. The old communist infrastructure has collapsed and the economy has ground to a halt. There has been a serious breakdown in law and order and the country has become totally dependent on foreign aid to feed its people.

In view of the daunting political, economic, and social challenges that lie ahead, the question is, will Albania, which has lacked a democratic tradition and was the last East European country (with the exception of Serbia) to depose its communist rulers, succeed in establishing a stable pluralistic democracy and a free market system? This is the dilemma confronting Albania's new leadership under Sali Berisha, a champion of bold and steadfast reforms aimed at creating a genuine multiparty system and a market economy. But whereas the citizens of Albania now have political freedoms, the devastated economy threatens to overwhelm the new democratic government. The downfall of communism has released long pent-up forces. The Democratic Party is now responsible for government policy and is determined to implement radical reforms. The reforms will undoubtedly contribute to severe economic hardship. Thus, other political forces, including the extreme right, will attempt to become the beneficiary of popular discontent. The Democratic Party's success in eradicating Albania's horrendous communist legacy will depend in large part on its ability to keep its election campaign promises. These include the restoration of law and order, privatization and marketization of the economy, luring foreign investments into the country, and obtaining foreign assistance to help revive its economy. The success of the process would certainly mitigate the social dislocations of market reforms and build democratic institutions.

Albania's Political Tradition

Albania is one of the most homogenous countries in Europe, with Albanians comprising 98 percent of the total population. There are more than 7 million Albanians in the Balkans, but only 3.3 million live in Albania. Some 2.2 million Albanians live in Kosovo, which has been under Serbian control since 1912; Macedonia has a large Albanian community, estimated at between 700,000 and one million. About 70 percent of all Albanians are Sunny Moslems, 20 percent Roman Catholics, and 10 percent Eastern Orthodox.

The Albanians are divided into two subgroups: the Gegs in the north and the Tosks in the south, with the Shkumbi River serving as a rough dividing line between them. They have had different historical experiences and levels of economic development, resulting in divergent political cultures. The Gegs, traditionally organized according to tribal groups and renowned for their independent spirit and fighting abilities, managed to assert a high degree of independence even during the worst periods of Turkish occupation. The Gegs traditionally had limited contacts with the outside world because of the inaccessibility of their mountainous territories. The Tosks, on the other hand, engaged in extensive dealings with foreigners and were more susceptible to western liberal ideas. Before the communist takeover of Albania, the Tosks lived in a semi-feudal society, with a small group of landowners controlling about two-thirds of the richest land and exploiting the peasantry, who accounted for the majority of the population. While in the south the aristocracy played an important political role, in the north a similar role was played by the clan chieftains, the *bairaktare*. The two subgroups have alternatively dominated Albanian politics—the Gegs during King Zog's reign (1925–39) and the Tosks under communism (1945–1992). While there have never been open Geg-Tosk conflicts, latent feuds have existed and seem to have been further fueled by the communist regime's ruthless attempts to homogenize the two groups.

The last Balkan country to liberate itself from Turkish occupation in November 1912, Albania has had a tumultuous history. Ruthless foreign suppression of the development of Albanian cultural and national identity, the loss of Albanian-inhabited territories such as Kosovo, economic and social backwardness, and regional, tribal and religious differences have obstructed Albania's political development. While the majority of its neighbors established at one time or another a parliamentary democracy, Albania never developed a genuine multiparty system.

The struggle against Turkish occupation, which had gained momentum after the congress of Berlin in 1878, ended with Serbia and Montenegro gaining large Albanian-inhabited territories. The struggle was waged by loosely organized nationalistic movements, led primarily by aristocrats in the south and tribal chieftains in the north. The focus of these movements was not only the liberation of the country from Turkish occupation but also the thwarting of Serbian, Montenegrin, and Greek designs on Albanian-inhabited territories.

The founding fathers of modern Albania devoted little attention in their political programs to the form of government they would establish after independence. However, there have been strong sentiments for the selection of a King or a strong leader in the mold of Gjergj Kastrioti Skënderbeu (Scanderbeg). This legendary leader united the Albanians in the fifteenth century and successfully fought the Turks for a quarter of a century. These sentiments were strengthened by authoritarian tendencies among significant sectors of the population. Albania lacked a well developed middle class imbued with democratic ideals. The majority of Albania's emerging political, cultural and military elites were educated in Turkey, a country that also lacked a democratic political tradition.

For a short period before the outbreak of World War I, Albania was ruled by a German prince, Wilhelm zu Weid, who was selected by the Great Powers. Albania saw the emergence of the first political groups resembling parties in other European countries only in the first half of the 1920s. But Albania's experiment with a multi-party system was short-lived. The two main political grouping, the "populists," led by Fan S. Noli, a Harvard-educated Eastern Orthodox clergymen, and the "progressives," led by Ahmet Zogu, a chieftain from the powerful

Geg Mati tribe, engaged in endless feuding and the parliament could not agree on anything of substance. Noli became Prime Minister in June 1924, after an uprising, but was ousted six months later by Zogu.[1]

Ahmet Zogu ruled Albania for fourteen years, first as president and, after 1928, as King. He restored law and order and laid the foundations of a modern state. However, Zog ruled with an iron hand. He prevented the emergence of opposition parties, thus stunting the country's political growth. The parliament played no significant role, the media and the judiciary were subservient to the King, and political participation was limited. Arguably Zog's dictatorial rule, which prevented the emergence of a loyal opposition and the development of a democratic civic culture, was largely responsible for the subsequent failure of the emergence of viable democratic parties.

The Italians annexed Albania in 1939, formed an Albanian Fascist Party, and installed a puppet government led by Zog's political opponents. In the wake of Italy's capitulation in 1943, the Germans in turn installed a new government which declared Albania's independence and neutrality in the war. In the early 1940s, three new political parties emerged: the Albanian Communist Party (ACP), *Balli Kombëtar* [National Front], and *Legaliteti* [Legality]. Formed with the assistance of Yugoslav communists and led by Enver Hoxha, a young French-educated communist, the ACP was modeled after the Soviet Communist Party. It operated in a highly conspiratorial manner, and downplayed its objectives of establishing a communist party-state system. It enlisted popular support with its armed struggle against foreign occupation and promises of democracy and respect for human rights. *Balli Kombëtar* advocated the establishment of a modern republic and opposed vehemently both the communists and Zog's followers. It also insisted that Albania retain its 1941 borders, which included the incorporation of Kosovo. Both the ACP and *Balli Kombëtar* had their strongholds in the south. In 1943, Zog's followers led by Abas Kupi, who had joined forces with the ACP in the communist-dominated National Liberation Movement, formed the *Legaliteti* party, which advocated the restoration of the monarchy. *Legaliteti* was not able to attract significant popular support outside Zog's native Mat district. As the end of World War II approached, the communists launched an attack against both *Balli Kombëtar* and *Legaliteti*, ruthlessly eliminating them from the political scene. The majority of non-communist elites were decimated;

others fled the country with whatever remained of their armed follow-ers. Remnants of *Balli Kombëtar* and *Legaliteti* survived in the West, but their anti-communist struggle was undermined by endless petty feuding. By the time the communist regime in Albania collapsed, these two parties could claim only an insignificant membership and were still led by the World War II generation. Despite continuous emigration from Albania and Kosovo, they had been unable to rein-vigorate their membership with new blood. Moreover, their programs were outdated.

From November 1944 until the sanctioning of political pluralism in December 1990, the ACP, renamed in 1948 the Albanian party of Labor (APL), held unchallenged monopoly over political life.[2] Under the rule of Enver Hoxha (1944–85), Albania became known as one of the most repressive communist countries in the world. After aligning and then dealigning his country in turn with Yugoslavia, the Soviet Union, and finally China, Hoxha embarked on a self-reliance policy, isolating Albania from the outside world. While other East European countries experienced periods of communist relaxation, experimented with limited economic and political reforms, expanded political par-ticipation by tolerating the existence of non-official groups and or-ganizations, Albania remained bound to a Stalinist system long de-nounced even by the Soviet Union. Unlike its former communist allies, Albania under Hoxha never went through a period of de-Stalinization process, which in all likelihood would have led to his replacement as First Secretary of the APL, this was one of the main factors that con-tributed to the break with the Soviet Union in 1961; the other main factor was Soviet leader Nikita S. Khrushchev's rapprochement with "revisionist" Yugoslavia.

Most East European regimes recognized and tolerated parties which were closely aligned with the ruling party and did not threaten communist monopoly of power. The Albanian regime not only refused to permit the formation of such parties but also prohibited any orga-nized activity outside its control. No other ruling communist party in Europe exercised a tighter grip on society and for such a long pe-riod of time as did the APL under Hoxha's leadership. Through its control of mass organizations, the Democratic Front, the youth or-ganization, the trade unions, the artists union, women's union, etc., the APL made sure that its power was preserved. Elections, whose only purpose was to legitimize the ruling party, were held every four years for the People's Assembly, the legislative branch of the government and the supreme organ of state. But deputies were elected from a single list of Democratic Front candidates and the voters had very little if any input in the selection of candidates. The APL Polit-buro, the locus of power, determined the list of candidates, which was then forwarded to the base. Before the March 1991 election, the first multi-party election since the 1920s, no candidate was rejected by the constituency or lost the election. All the members of the Polit-buro and many party Central Committee members were included on the list. The election law excluded the possibility of an independent candidate, let alone a candidate that opposed the ruling party. Vot-ing was compulsory and the campaign was short and usually limited to one general meeting between the candidate and his constituency. The fact that elections in Albania were a charade is reflected by the official results announced. Almost always, the authorities claimed unanimous popular support.

The Demise of Communist Rule

In the wake of Ramiz Alia's accession to power after Hoxha's demise in April 1985, Albania experienced few significant changes.[3] While Alia appeared to recognize the growing political, economic, and social crises facing his country, he shied away from radical political and economic reforms. He tinkered with cosmetic changes, apparently hoping they would suffice to turn around the stagnating economy, and failed to carry out a full decentralization of the centrally planned economy. In the political sphere there were few discernable changes and Alia continued to project an image of the APL as enjoying the unswerving support of the people. In the last election for the people's Assembly before the legalization of the opposition, held in February 1987, the Central Election Commission announced a voter turnout of 100 percent (1,830,053) and claimed all had voted for official candi-dates, with only one ballot in the entire country found to be void.[4] No other regime in Eastern Europe could claim such "widespread" support.

By the late 1980s, the Albanian regime was faced with serious problems, the result of a sharp economic decline and international isolation. The pressures on the regime increased dramatically fol-lowing the downfall of communism in Eastern Europe, particularly after the violent overthrow of Romania's dictator, Nicolae Ceausescu. There were striking similarities between the Albanian and Romanian regimes and apparently there was a widespread perception in Albania that Ceausecu's fate awaited Alia. Although chilled by the winds of democratic change in other communist countries and increasing domestic opposition, the APL's old guard dug in its heels and refused to budge from its monopoly of political power. Alia argued that yielding to demands for radical economic reforms and permitting the establishment of other political parties would exacerbate both economic and political problems. It could even lead to the collapse of Albania's socialist system. He made desperate attempts to reinvigorate the communist system.

Apparently, Alia hoped to succeed where other communist leaders had failed. He hoped to initiate a well-coordinated process of change, one which would result in the party retaining power. Simultaneously, he hoped to gain popular support by relaxing the party's grip on society, expanding popular participation, and gradually ending Albania's long international isolation. Alia realized that his hopes for greater international acceptance and broader economic cooperation required an immediate improvement in the human rights situation and opening of Albanian society. But he was confronted with the problem of how to deal with the possible domestic consequences. The regime correctly feared that increased contacts with the outside world would endanger the government's ability to maintain social order, discipline, and ultimately, its own survival.

Alia begun by taking measures to improve his regime's tarnished international image, apparently hoping that international acceptance would improve the regime's internal standing. An important aspect of his so-called democratization process, launched in early 1990 after the first anti-communist demonstrations in Shkodër and Kovaje, was the adoption of measures aimed at improving the deplorable state of human rights. Alia indicated that Albania would take steps to bring its human rights practices to the level of international standards. In May 1990, the People's Assembly revised the penal code to redress widespread human rights transgressions, and recognized the citizens' right to travel abroad. But the contradictory behavior of the authorities undermined Albania's efforts to be accepted as a full member of the international community. While on the one hand the government pledged to respect human rights and issue passports to all Albanians desiring to travel abroad, citizens trying to flee the country were killed by border guards or, received severe punishment. Such actions seriously embarrassed Tiranë and added ammunition to those in the West who argued for increased pressure on the only remaining bastion of Stalinism in Europe.

The regime's ideological commitment had left no room for pragmatism or compromise. After the break with China in 1978, Tiranë had sought to enhance its claim to world leadership of Marxist-Leninist parties by touting itself as the only truly socialist state in the world. It refused to engage in any dealings with superpowers, and strictly abided by its self-reliance policy, that prohibited the government from seeking or accepting foreign credits. In an about-face that underscored Albania's urgency of expanding relations, Alia in April 1990 expressed a desire to restore ties with the United States and the Soviet Union and expand relations with other countries, especially Western Europe. Albania's new foreign policy "realism," however, met with lukewarm reception. Western countries lauded the Albanian government for taking steps to improve the state of human rights. As an incentive to move in this direction they had granted Albania observer status at the Copenhagen meeting of the Conference on Security and Cooperation in Europe (CSCE) in the spring of 1990. However, they emphasized that Albania had a long way to go to become a full member of the international community. Alia's contention that Albania was different from other East European countries and that the communists in Albania enjoyed full popular support did not appear convincing to most Westerners. Albanian officials did not hide their anxiety that the West had made the strengthening of ties dependent on a major change in Albania's human rights policy and sanctioning of political pluralism.

Despite increased internal and external pressures, Alia continued to initiate only superficial political and economic changes and left no doubt regarding his intention to maintain one-party rule and centralized economic planning. He hoped to bolster his regime's popular support by asserting that the changes represented a commitment to the democratization and modernization of party and government structures. But Alia's inability or unwillingness to press ahead with major reforms only worsened economic conditions causing widespread disenchantment. In July 1990, five thousand Albanians stormed foreign embassies in Tiranë in an attempt to flee the country. The incident indicated how widespread the population's disenchantment with the regime had become.

The embassy episode represented a major setback for the APL and was a clear indication that the regime, despite its highly repressive nature, was not invincible. Alia's reluctance to use the armed forces to prevent the refugees from entering foreign embassies suggested that the government was sensitive to the political dangers of suppressing such a large number of people. Even at this eleventh hour, Alia hoped his regime would survive. Although faced with unrelenting domestic and international demands to permit political pluralism, he continued to reject the formation of other political parties, although he vowed to permit the free expression of ideas. The mass organizations, which had been used by the ruling communist party to mobilize support for the implementation of party decision, were declared independent. Alia also announced a series of economic measures, termed as the "New Economic Mechanism." A new election law, approved in November 1990, provided for multi-candidate elections. While in the past only the Democratic Front fielded candidates, the APL and the mass organizations were now given the right to put forth their candidates. The new law permitted independent candidates if they could obtain the endorsement of 300 registered voters. In conjunction with the new election law, Alia announced the formation of a commission to revise the country's constitution. He said the APL would give up its constitutionally guaranteed monopoly of power but would not sanction political pluralism.

Although in the Albanian context these changes were significant, they were too little and too late. Albania could not escape the reverberations of the East European revolution. Alia's controlled process of change was getting out of hand because he could not keep up with internal demands for reforms. Intellectuals took advantage of what appeared to be a mild relaxation of the APL's controls in the cultural sector to express views which until then had been considered anathema by the ruling party. Unrest began to spread among the students at Tiranë University, the nation's only higher educational institution attracting students from all over the country. Albania's relations with the West were practically frozen following the embassy incident. To Alia's great disappointment, the United States and the West European countries blocked Albania's acceptance as a full member to the CSCE at the Paris summit meeting in November 1990.

The biggest challenge to Alia and the ruling party came in the wake of student demonstrations at Tiranë University in early December 1990. After months of insisting that he would not permit the formation of other parties, on December 11, 1990, Alia accepted student demands for political pluralism.

Moves Toward a Multi-Party System

In an apparent attempt to regain the initiative, the communists took a series of well-coordinated steps. The official media launched a campaign claiming that it was the APL and Alia personally that had initiated the reforms that eventually led to the sanctioning of political pluralism. Hoxha's widow, Nexhmije, long considered as the leader of the conservative camp blocking changes, was replaced by Prime Minister Adil Çarçani as chairperson of the Democratic Front, the country's largest communist-controlled mass organization. Çarçani's nomination to this post, which ran counter to Alia's insistence that the mass organizations were no longer transmission belts for the APL, was a clear indication that Alia intended to replace him as Prime Minister. The authorities removed from central Tiranë the last statue of Stalin and the Council of Ministers issued a decree removing the name of the Soviet dictator from all institutions.[5] In addition, the APL approved a new program, breaking with many traditional Marxist-Leninist principles and moving closer to the ideals and organizational principles of a social democratic party. These belated measures, however, failed to improve the APL's image. The depth of revulsion against the regime was reflected by the outbreak of violent anti-communist demonstrations in several cities. Burdened by close to fifty years of Stalinist ideological baggage, the APL had become so discredited that its claims of renovation could not reverse its decline.

The first opposition party to be formed was the Democratic Party, a center right party, led by Sali Berisha, a former member of the APL and one of Albania's best known cardiologists. The Demo cratic Party called for the establishment of a pluralistic democracy based on the rule of law, full respect for human rights, and a market economy. The Republican Party, which took a stand to the right of the Democratic Party, was formed in January 1991. It was followed by the formation of the Ecological, Agrarian, Social Democratic, and several other parties.[6]

As the first opposition party, the Democratic Party enjoyed an unquestionable advantage. Resembling more an umbrella organization than a traditional party, it rapidly attracted a massive membership, with diverse political interests. They included former APL members, individuals who had been politically inactive until then, remnants of *Balli Kombëtar* and *Legaliteti*, and former political prisoners. The Democratic Party came to be viewed as the most viable alternative to the APL. But despite the presence among its members of many die-hard anti-communists and former political prisoners, who might be expected to take a more conservative stand on many issues than former APL members, the Democratic Party rapidly rallied around common objectives of establishing a genuine multi-party system and a civil society. However, the most radical members of the party, eager to see a speedy dismantling of communist structures that permeated all levels of Albanian society, were soon disappointed with the leadership's gradual assault on the communist regime. Initially, the Democratic Party as well as its sister Republican Party praised Alia,[7] put forth only moderate demands, and were careful to distance themselves from those advocating immediate radical reforms. Opposition leaders, recognizing their parties' weaknesses and concerned about the danger of a backlash by conservative communist forces likely to lead to a popular revolt or even civil war, emphasized reliance on peaceful means. They tried to reassure the communists that they had nothing to fear from the establishment of a multi-party system.

During the period preceding the parliamentary elections on March 31, 1991, the political situation deteriorated, with the outbreak of widespread politically-motivated strikes and demonstrations, violent confrontations between Democratic Party and APL supporters, and the emergence of a communist organization of "volunteers" committed to defend Hoxha's legacy.[8] Alia came under attack from both the reformers and conservatives within the ranks of his own party and seemed to be losing control. In late February, he dismissed Prime Minister Çarçani, replacing him with a young economist, Fatos Nano, and formed a Presidential Council, assuming personal control over the country in contravention of the Constitution. The elections were held in a climate of fear and repression. The APL used the enormous resources at its disposal to impede opposition campaign activities and access to the media. The opposition parties were largely unable to spread their message to rural areas, which accounted for 65 percent of Albania's population. Election results were not surprising: the APL won 169 of the 250 seats in the People's Assembly. The Democratic Party won 75 seats, while the Republican Party, the second largest opposition party, failed to win a single seat. The communist-dominated National Veterans' Organization won 1 seat, and *Omonia*, an organization representing the ethnic Greek minority, five seats.

Although the APL scored a big win, it turned out to be a Pyrrhic election victory. Nano, who formed the new government, was soon faced with mounting labor unrest and it became evident that the communists had lost the ability to govern the country. The newly founded Independent Trade Unions, with the blessings of the Democratic Party, launched a nation-wide general strike, forcing the resignation of Nano's government in early June. The Democratic Party, which only two months earlier had rejected Nano's offer for a coalition, agreed to participate in what was termed as a Government of National Stability, headed by Ylli Bufi, a relatively unknown communist and Food Minister in Nano's government. The democrats received seven portfolios, including the economic, finance, and defense ministries. Gramoz Pashko, a senior member of the leadership of the Democratic Party, became deputy prime minister and minister of economics, and his brother-in-law, Genc Ruli, minister of finance.

The decision to enter into a coalition with communists presented both opportunities and risks for the opposition. It confirmed the fact that only six months after its creation the Democratic Party had become a key political force. But the democrats now shared responsibility with the communists for the nation's problems. They had taken over the two most critical posts in the government—the economics and finance ministries—at a time when the country was practically bankrupt. It soon became evident that the communists, who in June 1991 renamed the APL as the Socialist Party and repudiated Hoxha, were not seriously interested in implementing reforms advocated by the Democratic Party since they would undermine their dominant position. The coalition government turned out to be grossly incompetent, and the crumbling of the economy and growing social strife further destabilized the situation, with an increasing number of Albanians blaming the Democratic Party. Growing official corruption impaired foreign relief efforts, with humanitarian supplies diverted into the black market or repositories for bureaucrats and their underlings. Even Democratic Party ministers, including Pashko, Ruli, and Preç Zogaj, the ministers of culture, were accused of corruption. By the end of the summer 1991, there appeared to be widespread disenchantment with the Democratic Party.

Meanwhile, other forces attempted to take advantage of the perceptible decline in the support for the Democratic Party. In the early stages of political pluralism, the APL had prevented the creation of parties of the far right, terming them as "fascist" and "anti-national."

The decree on the creation of political parties, issued in December 1990, had specifically prohibited the establishment of "fascist, racist, warmongering, [and] anti-national" political organizations and associations. This was aimed at preventing the creation or revival of parties in the mold of *Balli Kombëtar* and *Legaliteti*, but in addition to legal constrains, the emergence of rightist parties was inhibited by lack of leadership.

The opposition to communist rule had been spearheaded by intellectuals and students, the overwhelming majority of whom were either members of or had close contacts with the establishment. After all, given the communist regime's brutal treatment of its opponents and lack of any independent organizations, only intellectuals and students who had benefited from the establishment could organize opposition groups in the initial phase of political pluralism. The few survivors of the pre-communist elites and their heirs were still being held in prison or internal exile, while leaders of Albanian political parties in exile were not yet permitted to return to their native land and participate in the political process.

But the parliament's approval in the summer of 1991 of a more liberal law on the organization of political parties led to an explosion of their numbers. By the end of the year there were more than twenty parties, several of them Rightist. King Zog's supporters created the National Democratic Party. Its leaders questioned the Democratic Party's commitment to eradicate communism and said they would not open their ranks to former communists. Advocating the return of the monarchy, the party called for a national referendum to decide whether King Zog's son, Leka, should return to the throne. Leka was two days old when his parents fled Albania in the wake of the Italian invasion in 1939 and has never set foot in his native land. When his father died in Paris in 1961, a group of loyalists proclaimed Leka King. After his expulsion from Spain in the 1970s for alleged arms trafficking, the pretender to the Albanian throne moved to South Africa. He has repeatedly expressed a desire to return to his native land. Initially, founders of the National Democratic Party had the support of *Legaliteti* followers in the West. Subsequently, however, *Legaliteti* applied to the Albanian Ministry of Justice for recognition and in early 1992 it was legalized. Nevertheless, there are no discernable differences in the programs of the two monarchist parties.

Supporters of *Balli Kombëtar* have also formed a party—the Nationalist Party Albanian Democratic Union. In addition, there are at least three other parties that consider themselves Rightist. With the exception of the National Democratic Party's and *Legaliteti*'s demands for the return of the monarchy, the parties of the right have strikingly similar programs. They have emphasized the need to instill their fellow citizens with notions of "Albanianism," claiming that under communism the Albanians had lost their true national identity. They insist that Albanians have always been poor but they were proud of their ethnicity, while now they display little respect for their national symbols.[10] While these parties recognize that Albania has become dependent on foreign aid, they are resentful of the growing presence of foreigners, especially Italians, and emphasize the importance of the Albanians regaining their dignity. The mistreatment of Albanian refugees in Greece has received wide publicity in Albania and has lead to widespread anti-Greek sentiments. The increasing presence of Greek Orthodox clergy in southern Albania has also been seen as a violation of Albanian sovereignty and an indication of Greek designs on southern Albania. The outbreak of war in former Yugoslavia, increased Serbian repression against Albanians in Kosova, and Greek support for Slobodan Milosevic, the chauvinistic Serb premier, have raised the specter of a Serb-Greek encirclement of Albania. Many political parties have used Kosova as a rallying point. While the Democratic Party has insisted that Serbia recognize ethnic Albanians' right to self-determination and has not demanded border changes, the parties of the right insist on outright union of Kosova with Albania, contending that the injustices heaped upon the Albanian nation by its more powerful neighbors must be corrected.

The efforts of the rightist parties to capitalize on the increasing disenchantment with the Democratic Party met with limited success. They attracted only a small membership, could not build a nationwide organization and, perhaps more importantly, were unable to come up with a detailed action program to arrest the deteriorating economic situation. Moreover Berisha, concerned with the ineffectiveness of the coalition government and the declining popularity of his party, laid out a carefully crafted position evidently intended to attract support from the political right. He dismissed the claims of Socialist party leaders that they had repudiated communist ideals, accusing them of blocking the country's democratization. Berisha formed a united front with the Republican and Social Democratic parties, the powerful Independent Trade Unions, and the influential Society of Former Political Prisoners. Through a series of joint organized activities, including massive rallies, the opposition forces stepped up demands for the eradication of communism, the arrest of former Politburo members, and early parliamentary elections. But while Berisha's new strategy attracted almost instant popular support, it met with opposition from some elements within his own party. Pashko and other Democratic Party ministers in the government, supported by some members of the party's top leadership, criticized what they termed Berisha's "street" tactics, and accused the party leader of having usurped too much power in the leadership.

The national convention of the Democratic Party, held at the end of September 1991, became the scene of a fierce battle over the party line, as the split between Berisha and Pashko, which had been brewing for some time, burst into the open. Pashko and his supporters, referred to as "the intellectual group," launched a blistering attack on Berisha, forcefully indicating to the nation that their party should stay in the government coalition. Although Pashko's group evidently enjoyed a majority in the party's presidium, its zesty efforts to gain a dominant voice in determining the party line failed. With the support of local party branch leaders and activists discontented with what they termed Pashko's "neo-communist" policies, Berisha successfully undercut his opponents and was reelected party chairman by an overwhelming majority.

During the next two months, Berisha capitalized on his recent victory at the party convention. Support for his policies and leadership expanded at all levels of the party. His opponents had been put on the defensive and, although conflict within the party leadership remained intense, Berisha had seized the high ground and had become unquestionably the dominant voice in laying down the political line. In early December, Berisha sent an ultimatum to President Alia threatening that the Democratic Party would withdraw from the coalition unless a series of demands were met, including arresting former APL Politburo members and Hoxha's widow, accused of crimes, and holding early elections. Berisha's stand followed a series of public brawls with his ministers, who strongly opposed withdrawal from the government. When Alia refused to fully meet the demands, Berisha carried through his threat and the coalition government collapsed. The Democratic Party's withdrawal from the coalition was followed by an unprecedented outpouring of popular support for Berisha.

Alia named a caretaker government and set elections for March 22, 1992. The Democratic Party launched a well coordinated campaign, promising to implement radical economic and political reforms and to restore law and order. The democrats mobilized large segments of the population and won a landslide victory, capturing 92 seats in the 140 seat parliament. Their allies won 8 seats (the Social Democratic Party 7, and the Republican Party 1, giving the opposition bloc the two-thirds majority necessary for constitutional changes. The Socialist Party won 38 seats and the Human Rights Party, the successor of the ethnic Greek society Omonia, 2 seats. One of the biggest surprises was the Republican Party's poor showing; it failed to reach the 4 percent threshold, that would have made it eligible for seats in parliament. The Republican Party's prospects were apparently undermined by poor leadership and organization as well as the Democratic Party's swing to the right.

Within days of the Democratic Party's election victory, Alia resigned and the parliament elected Berisha as president. The formidable task of reviving Albanian society atomized by close to fifty years of communist misrule now fell on the democrats. The new government, headed by Prime Minister Alexander Meksi, lost no time in beginning to implement the electoral program of the Democratic Party. It introduced legislation aimed at attracting foreign investments, liberalized prices and wages, took measures to make the Albanian currency, the *lek*, convertible, reduced or eliminated subsidies for unprofitable state enterprises, and announced plans to speed up the privatization of agriculture and the state industrial sector. Berisha called for increased foreign assistance. He attempted to convince Western governments and international institutions to treat Albania as a special case because of the very repressive nature of its past communist rule and long isolation from the outside world. He insisted that his country will have to start figuratively from scratch. Although tiny Albania has had to compete with other East European countries and former soviet republics for Western aid, it has received considerable attention. By August 1992, the United States and the European Community had committed some $900 million in direct economic and humanitarian assistance. In addition, the World Bank had granted Albania a $40 million loan to help its agricultural sector. Although reforms are off to a rocky start, with fast rising inflation and labor unrest, Albanian officials have expressed optimism about the future.

Prospects for the Future

Albania's political tradition has not been conducive to a democratic order. It will take years if not decades to eradicate the legacy of communism. In the view of many Albanians as well as outside observers, the communist regime devastated everything, including national traditions, leading to a loss of a sense of personal dignity and responsibility. In addition to the economic crisis and lack of a democratic tradition, the absence of entrepreneurial elites, assertive middle classes and political forces and ideas associated with them, will complicate the drive for a genuine democratic system and market economy.

Two years after the end of the communist monopoly of power, Albania has seen the emergence of a volatile multi-party system. Party identification remains weak, primarily because of striking similarities in the programs of most political parties. The demise of communism was followed not only by a revival of nationalism and cries to correct the injustices inflicted by neighbors on the Albanian nation, but also to an increase in crime and to a revival of regional differences. The removal of communist shackles was followed by a dramatic increase in the number of murders, robberies, assaults and other violent acts as well as blood feuds in some parts of the country. The explosion of crime was due to the general relaxation of authority, as well as to the inclination of some people to take advantage of the new democracy. What further complicated the situation was the rise of new types of crimes, such as fraud, profiteering, illicit trade, gambling, and printing of forged currency.

Albania has also witnessed an increase in regional differences. While in the inter-war period, the Gegs had dominated Albanian politics, under communism the number of Tosks who enjoyed upward mobility in the party and state hierarchy was extremely high. Hoxha also pursued a heavy-handed policy against the Gegs (especially against Roman Catholics who had forcefully resisted the imposition of communist rule), neglected their economic and cultural development, and imposed on them ostensibly a standard language, heavily dominated by the Tosk dialect.

Communist policies resulted in major differences in the educational and economic levels between north and south. Many Gegs resented what they saw as political, economic, and cultural domination by the more modernized and prosperous southerners. The political elites from both sides have in general avoided inflammatory rhetoric on the north-south issue. But after the elections the socialists attempted to fan the tensions, evidently hoping to exploit the resentment of some southerners that Berisha, a northerner, had become president.[12] The possibility of Kosova's eventual union with Albania also seems to have created apprehension in some parts of the country. While the number of Gegs and Tosks in Albania is about equal, the addition of about three million Albanians from Kosova and Macedonia would tip the balance in favor of the north. Some have expressed concern that because of the woeful state of the economy, the Kosovars could easily "take over" Albania. Berisha's decision to grant dual citizenship to all Albanians abroad, including those in former Yugoslavia, was criticized as making the natives' second-class citizens in their own country.

Although the history of relations between the Gegs and the Tosks is not fraught with conflict, the possibility cannot be excluded that demagogues and extreme forces of all sorts might attempt to exploit the issue. This would have serious repercussions for the viability of the Albanian state.

In spite of the fact that large masses, threatened by the new government's radical reforms, are available to be mobilized, the Rightist parties have been unable to develop clearly defined programs and emerge as viable political forces. However, several factors could lead to an increased support for the right. The implementation of radical economic reforms the democratic government considers necessary for the reinvigoration of society will be very painful and will likely lead to a disenchantment with democracy. The quality of life during the next two to three years is likely to be significantly worse than it was in 1990. If the new government turns out to be ineffective, severe economic hardships will continue indefinitely. If law and order are not restored, some Albanians may be tempted to look to more authoritarian solutions. The political left has been discredited and there appears to be little chance of its resurgence. Therefore, the disaffected are more likely to turn to the Right.

For the foreseeable future, however, the Democratic Party will most likely maintain its key role in Albanian politics. It remains the only party which has a concrete plan of action and has displayed the ability and determination to embark on the difficult road of fundamental reforms. Assuming the Democratic Party keeps, as it has successfully done until now, its diverse membership form splitting into different factions, Albania is less likely to see the emergence of the political Right from outside the political spectrum. It is more likely that President Berisha and his party will move to the Right.

Parliament is composed largely of inexperienced members and has become obstructionist, resembling more a contentious debating club than a law-making body. Berisha might find it necessary, as have his colleagues in other emerging democracies in Eastern Europe, to seek enhanced powers to tackle grave problems facing his nation. Albania's fledgling democracy will depend to a large degree on Western business training, educational assistance and aid for the development of independent media, judiciary and parliamentary procedures and training in building and upholding democratic institutions and standards that will maintain sufficient checks on any chief executive.

NOTES

1. See Stavro Skendi, *The Political Evolution of Albania 1912–1944* (New York: Mid-European Studies Center, 1954); Arben Puto, *Demokracia e Rrethuar* [The Besieged Democracy] (Tirane: "8 Nentori," 1990); Bernd Jürgen Fischer, *King Zog and the Struggle for Stability in Albania* (Boulder and New York: East European Monographs/Columbia University Press, 1984); and Nicholas C. Pano, "Albania," in Joseph Held, (ed.), *The Columbia History of Eastern Europe in the Twentieth Century* (New York: Columbia University Press, 1992), pp. 22–23.

2. For background information, see Nicholas C. Pano, *The People's Republic of Albania* (Baltimore: The Johns Hopkins Press, 1968); Anton Logoreci, *The Albanians: Europe's Forgotten Survivors* (London: Victor Gollancz, 1977); Peter R. Prifti, *Socialist Albania Since 1944: Domestic and Foreign Developments* (Cambridge, MA: M.I.T. Press, 1978); and Arshi Pipa, *Albanian Staninism: Ideo-Political Aspects* (Boulder and New York: East European Monographs/Columbia University Press, 1990).

3. Elez Biberaj, *Albania: A Socialist Maverick* (Boulder: Westview Press, 1990).

4. *Zëri i Popullit* (Tiranë), February 3, 1987, p. 1.

5. Ibid., December 22, 1991, p. 1.

6. It was widely believed that Alia was instrumental in the creation of the Ecological and Agrarian parties to mitigate the rapid rise of the Democratic Party. In the disputes between the opposition and the APL, these two parties tended to side with the APL.

7. While Democratic Party leaders went out of their way to praise Alia in the days immediately following his decision to meet

the demands of striking Tiranë University students to permit the creation of other political parties, the Republican Party continued to maintain a baffling attitude toward the communist president. Sabri Godo, leader of the Republican Party, described Alia as the only personality that could preserve the country's stability and on the eve of the March 31, 1991 elections urged voters in Alia's district in Tiranë to cast their votes for the president, who still was First Secretary of the APL. Alia lost to a relatively unknown Democratic Party candidate.

8. Members of the organization of Hoxha's "volunteers" terrorized Democratic Parry followers throughout the country following the dawning of the former dictator's monument in Tiranë on Feburary 20, 1991. The leader of this organization, Hysni Miloshi, in November 1991 formed the Albanian Communist Party. In July 1992, the Communist Party was outlawed.

9. *Zëri i Popullit*, December 19, 1990, p. 1.

10. When U. S. Secretary of State James Baker visited Tiranë in June 1991, he was met by hundreds of thousands of Albanians wielding American flags, but very few Albanian ones. And many Albanians who have sought refuge in Greece and Italy are said to be "ashamed" to admit their ethnic origin, and some have changed their names and religion. See *Drita* (Tiranë), June 2, 1991, p. 3.

11. An estimated 150,000 Albanians have crossed illegally into Greece in search of jobs and a better life. Greek officials have complained of difficulties in dealing with such an influx and have accused many Albanians of committing crimes and engaging in illegal activities. A number of Albanians have been killed by Greek border guards.

12. The Socialist Party newspaper, *Zëri i Popullit*, the country's only daily newspaper, launched a campaign against Berisha, accusing the President of appointing too many Gegs in high positions. In a highly polemical article, the former president of the parliament, Socialist Party deputy Kastiot Islami, suggested that Berisha's campaign of purging communists from the state bureaucracy was allegedly being directed primarily against Tosks. See *Zëri i Popullit*, May 31, 1992, p. 2. A well known journalist, Faruk Myrtaj, vehemently criticized Islami, accusing him of fanning regional differences. Myrtaj said that a "balance" existed between the Gegs and the Tosks in Meksi's government and posed a rhetorical question: Why should Albania's president be from the south and not the north? See *Rilindkja Demokratike*, June 6, 1992, p. 1

CONCLUDING THOUGHTS ON THE REVIVAL OF THE
POLITICAL RIGHT IN EASTERN EUROPE

Iván Völgyes

It is relatively easy to offer introductory remarks to a conference on any given subject. The old, time-tested method is to outline the conference, offer a few methodological hints, establish the vocabulary of discourse, and offer good wishes for those about to be engaged in diverse attempts to delineate their subjects. All in all, writing introductory speeches is one of the more fun activities of participating in a conference.

Writing concluding remarks to a volume is vastly different and far more trying. Summarizing the papers presented is at best a sophomoric activity for anyone interested in serious scholarship, while writing something new, radical, or unmentioned is not really the task of the author writing a conclusion to an edited volume. Consequently, in order to stay close to the charge of writing a summary, or a conclusion, the author must attempt to judiciously balance the two approaches: a task bound to be difficult for an academically minded "objective" scholar. This essay, however, will at least try to come close to examining the revival of the Right in Eastern Europe, precisely from the standpoint of that elusive "objectivity."

The usual *caveats*, of course, are in order. In this concluding chapter I am using Eastern Europe to include Bulgaria, Croatia, the Czech and Slovak Lands, Hungary, Poland and Roomania. Furthermore, the generalizations that are about to be made will not fit any single country to the T, rather my efforts will attempt to deal with the "modal," the "universal," if that is possible at all.

Consequently, this chapter will (1) attempt to identify what the political "Right" in Eastern Europe is; (2) discuss the differences between the "old" and the new "Right" in the region; and (3) analyze the characteristics of the political Right in contemporary Eastern Europe.

The Political Right in the New Eastern Europe

It is an interesting phenomenon that literally thousands of tomes have been written to date—or at least, until the demise of the Communist ideology and its intestate system—about the Left, but very few such works were ever really published about the "Right" in history.[1] That this is really so may be due to a number of causes. First, the study of the "Right" has been exceedingly amorphous. Unlike the "Left," the "Right" never had a coherent ideology that was unique to the Right as a movement. Though it was assumed that the Right was authoritarian, though it became clear that it had some orientations that would more likely show up on the Right, the fact that a set of interconnected ideas providing explanatory variables for all "rightist" phenomena was nowhere to be found rendered the Right far less "researchable" than the Left.

A second reason for the lack of interest in the political Right was its boundary problem with communism. Such studies as those by Adorno, Arendt, or Brzezinski dealt with "authoritarianism" or "totalitarianism" as a behavioral and not as an orientational problem. In such an approach the Right became meaningless, unless it identified with a particular kind of authoritarianism or totalitarianism. Moreover, within such categories the Right only made sense in contrast to the Left; Fascism was important as a variety of the Right, especially as it was contrasted to communism.

A third reason for the understandable reluctance of scholars to engage in generalizations concerning the Right was the fact that part of the Right received such enormous, negative attention. Fascism, in all its varieties and manifestations, garnered all attention away from more generic treatments of the topic. Right, in short, in many people's mind became synonymous with Fascism, and with Fascism dissipating into historical memory, interest in the Right also began to wane.

Yet, the Right appears to be a meaningful philosophical and political category, even if it cannot be used as a contrast with the Left in the sense of being located at opposite ends of the political spectrum. Though it defies easy description, though it stretches from a moderate to an extremist spectrum, the Right exists in every society in its own peculiar form, with its own separate identity, with its sharp differences from other "Rights" elsewhere, in other lands, and at other historical times. Unlike the Left with an "international" message—albeit a moribund one as of now!—the Right exists without international symbols and messages.

It is even more difficult to identify the political Right in Eastern Europe than elsewhere, since in this region it was generally Left-wing intellectuals who identified their opponents as being on or of the Right. While the Left envisioned itself to be the inheritor of the historical mantle of progress toward a rationally based human Paradise, the Right was viewed—especially by those who claimed that inheritance—as that part of society that was most "retrograde," "reactionary," or "counterrevolutionary." Working against the Right, therefore, meant to follow the "inevitable" march of "progress" toward victory. Especially in the minds of those convinced of the righteousness of the cause of the Left—whether manifest in communism, socialism or in the support of the welfare state—the Right could offer no "redeeming human values" or desirable solutions for the "progressive," or "thinking" part of mankind.

It is worthwhile to reiterate briefly here, that the Right in Eastern Europe has always been used in contradistinction to the Left; e.g., as time went on, all those opposed to communism in its manifestations were viewed as "Rightists" by the communist regimes in power. On the part of the ruling communist elites, little differentiation was made between the members of the "democratic" opposition, the "royalists," or even the "Fascists." And while the population may not have identified the Right as negatively as the elites, "being on the Right" remained a negative distinction at best.

Old Right – New Right – Even Newer Rights

The historical literature identifies the old Right in Europe as the aristocratic, monarchic, semi-feudal holders of power; people who, generally, ruled before the fall of the dynasties in the aftermath of World War I. Whether they were embodied in a Bismarck, the Tsar, or Emperor Franz Josef, the Right was identifiable with relative ease. Together with such supportive organizations as the Catholic Church, the Imperial armies' officer core, or the landed estates, the Right stood against popular rule, parliamentarism and even social justice. Coupled with the power of the large commercial barons and the captains of industry, the Right in short was viewed to stand in the way of democracy, broadly defined.

In Eastern Europe the identification of the old Right was a little more complicated than in the West. The landed aristocracy in Hungary, for example, clung to the "Right," though not necessarily to membership in the Empire; being a Rightist and a nationalist at the same time may or may not have been contradictory terms. In Poland, being on the Right, largely meant an identification, however, with the ruling elites, be they from whatever partitioning power. And, as history evolved, in the Czech Lands, too, being on the Right meant being affiliated with the forces against independence and a preference for maintaining the old order. In short, preferences for a special type of domestic, internal power allocation were intermixed with preferences for arrangements of national existence.

World War I changed all that. The empire-oriented dynastic, aristocratic Right disappeared in most places, and even in places where it was preserved it was shorn of its great power/empire orientation; in short, the aristocratic Right—as well as many other parts of society—became "nationalized." Territorial or other grievances also helped to create a movement on the Right. This was, of course, understandable, since the Left was expropriated both by the "socialist" parties and movements, as well as by the governing elites of the new democracies—where, in fact, such democracies existed (e.g., Czechoslovakia, and, for a while, Poland). I hasten to add that it was not the political intention of the victors at Versailles to create democracies with a Left-wing orientation, nor was it their intention to force the nationalists into the camp of the Right. Intentions, however, are no guides to policy; the direct and unfortunate net result of the settlements of Paris on Eastern Europe was to force the coagulation of the national cause with that of the Right.

The new Right soon became a mixture between the populist, nationalists, and the upper-class nationalists. Though representing widely different trends in regards to economic and social goals, the Right willy-nilly agreed on the cause for virulent nationalism. And whatever the eventual outcome—whether populist Fascism in Slovakia and Romania, or upper-class authoritarian Right-wing rule in Hungary—the new Right everywhere rode the crest of nationalism to power. Whatever the "Right" meant in a given language, in historical terms it meant authoritarian rule versus democracy, nationalism instead of globalism, and in all instances a virulent rejection of the "Left."

As noted earlier, World War II, the tragedies of the Holocaust, and the defeat of Fascism, relegated the "Right" to seemingly histor-ical oblivion. The "Right" was now condemned for all the ills of the past; the "Left" was victorious in the form of welfare-statism in the West and communism in the East. The supporters of the "Right," the Catholic church, the "capitalists," the merchant class, and the aris-tocracy, were discredited, scattered, and often even destroyed. The claim of the Right to be the voice of the nation, and of nationalism, was ridiculed, berated and squelched; "this is what you wanted?" proclaimed the huge posters showing the horrors of the war. From now on, so the communists reasoned, since communist ideology was internationalist, there will be no need to discuss issues of nations, minorities, nationalities, and nationalism; *de mortibus, nil et nisi,* so went the communist logic. The Right had no rights anymore. And, although the communist rule was based on totalitarian precepts, it was the totalitarianism of the Left and not of the Right that came to rule.

The fall of communism—its sorry record in the past and the sad legacy it left behind—however, in turn, discredited the Left. The self-identification of the communists with the Left, and often of the Left with ideologies and ethoses that were close to those held by the communists, added to this discrediting. The world-wide trend to the Right, the resuscitation or reinvigoration of the Right that had its international manifestations in the near simultaneous elections of Reagan, Thatcher, and Kohl added further fuel to the rebirth of the Right in Eastern Europe as well. The revolutions of 1989–1990 created a new "Right" in the region again.

In this sense, the newest political Right that has emerged exists on two levels. First, it exists in contradistinction to the Left; anything that is anti-Communist is on the Right. In this respect, then the Va-tra, the Civil Forum or Solidarity represent the Right alike. Second, the Right also exists as an ideology with fuzzy ideals that are not shared—today, anymore?—by the Left. While there are obviously a great many gradations among the various groups that are a part of the right in Eastern Europe today, this aspect of contradistinction should be borne in mind in our delineation of the various Rights in the region.

It is also worthwhile to note that a great many observers of the re-gion identified the actual "revival of the old Right" in the region. The Vatra or Matica are obviously not new organizations; they originated in the shadows of World War II. Indeed, it is true that today many parties and movements on the East European Right populate their philosophies with references used in earlier times, pepper their proclamations with a vocabulary clearly reminiscent of those same eras and, indeed, utilize political categories that appear to come straight from the 1930s. Thus, for example, the "nostalgia politicians" of Hungary utilize terminology from the 1930s, appeal to ethno-territorial Hungarian nationalism by claiming to be the rightful representatives of Magyars from all of the neighboring states, appear to bring back outmoded and once outlawed socio-aristocratic hierarchies, titles and ranks, and once again seek to place Magyars on a national scale higher than others from the region. Or alternatively, the self-identification of Croatians versus Serbs, Czechs versus Slovaks, Romanians versus Gypsies, Poles versus Jews, all utilize concepts and employ vocabularies that were used during the 1930s.

Yet, the fact is that 1992 is not 1920 or 1940; those periods are gone from history irrevocably. The politicians and the people alike are at a loss as to the vocabulary utilized to describe their own values and interests. It is clear that Walesa is not Pilsudski, Csurka is not Szálasi, Mečiar is not Tiso, and so on. What the people "on the Right" want is not a return of the bygone political eras of the 1930s or 1940s, but the translation of their current goals into a vocabulary that is comprehensible. Unfortunately for the region, however, political discourse to be meaningful must have a commonly accepted political vocabulary where at least the concepts are not muddled; that language has yet to develop in the region; hence the politicians of the Right employ the only vocabulary they know, the one that they used during the interwar-era.

The Right in Contemporary Eastern Europe: Instead of a Conclusion

In contemporary Eastern Europe, belonging to the Right means identifying with three major elements of the value system. The first refers to the desired domestic power arrangement, the second to the manner of reaching the desired goal, and the third, refers to the value of the nation.

Of course, it is relatively easy to identify the "extreme Right." In Eastern Europe the commonalities are enormous. For the Right, the centrality of the nation as an overarching phenomenon is essential. Defining the nation and not the state as central to its concerns, *eo ipso* puts the East European Right in conflict with the modern prerequisites of contemporary liberal Europe and the liberal, universalist, global order. Insisting on either defending the survival of the "ethnic nation," or extending the "rights" of the nation at the expense of others, clearly focuses the attention of the extreme Right on those who would detract from the "sacred cause." Suffusing that cause with a zealotry, populating it with ancient symbols that seem to be *passé* in a modern age, but for which the limited imagination found no replacement as yet, the extreme Right embarks on a crusade to remedy wrongs perceived to have been committed against the nation. Hence, its opposition to liberalism with its emphasis on universal human rights and respect for tolerance. Hence, its opposition to "urbanism," "cosmopolitanism," "universalism,"—in short, hence its xenophobia and horrendous anti-Semitism. Hence, its preference for autocratic solutions that would both subordinate the rights of the individuals to group rights and would opt either for an authoritarian domestic power arrangement, or an autocratic leader who would accomplish the goals preferred by the Right. And hence, the fact that the extreme right has no unified economic platform; as far as they are concerned, the economic system of the future domestic order they prefer can be anything as long as it serves the nation.

Beyond the "extreme Right," however, a center-Right or just a "Right," still exists, pretty much as it exists in other parts of Europe as well. The hues vary greatly from Thatcherites to supporters of the CSU, from Italian types of Christian Democrats to those who think that Kohl's CDU has the only answer. Belonging to the Right in this European sense, separates the socio-political spectrum only from the "Left." In Western Europe those on the Right are often as separate from each other as they are from their domestic opponents on the Left. Generally, however, those on the Right elevate the rights of individuals above group rights, emphasize their preference for private competition as versus the constant guiding hand of the state, and prefer to limit the overwhelming influence of the welfare state.

Unlike in the West, in Eastern Europe, in general, belonging to the Right is a matter of degree in commitment to the singular cause of the nation. The farther to the Right the more vociferous and vituperative the manifestations of nationalism, the greater the anti-Semitism and other elements of extremism noted above. The authoritarian bend of the Right is clearly aimed at insuring the centrality of the nation and not as a justification for the nation to support authoritarian solutions. Our task in delineating the "Right" in Eastern Europe, however, is made all the more difficult by the fact that aside from the parties of the Left, all political parties and movements in the region are generally catch-all affairs at the best. Identifying them with any orientation stretching from Right to Left, therefore, is a somewhat awkward task, except insofar as separate single issue orientations are concerned. Self-identification, in regards to their stance *vis-à-vis* communism is, of course, not much help here, for aside from the successor communist parties, all the current parties claim to be parties of the Right.

Consequently, at this stage, we may draw the following conclusions concerning the right in contemporary Eastern Europe:

1. As far as the desired power arrangements are concerned, those belonging to the Right are assumed to desire a generally statist orientation, somewhat reminiscent of attitudes of former national socialists.

2. As far as the desired manner of reaching the desired goals are concerned, people on the Right may be identified by their excessive reliance on the state—as versus the individual—to reach the expected goals; a person on the Right of the political spectrum is potentially more likely to favor authoritarian methods of rule than a "libertine" individualist.

3. The value of the nation appears to split the Right from other parts of the body politic. People on the Right give far more value to the nation, to its survival, its integrity, aspirations, and intrinsic value, than those not on the Right; the ethno-nationalists are clearly located on the Right end of the political spectrum. The extent to which they possess negative values toward others around and in their midst—other nationalities, Jews, Gypsies, etc.—differs from state to state, as does the manner in which they act out their values. But their intolerance of others in regard to the extreme value of the nation is uniform among the Rightists of the region.

4. Finally, the difference between the "extreme Right" and the "center Right" is both a matter of degree and a matter of commitment; while the center Right is, generally, willing to fight for its avowed principles based on the ground-rules of democracy, the extreme Right is willing to use extreme, even extra-legal, measures to reach its desired ends. Though the extreme Right is willing to use the ballot box in its quest for power, it also does

not hesitate to use extra-legal means to reach its desired end. It is, thus, its zealotry, its convictions and willingness to step outside of the bounds of the established democratic game, that makes the existence of the extreme Right in Eastern Europe such a dangerous phenomenon.

It is, of course, too early to tell whether the extreme Right has the popular support most observers of the region fear they possess. In fact, my own haunch is that they do not possess the kind of backing their leaders claim to have. Except for a small number of vociferous extreme Rightist organizations to date, it looks to me as if the people of the region have yet to support the emotion-ridden and hate-driven campaign of the *Vatra*, the *Matica*, or even the returning *Ustasha*.

The future success of the extreme Right will depend on several factors. First and foremost among these factors is the ability of the existing governments to mitigate the greatest harms of the transformation to a market economy: massive unemployment, massive impoverization, massive socio-economic displacement. The ability to handle that displacement within acceptable bounds is the single most important indicator of the potential success of the extreme Right.

Secondly, the success of the Right will depend on the efforts of the current governments to separate themselves from the workings, the zealotry, the verbiage of the extreme Right. Whether the existing governments are of the center Right or coalition affairs, they must denounce the efforts of the extreme Right to use extra-legal means, to use demagoguery and incitement to riot in order to accomplish their own ends. By separating the "respectable Right" from the "extreme Right," and by identifying the former with all of the forces arrayed against the extreme Right, the center Right can gain respectability and success in limiting the extremism of the Right.

Thirdly, much will depend on the response of the forces of the Left. Beaten, demoralized and lacking in solutions that are not discredited, to date the "Left" has been rent by internal dissent, incoherence in goal orientation and an inability to mount common platforms. The old ideology of either "socialism," or "welfare statism," simply will not work in Eastern Europe for some time to come; the Left must provide a platform that will enable it to work with the center Right on issues and concepts of mutual interest. Unless the Left does so, willy-nilly, it will force the center Right to seek alliances with the extreme Right, rather than the moderate Left; this is one of the greatest historical responsibilities placed on the Left in Eastern Europe today. Finally, the international environment may also influence the "game." Though in Western Europe the rise of the extreme Right is also a phenomenon that should not be neglected, the fact is that the structure of the governance of Western Europe has major tools available to influence the further development of the extreme Right in Eastern Europe. Without interfering in domestic power-arrangements, Western European assistance could be tied to the strict observance of human and minority-rights protocols, and these, in turn, can influence the governments in power to take steps in limiting the undue influence that may be exercised by the extreme Right today.

In short, by way of closing this volume, it is easy to note that there exists a revival of the political Right in Eastern Europe. Throughout the volume, however, we noted that the "new Right" that emerged after the Great Transformations of 1989–1990 is a potent force, but clearly different from both the extreme Right of today and the old Right that existed in the 1930s. The great question—whether the post-communist Right will become similar to that seen in the mainstream of the political life of contemporary Western Europe, or will merge with the extreme Right of today and form a coherent and potent nationalist-extremist force—cannot yet be answered with any certainty. Let us simply hope that the men who lead the centrist forces of today will be better students of history than the leaders of the extreme Right during the inter-war era were.

NOTE

1. The single most important work on the topic is, of course, Hans Rogger and Eugen Weber (ed.) *The European Right: A Historical Profile* (Berkeley and Los Angeles: University of California Press, 1966). To illustrate this hiatus in the literature, readers are urged to look in such catalogues as the University of California system, where, for instance, out of 684 titles on the "Left" and "Right," only 62 deal with the Right.